"The music has to be by the musicians, and there's too much changing things by the record company. I got a message for everyone in a record company: We don't care if you lose your job! You ruin music and I'll get all of the smoothers out of the way, the people who smooth the sound off. Let the musicians have the music the way they want it, and not the way you think the grandmothers and 3-year olds will gonna buy it. 'Cause this is not about 3-year olds or grandmothers... This is Rock and Roll"

Joe Strummer

All the groups and individuals that I am aware of as appearing in Burton throughout the period covered by the book, appear in the first instance in **bold lettering** in the text. Though I have tried to be as thorough as possible during the research there will inevitably be some omissions, the same goes for the appendices listing the performers in the town through the 1950s, 60s and 70s.

(Front and back cover photographs courtesy of John Chambers, Champ Electronics, The Vintage Tube Amp Hospital, Nottingham, England).

Number 76 High Street, Burton-on Trent.

IS THIS IT?...

I guarantee that this is what the visitor will say when confronted with what remains of the old, legendary, **76 Club** in High Street (above).

Head off towards town, peer down the alleyway down the side of the Lord Burton, and there is the former **Paradise Club**. What happens in there nowadays? I don't know, I don't really want to know.

Move along a bit further, see the solicitors? That was a pub once, with a back room called by its patrons the **8 Bar Rest**, a jazz club - modern, not trad! Some of the finest musicians to be found in, and around, the town.

That's just the High Street: want to dance to a big band? Try the **Kevin Ballroom** or the **Town Hall**; see The Kinks in all their pomp? The **Jubilee Hall**'s the place. Over the water you could see any number of renowned 'folkies', performing for the **Burton Folk Club**, in the back of a pub, on a stage about 3 ft square.

You will not see any blue plaques outside these places informing the casual observer that "one of the finest drummers that ever stood upright, a Burtonian, regularly played here", or that "15,000 people once crowded into this small club to see the early *Sex Pistols* perform" (that's my estimate, and the numbers still growing!).

These clubs have all been and gone, the beat groups grown up. They provided the sense of belonging that we need when we are young; all who were there can reference events to a particular night, a particular group. The music and the place was the soundtrack, and backdrop, of our lives, be it *skiffle, rock and roll, jazz, folk, prog rock, Northern soul, heavy metal, punk,* or *reggae*. Gone they may be, but forgotten they are not.

In a town where even the much heralded brewing heritage now seems to be up for the highest bidder, we can at least point out that we have the legacy of live music, in real clubs, played by real people, many of whom went on to great things. Our town - and its people's part in the history of popular music - are secured. Not by screwing discs to a wall, but in the memories of those who were there, those who played their part.

Is this it? This is it. Want to find out what it is?

All the best,

Robert Cox

Contents...

BEST WISHES from JERRY ALLEN & HIS TRIO

The Jerry Allen Trio   (Chris Roe)

I know you lot, you're Teddy Boys...

There's always been music; it accompanies us all the way through our lives. Clever people have worked out that we are aware - and can sense - musical rhythms whilst in the womb (apparently we are that fond off it that we don't really want to leave). Birth, Marriage, Death; its all accompanied by music.

There have always been young people: you cannot get from being very young to being very old without going through the bit in the middle.

During the 1950s these two elements came together. Prior to this, music of all styles had been shared by all age groups. Whole families could go to a Saturday night dance, partners for the dance were politely asked if they would care to, and the set rules for a particular style, be it foxtrot or two step, were meticulously followed.

Then it happened: drifting in from the States came what many oldies at the time called 'Jungle Music'. The kids loved it and rock and roll was its name. Immediately the new music providing a vehicle for teenage rebellion: it was their own sound, played by people of their generation (Bill Haley is conveniently overlooked here), and their parents hated it - result!!

In 1950s Burton the place to head for on a Saturday night was The Kevin Ballroom, later known as the Drill Hall, a large tin roofed building, which saw many bands performing; local lads and lasses as well as those from further a field. **Joe Loss** appeared there, but it was mainly local, well established bands like **Len Reynolds** and **Ronnie McRae** who were providing the entertainment. It was a favourite place for recent conscripts, home on leave, to try out their newly acquired fighting skills on anyone that looked at their girl, knocked over their pint, looked at their pint, knocked over their girl, that sort of thing. During this time a number of people were banned from the hall for fighting, and not for nothing did the adverts stress that it was 'The Ballroom with atmosphere'. The fact that the place was situated right behind the police station didn't seem to deter them at all. Though fighting at dances was hardly something new; during the Second World War many local dances were livened up by beer-fuelled exchanges.

Many more local dances during wartime were perked up by the presence of a mischievous looking (and possibly slightly bored), young lad occupying the drum stool for the Len Reynolds Orchestra, **Phil Seamen** explained some years later that all he had to do was "keep time, that's all, just keep time", at his peak, as one of the most acclaimed jazz drummers in the world he would later give free rein to his inventiveness, and his spontaneous drumming style. We will be hearing more of him later.

KEVIN BALLROOM, Burton-on-Trent

CONTINUOUS
DANCING
EVERY   WEDNESDAY

VALID **3** APR 195?

Dancing 8-0 till 11-30 p.m.

ADMIT the BEARER and ONE FRIEND
for 3/6

(Chris Roe)

The Kevin Ballroom had a grand re-opening night in December, 1956, after a £2000 re-fit, which included a cafeteria and 'romantic lighting' ("who you lookin' at?" would have sounded so much better under this). Providing the music on the night was **Roy Tilley**, a Derby man, and his band, who would later become resident at the hall.

Roy Tilley   *(Burton Mail)*

Another very popular venue in town was the Town Hall. Regular events were held here, and **Victor Silvester** and his band appeared, but again the likes of **Roy Norton, Bill Roulstone** and **Joe Fearn** were regular entertainers, all members of the Musicians Union (at this time only members could perform in Burton). They would hold an annual Jamboree, often at the Town Hall, with a number of bandsmen playing together.

***Burton Musicians Union**, 4th Annual Dance Band Jamboree at **Swadlincote Rink**, September 1955. (l-r) piano: **Joe Fearn**, guitar: **Allan Locker**, accordion: **Freddie Lawrence**, clarinet: **Roy Norton**, saxophone: **Tom Smith**, double bass: **Jack Harrison**, drums: **Norman Dowson**. (trombone: unknown).*
(Burton Mail)

The Town Hall hosted many visiting orchestras and 'big bands', **Ricky Thompson**, from Coalville recalls appearing there with his band, though he points out that "Burton was a very closed shop as far as big bands were concerned, due to the Musicians' Union looking after their own". He does state that the Town Hall was a very good venue (for big bands, although not for rock bands, as we will see later). Ricky was once approached by a young man by the name of *Gerry Dorsey*, who wanted to try out as the singer for the band, he was turned down as he was mainly a ballads singer - a very popular one too, as it turned out, as *Engleburt Humperdink*, who he later became, will testify.

Many of the bands were now providing the right sounds, in small doses, for the punters to try out their moves: "jitterbugging, rock and rolling and hand jiving". How you dressed was now becoming a very important part of young life, many of the men sported the quiff and 'Ducks Arse' hairstyle, while the ladies were topped off with a bouffant, and of course, the billowing skirt for all those twirls during the jive.

Some of the bandsmen were perhaps looking even further ahead at the time. Ricky Thompson's band now had a bass player, a young Leicester lad who would turn up at band practice on a scooter with the bass over his back. Have a look at the picture: does it remind you of anyone?

Ricky Thompson Big Band.....that fella in the centre with the glasses looks familiar.   (Ricky Thompson)

Well if video did kill the radio star it didn't stop Trevor Horn from becoming one of this country's top record producers.

The publicity and hype emanating from the screenings of 'Rock Around The Clock' in cinemas all over the country, and the alleged seat trashing incidents, were beginning to have an effect. The seemingly terrified infrastructure of the law was already 'nipping it in the bud' locally. The *Burton Daily Mail* fired off a 'warning to rock and roll fans' in 1956; the newspaper reported that Police Superintendent W E Hinckley of Burton Police had stated that they would be out in force to prevent "Rock and roll fans at *Burton Statutes Fair*, who might attempt to start a rock and roll session".

Not wishing to be outdone in displaying intolerance towards young people actually enjoying themselves, Burton Markets Inspector Mr Hicken went on record stating that "if rock and roll records were played at any of the side shows he hoped they would be replaced by something else" - presumably not the *Eddie Cochran* classic.

Tutbury has, over the years, been witness to many scenes of violence and debauchery, with skirmishes at the castle and bull running to name but two, but the sight of "six Burton boys engaging in a 'rock and roll type dance' in Duke Street" was beyond human endurance. Five people complained immediately to the police, while another complained the next day as she was 'too terrified at the time', the culprits were hauled up in court and fined £1 each. I'm sorry, and perhaps one of our learned friends can enlighten me here, but since when has dancing in the bloody street been against the law?

Another youngster in Burton was easily identified as the culprit behind stealing milk money off doorsteps in Horninglow by his 'rock and roll appearance'. To make matters worse, some of these people were discovering the delights of alcohol, though they were loath to pay the sort of prices some of the venues were asking - or maybe they were too young to be served. Whatever the reason, in 1956 the Jubilee Hall banned the wearing of overcoats on entry to 'prevent the sneaking in of drink'.

The impact of this new 'fad' on the town was restricted to recorded music and films at first, but in the minds of some of its young fans ideas were beginning to form, "if they can do it so can I," thought many budding, would be, rockers, and they set about their aspirations with a vengeance: some with a bit less vengeance than others, though: one young lad held the audience enthralled at an *Entertainment Committee Dance* at the Town Hall by playing a blistering version of 'Rock Around The Clock'....on the bones!

See, you just can't stop the rock.

(Burton Mail)

Old Nick and Mocambo...

Please pity this nitwit, who tells you the tale,
Of fabulous sums, and completed sale,
A very small mind, and a big long stick,
Can stir it up, and take the 'mick',
But goons like this, should tread with care,
Old Nick and Mocambo, are very much there?

The little ditty above was placed as an advert in the *Burton Daily Mail* at the time the Mocambo Café in the High Street was put up for sale. The little café plays a key part in the tale of live music in Burton. Starting out as a meeting place for some of the town's youngsters, it went through a transformation after the sale and eventually became an integral part of the, much vaunted, 76 Club. Why was the piece put in the paper? I've no idea. Obviously it was in some way connected with the proposed sale, but who placed the ad, and why, will have to remain a mystery.

The Mocambo was always popular with those that preferred the motorbike as their transport of choice in Burton. Rows of them were often lined up outside, although, contrary to popular belief, they were not involved in attempts to terrorise the neighbourhood. It was all a great deal simpler than that, as one of the old Mocambo regulars, Tim Emmerson, informed me, "having a bike was a fantastic way of pulling the birds!"

With much the same idea in mind, many boys from the Burton Grammar School (then in Bond Street) frequented the place, at lunch times, after school and Saturday mornings. Ken Bell and John Smith both recall going down there, and especially the juke box, "which was well fed with sixpences and consequently blasted out rock 'n' roll music all the time".

Tim Emmerson outside **The Mocambo Cafe**
(Tim Emmerson)

By the fall of night the café became a hang out for the *Teds*, who *were* out to terrorise the neighbourhood as we have already heard. They would often use it as a halfway house between the *Golden Eagle*, just up the High Street (complete with resident macaws and monkey!), and Dances at the Town Hall. It was here the *Teddy Boys* came into their own. With no opportunity to show off their bikes, the Mocambo lads had to take second place as the *Teddy Boys*, dressed to kill, took their choice of dancing partners.

Despite these odd Town Hall and Kevin Ballroom functions, many people describe Burton in the mid to late 50s as 'as dead as a dodo' (good job it's no longer like that eh?), and many opted to travel along the old Derby Road for a night out. However, due to ill health, Mr & Mrs. Nicholls, the Mocambo proprietors, were selling up. They had already started to offer the youngsters a little bit more than just refreshments, the café's juke box provided the chance for the youngsters to let off a bit of steam.

One of the prospective purchasers, no doubt taking into account the adverts blurb about the place being 'in a wonderful position, with possibilities for expansion', decided to check the place out. Gordon Band, from Walsall, was already in the catering trade. Having an eye for a business opportunity as well as having kept a close watch on what the youngsters were interested in, he saw the potential of the place. He also knew that, due to the emergence of, first the skiffle groups, then their natural progression to what would now be termed 'pop' groups, he would have a supply of entertainment, both from outside sources and others much closer to home.

The Mocambo Café   (Burton Mail)

If you needed a date for the start of home grown British Pop music, then 1957 would be it. We had already had our appetite wetted by *Elvis, Bill Haley, Little Richard* and *Jerry Lee Lewis*, who we imitated to a certain extent, but, as ever, British ingenuity was able to add an element that made it ours. *Lonnie Donegan*, a Glaswegian, had his first top ten hit with 'Rock Island Line' in 1956, and was one of the original performers beamed out to the nation's eager youths on the *Six – Five Special* television show, the first music show aimed specifically at teenagers. He played in a style that mixed the sound of American *country* music, British folk and elements of rock 'n' roll. In his live shows he would utilise everyday household items to produce cheap, but effective, music. A washboard, combined with thimbles on the fingers would provide a rhythmic accompaniment, an empty tea chest with a broom handle secured to one corner and a length of washing line, or string, would give an instant, elementary bass sound. Lonnie himself would often strum a cheap Spanish guitar, and the message was clear and simple: in a mantra that would be taken up by youngsters all over the land 20 years later via the punk uprising, Lonnie was telling everyone 'it was easy, it was cheap, go and do it!' which the youth of Britain duly did in their droves.

Donegan is quoted as _the_ major influence on just about everyone involved in pioneering British pop music from *The Beatles* to goody goody Botox merchant *Cliff Richard*: all over town the sound of painful, blistered fingers attempting to hold down strings that were so far away from the fret board they could have sent it a postcard, could be heard. There were no websites providing easy tabbed run downs of the latest big thing, all had to be either learned from listening on the radio, or buying, borrowing or stealing the record, and trying to re-create what you heard, or thought you heard, or by being taught by those who were perhaps older and wiser.

Many budding Burton musicians, who were later to show up in some very successful local bands, began by following Lonnie's lead. Ken Ratcliffe started out doing regular spots at *The Crown* in Yoxall on Tea Chest Bass, accompanied by Mike Smith on the washboard and Doug Perry on Banjo, with Mick Kersey providing the vocals. Tony Tipper, who would later team up with Ken in one of the town's top groups, **The Alpines**, followed the 'do it yourself' ideal faithfully: his brother made a set of drums for him from cardboard boxes obtained from Wesley's printers, topped off with a cymbal made from tin.

The Blackjacks, *rehearsing at Byrkley Street Church Rooms, 57/58*
(l-r): **John Bott, John Butler, Barry Dale, Pete Youngman.**

(Pete Youngman)

Skiffle was, by necessity, a young mans music, and very often the group members were actually too young to be legally admitted to the venue they were appearing in. Pete Youngman recalls appearing with **The Blackjacks** at the *Star and Garter* in Grange Street. His payment for the nights work was 2/6d (about 13p) and a bottle of lemonade, well he was only 15! Pete had already had some musical grounding before taking up the guitar, he had started to learn the harmonica at eight years old, appearing at a benefit concert for Hungarian Refugees as part of an harmonica trio at the Jubilee Hall alongside a jazz trio who's guitarist, Trevor Mears, taught Pete a few chords - "and that's where it started".

Others followed what might be called a more traditional route to learning their instrument. Tony Leech took lessons on guitar at Burton Accordion Centre, which was run by *Abbey Music*, a firm which for many years had a music shop in Burton Market Place. The accordion centre was in Uxbridge Street, a number of local guitarists learnt their stuff here, many starting out on banjo, a much more popular instrument in those days. It's well documented that a young fellow by the name of John Lennon was doing exactly the same thing in Liverpool. Tony's father ran the *Swan Inn* in Newhall, and Tony would play in the pub as part of the **Red Rockers** along with Henry and Joey Parr, his nephews, and the pubs resident piano player (most pubs had them at this time), Trevor Barnett. They would initially perform skiffle style, accompanied by Eric Palmer on tea chest bass, progressing as they became more proficient, like many others, on to the well known hits of the day.

Eventually they began to get gigs further from home, mainly around the South Derbyshire area, though they did perform at the *Star* and the *Leopard* in Burton. By this time they had replaced the piano player with a chap by the name of Keith Bowler, his debut gig was at the *Star* on Burton's High Street. The *Star* was a very traditional Burton pub, with traditional Burton pub pastimes like darts and dominoes and, when the occasion called for it, the clientele attempting to punch each others lights out, which they duly did on the night of Keith's first appearance. Keith wisely took refuge behind the piano until things had calmed down a bit, these things didn't just happen in the movies, they really did happen. Most bands would get used to playing on as the assembled happy gathering would erupt into violence, and only very rarely did it involve the band themselves, though it did, invariably start out over an argument about the female of the species.

Tony eventually bought a Hofner Club 40 guitar which he played through a 10-watt amplifier (10-watts!), with a home made speaker, Tony having to go to Birmingham to fetch the guitar. Later both *Abbey Music* and *Normans Music* in New Street would be the mainstay for local musicians, and Norman Willey would become a very good friend to many of the shop's customers. Tony remembers Norman phoning him whenever a new record came into the shop. He would quickly get hold of the disc and work out the chord progression, sharing it with the rest of the lads at band practice.

Tony Leech with his Hofner Club 40

(Tony Leech)

Emerging out of this local skiffle boom was another South Derbyshire lad, one of the most respected local musicians, who is still revered amongst Burton's guitar fraternity. Maurice Hall used to listen to the *Saturday Club* on the radio and loved what he was hearing - so much so he decided to make his own guitar. Okay, it was only made of cardboard, but it wasn't long before he had the chance to try out the real thing. One of his friends had been bought a guitar by his parents, but not having the patience to sit and learn it, he gave it to Maurice, who set about the instrument with a tenacity which would soon pay off. Completely self-taught he practised faithfully. He was encouraged to check out some of the Burton groups on the go at the time, dropping by at *St. Margaret's Church Hall* in Shobnall Street, he found himself invited to join in the practice with Bernie Prince's **Dolphins**. Leaving no one in doubt that 'the boy could play' he soon became a permanent member of the group.

The school system during this exciting period meant many young lads and lasses were kept apart from each other for the best part of the day, only meeting up after the school bell at one of the local cafés, such as the aforementioned Mocambo, or perhaps the *Harlequin* in Station Street (later also owned by Gordon Band), or at one of the neighbourhood dances. Many local groups were formed amongst the boys' own atmosphere of the Grammar School. Performing at venues like *St. Aidens Church Hall* in Shobnall Road, these rock 'n' roll dances emerged from bible classes at the hall, mainly organised by Girls' High School pupils such as Judith Aldous, Patricia Ford and Yvonne Andrews. Their invitations to the boys' grammar kids were taken up enthusiastically.

One group of Grammar boys formed up as the **Trent River Ramblers**, appearing at some of the aforementioned dances as well as other venues like the Town Hall, which hosted a skiffle contest in 1958, with **The Rockets** from Nottingham eventually running out as winners.

Outside influences were also at work in the town. The Kevin Ballroom hosted a visit from 'British Skiffle Champions' **The Black Cat Skiffle Group**, and the Jubilee Hall proudly advertised in September, 1958:

'Billy Shinfield presents dancing at the Jubilee Hall.. **Cy Laurie** *and his band supported by* **The Worried Men** *Skiffle Group'*

It was a chance for Burtonians to catch **Adam Faith** with his *Worried Men* before he hit the big time.

The two venues mentioned above, along with the Town Hall, were still the mainstays for local and touring groups, with church halls mainly providing the alternative site for music fans. This was soon going to change, and we were to get a new place for our music fix that was to be part of the town's modern music folklore.

Big Beat...

The Alpines at **The Cambo**
(l-r): **Ken Ratcliffe, Doug Perry, Johnny Butler, Mike Smith, Bob Bishop, Barry Farmer** and **Gary Fletcher**. *Count 'em: four guitars, two drummers and a vocalist - 20 years before Adam Ant 'thought' of the idea.*

(Ken Ratcliffe)

Number 76, High Street, Burton, had seen a number of occupants over the years; in 1900 it was the home of one Henry Lea, a sanitary engineer (who said the 76 was a toilet?). By 1957 Thomas Mansfield, shoe repairer, who's shop stood next to the 76 alleyway throughout the club's history, was in residence. The address itself fronted on to the High Street, though round the back of the property stood a block of small cottages. These were accessed via a narrow alleyway that would eventually become the entrance to the club, an access fondly remembered by all except roadies, who soon became fed up with ferrying equipment up and down it.

The Mocambo was still listed at number 76 in 1960, though the occupier of one of the rear cottages was Gordon Band, the new proprietor of the café. He took the logical step for the meeting place and opened up an area specifically for entertainment, mainly for the youngsters. At first it was still unlicensed, giving it the title of the Cambo Club. Gordon was able to provide musical entertainment, initially by the use of a record player, but soon progressing to showcasing some of the growing number of Burton bands.

The Red Rockers were one of the first groups to appear there, with Christmas Eve entertainment in 1959 being layed on by The Alpines, while a chance to dance away some of the Christmas excess was provided by Pete Youngman's Blackjacks a few days later.

The dawn of the 60s - a recognised golden era for British pop music - was heralded in by **The Bartenders** at the Cambo club, though whether these were a group or just the people who served the drinks I'm not sure.

The club was proving a big success, and, with everyone from **The Vigilantes** to **Colin Storm and his Whirlwinds** giving it some, it became obvious to Gordon that he would need to expand. He saw the need to provide somewhere where townspeople could meet, be entertained and enjoy the benefits of alcohol at the same time and needed a purpose-built place to provide the type of entertainment he had in mind.

*The new **Cambo/76** interior, 1961. The door was the entrance from the **Mocambo Café**.*
(Arthur Phillips)

Having already sold off the *Harlequin Café* in Station Street to a group who promptly re-opened it as *The Lee Yen*, the first Chinese restaurant in Burton. In March. 1961, Gordon set about demolishing the cottages at the rear of the Mocambo and built what was to become the 76 Club. In 1962 it became one of the first clubs in the country to be granted a license to sell alcohol.

Throughout the summer of 61 The Alpines were regulars on stage at The Cambo. In October the club was closed for a short time while the necessary alterations were carried out, re-opening on Friday, December 1st, as the 76.

The club was to be open every night of the week, catering for the needs of as many people as possible. The décor was along the same, African theme as the Mocambo Café, including the mock African shield which many people remember gracing the front of the Mocambo. The club boasted a TV lounge, not yet a fixture in every living room in the land, with regular dancing on Saturdays and Sundays. Bernie Prince's **Dolphins**, who had performed at the opening night of the 76 Club, took over the regular Saturday night-spot, with others, including **Joe Fearn and his Ambassador Trio** providing the ambience on a Sunday.

(Burton Mail)

To show just how diverse the entertainment was at the time in the club, here's a selection of some of the performers and activities that were going on:

Monday: **Big Film Night** – *'Voodoo Woman'*.

Tuesday: **Tape Night**, "for those interested in Taping", (or 'Rave' in the new outside lounge).

Wednesday: **Ron's Record Hop**

Thursday: **Jazz night**

Friday: **The Dolphins**

The mention of 'Ron's Record Hop' above brings us on to one of the early 76 Club's principle characters. Arthur Phillips was, for a time, Gordon Bands right hand man at the club. He had worked at the *Golden Eagle*, over the road, but Gordon persuaded him to move to the club. Here he would put on records for the youngsters to dance to, becoming one of Burton's first DJs in an era when there were no "Superstar DJs". The records were all borrowed from electrical retailer *WT Parker*, whose management was happy with the arrangement as, the theory went, kids hearing a sound they liked would hot foot it down to the shop the next day and buy a copy. Like many theories it was slightly flawed; many would wait until they had saved up enough for the single (for younger readers, a single was a 45 rpm, seven-inch disc, the standard musical format for the 60s and 70s, played on a record player or stereogram - ask your Granny about them), but many of those pesky kids would head for *Broadmeads* in the High Street, one of the first record shops in Burton to have a "Listening Booth," where you could request the record of your choice and go and have a furtive listen (several times over, if you were just taking the mickey, up until the point where the harassed assistant realised what you were up to and pulled the plug). Most record shops had them, or something similar, though *W. T. Parkers* themselves had, at one time, a set of Bakelite headphones, put to the same use, with the added bonus of the Top Five being played on a constant loop.

Arthur, equipped with only the most basic *'Dansette'*-type record player (mono only in those days, stereo was only for recording studios) would encourage the kids to get up and dance, sometimes more successfully than others. On occasions he would threaten to put on classical music if they didn't get up and cut some rug. Calling his bluff they remained seated, so on went the classical stuff, marking a moral victory for Arthur, and they would soon be begging for a return to the hip stuff, making sure they all got up to dance. He was also responsible for running the film shows on Monday nights, such as the *Voodoo Woman* listed above, mainly he says 'for the motorbike crowd from the Mocambo'.

*The **76** Bar area 1961/2*   *(Arthur Phillips)*

On most nights the club would be shutting its doors by 10pm or 10.30 pm, for this was an era when the only late openers were in the big cities. To certain elements of our society opening times are irrelevant, such as the individuals who decided to break into the club one night and help themselves to the takings. Once all the formalities with the police were done with the club needed to be secured for the rest of the night as best as possible, and so it was that Arthur found himself in the new role of resident club security guard, spending the night in the building to deter any other would be burglars. Arthur recalls it well: "it was absolutely freezing".

The 'Big Beat' boom gathered pace with such momentum during this period that every available premises, from the smallest church hall, to the Jubilee Hall at the Working Men's Club on the corner of Orchard Street and New Street, was put to good use showcasing bands and performers from all over the U.K. *Rock Jamboree* nights were organised at the Jubilee, with the first one, in January, 1961, mainly a showcase for some of the many local bands that had recently been formed. Taking the stage that night were The Alpines, **Atlantix, Crusaders** and other guests.

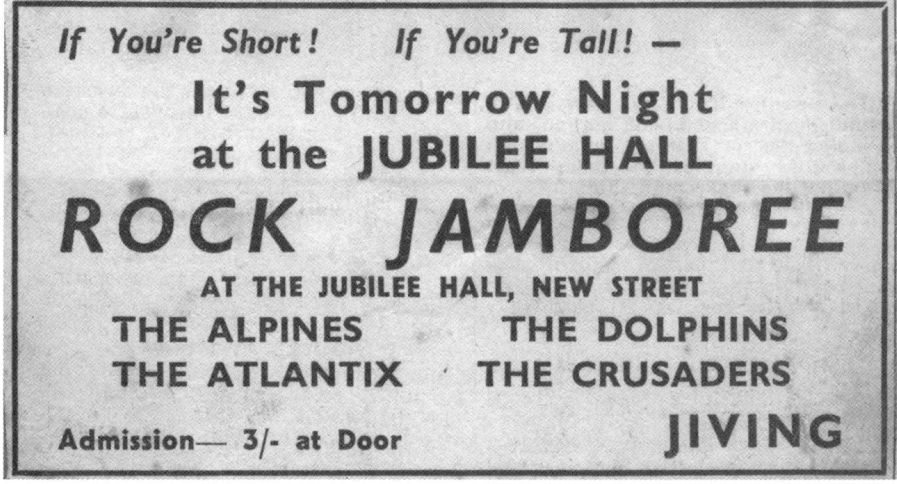

(Gary Barnett)

By far the biggest influence on both bands and audience were Cliff Richard's new, all conquering Shadows, a by product of the skiffle boom centred on the *2 Is Coffee Bar* in London's Soho. Every band seemed to contain at least one Hank Marvin 'wanabee', *Norman's* and *Abbey Music* were getting requests for Fender Telecaster guitars, or at least the nearest affordable copy. Some groups even had a Hank Marvin look-alike who actually physically looked (and played) like the man, all this in an age before *Stars in Their Eyes* where, no apologies to anybody, but it has to be said, mainly talentless chancers spend days in television make up departments, possibly receiving face altering plastic surgery, only to emerge through the dry ice looking, and sounding, like some cheap karaoke version of their hero/heroine. Many involved at the time quote 'Mas' Mason of The Dolphins, as the most authentic looking of the Burton bands *Hank* imitators, possessing both the looks and the talent. Maurice Hall says emphatically: "he *was* Hank!".

Within a few months the term 'Teen Beat' was the Jubilee advertising hook, obviously aimed at a specific age group. The venue was also attempting to lay on some of the more well known groups who were touring the country at the time. Many groups contained elements of what were to become part of the British rock music ascendancy to the World conquering stage during the next decade. **Buddy Britten and the Regents** (who we will meet again later on), had on bass Nick Simpler, later with heavy metal pioneers *Deep Purple*, while when **Danny Storm** paid a visit from up the road in Leicester and let rip, the audience were treated to one of the most powerful and instantly recognisable voices in British music. The man behind the voice, Roger Chapman, would later return to the town some years later, fronting **Family** (*"lay down easy, stars in my eyes"*.- terrific lyrics), armed with, if anything, an even more powerful vocal range. Top geezer **Joe Brown with his Bruvvers** played both the Jubilee (with support from the fast rising Alpines), and the 76 Club in 1961, bless his cotton socks, he's still doing it live now.

Screaming Lord Sutch was one of life's great characters. We need people like him; those of us who have to live out the everyday normal life look to the likes of Sutch, Keith Moon and Keith Richards or (insert 'hell raiser' of choice here) to do what we have neither the money or the balls to do ourselves, much as we would deeply like to.

A great deal of Sutch's act was based on what he had gleaned from others (*Screaming Jay Hawkins* being the most obvious), but you show me somebody in his business who hadn't taken elements of other peoples ideas, in some cases the whole idea, and presented it as their own. There is nothing new in rock 'n' roll. Not only did he provide a complete entertainment package show himself, he took along with him some exceptional musicians, known as **The Savages**.

Although he was not with the band on this particular visit to Burton, Ritchie Blackmore was a regular; what we had to make do with was a fella by the name of Nicky Hopkins on piano – Hopkins later became virtually a permanent fixture on the Rolling Stones tours and studio workouts. Another part of the entourage on one of the *Lord's* fairly frequent visits to Burton (he also played the 76 and the Paradise Club) was a young Paul Nicholas. Nowadays a well-known actor, by the time of his visit Nicholas was already planning the next stage of his career. Warming up his vocal chords, and loosening up his joints with a drink or two in the nearby *Green Man* pub, he let slip during a chat with Kevin Kent, the rhythm guitar player with local support act The Crusaders, "I don't want to do this any more, I'm going to pack this in and become an actor". We now know that's exactly what he did, though not without some Lord Sutch style visual and audio terrorism in the form of the cheesiest of cheesy songs, 'Dancing With the Captain', accompanied by a bowler hatted dance 'routine'. I think we'd best leave it at that eh Paul?

The Savages went through several routines during the show. At particular points they would all break out into a very choreographed version of the can-can while still playing their instruments, at other times the guitarists would keep spinning round until they were completely entwined in their leads. All pretty innocent stuff nowadays, but nobody had done it before them, and the name of the game was entertainment from the off.

No part of the town during the early 60s went without their weekly supply of live music. In addition to the Jubilee and the 76 there were regular music nights at the Town Hall, run by *Municipal Entertainments*. On Saturdays this would normally be a combination of a live 'beat' group' supporting a more established dance band, while alternate Sunday nights would see live bands and recorded music, either as Swing Time or Top Tune Time. with the vinyl being provided by either Normans or The Accordion Centre, again bashed out on the old Dansette, usually by one of the record stores' female assistants. MC for the events was usually another well know figure around the town, Ivan Parker. The house full signs were up most weeks as it was all seating.

The Crusaders *outside Burton Town Hall, Sunday, October 8, 1962.*
(l-r): **Eric Andrews** *(Bass),* **Glyn Newborough** *(Lead Guitar),* **Kevin Kent** *(Rhythm Guitar),*
Roger Anderson *(Drums).*

(Kevin Kent)

We're a Church Hall band.....

The Dolphins *rehearsing at the old Derby Turn*
(l-r): **Brian Hallam, Bernie Prince, Alan Thompson** *(later Shane Spencer) and* **Maurice Hall**.

(Bernie Prince)

Church halls would be unused for the best part of the week, only really serving the purpose they were built for on Sundays, those groups that had not yet secured a pub backroom were on the lookout for a place to practice. The church authorities, always on the lookout for a way to boost their coffers, saw the opportunity and invited the bands to use the rooms for practice as well as regular performances nights. Though money was tight for the church as well as everyone else, anyone who has ever practiced in a freezing cold hall, attempting to play instruments with fingers that are blue with cold and refusing to move at anything other than turtle pace, will surely recognise The Dolphins predicament.

They used to put on dances at the St. Margaret's Church Hall in Shobnall Street, an unusual place (now long gone), which had a stage either side of the room.

Bernie Prince recalls: "There was no heating in the hall, so the band used to take their own paraffin heaters, which we used to leave in the hall overnight, ready for the church service the next day".

You see, rock and rollers are nice people! Mind you, you had to be careful where you left your instruments. Bernie once left his guitar in the kitchen, and while it was difficult enough to keep the instrument in tune in the Arctic air of the hall, it was made somewhat harder the day he left it near the kettle. The steam from the kettle bent the neck - "no truss rods in those days" says Bernie – and it was exit one guitar.

St. Margaret's Church Hall - Shobnall Street.

In Stapenhill, in order to alleviate the 'we've got nowhere to go, nothing to do' attitude that is simply part of growing up, like-minded citizens attempted to help out by organising a youth club, probably one of the first of its kind in or around Burton. It was, of course, in another church hall (this one is still there, in Ferry Street), it was named The Norman Cochran Youth Club in memory of a local doctor who went missing on a climbing trip in the Swiss Alps. The locals started to raise the money to set up the club in 1960, with the official opening taking place in April, 1962. The flood of membership applications before opening night was encouraging, partially because the leaders behind the club also had the foresight to provide regular live music nights as well as all the other youth activities.

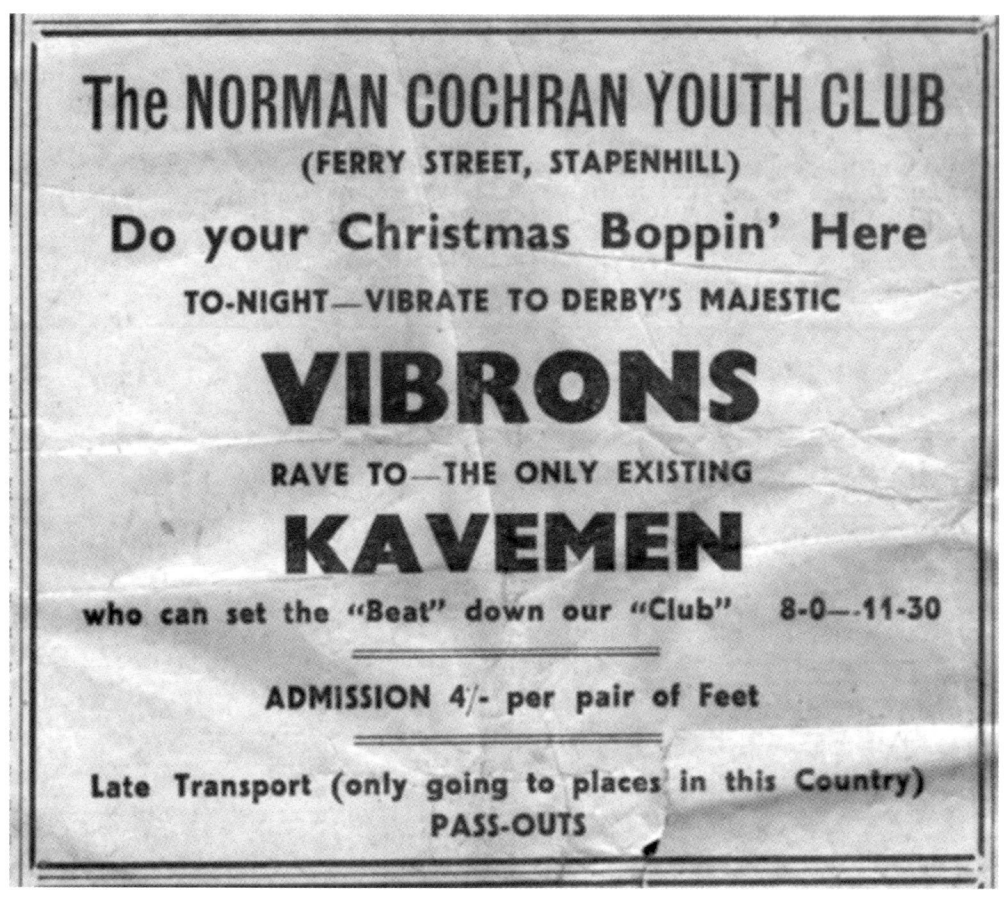

(Dave Hughes)

Many local groups appeared there, including **The Zodiacs**, **The Sapphires** and Derby band **The Vibrons**, while on more than one occasion they managed to book one of the top groups in the area **Shane Spencer and the Casuals** (more of whom later!). Supporting them, playing their debut gig, were a Stapenhill band by the name of **The Kavemen** whose manager, Rob Golding, helped run the club. The night was an absolute sell out: 300 bodies crammed into the hall, all keenly anticipating the night's entertainment ahead.

The Kavemen's drummer, Dave Hughes, proudly recalls the group: over 40 years later the memory remains undimmed. "We used to practice Shadows' stuff in my mums front room, plugging the amps into the light socket!"

On the bands debut night at the club, the already nervous young lads had to overcome some hazards of the business they were in. Occasionally groups would help each other out by borrowing each other's equipment, which would save time and effort setting up. On this occasion, though, the headliners' drummer refused to let Dave use his kit, so he and the rest of the lads, dressed in their stage attire of matching black polo neck sweaters, had to make their way from the back of the hall through the 300 punters to the stage with Dave's drum kit carried above their heads. It didn't put them off in any way, "the (musical) atmosphere at that time was infectious", and they had in their number a very talented lad by the name of Nick Pallett, who later appeared with **The Skillets**.

The Kavemen at Norman Cochran Youth Club
(l-r) **Andrew Fern, Nick Pallett, Paul Brister, Dave Hughes.**

(Dave Hughes)

The club itself prospered, but events were increasingly disrupted as, in the *Burton Mail's* words, 'hooligans and vandals appeared on the scene.' Dances, and other functions in the centre became 'chaotic' and parents became worried about letting their children attend a place where 'rough necks' gathered. An influx of what were termed 'outsiders' (you're not from these parts are you?) was seen as part of the problem, and by 1967 the place had been shut down after the town's education committee refused any more financial backing, although it did re-open later as a 'Stapenhill only' club.

Some other venues also managed to gain an unwelcome reputation for trouble, both inside and out. Winshill Church Hall was host to bands, but unfortunately the quality of the bands was overlooked because of events that took place around them. The place soon gained a reputation as a location where things were likely to kick off amongst the audience, over the usual girl trouble or sometimes territorial disputes or maybe just because one or two in the audience were spoiling for a fight.

Janie and the Silhouettes, a Derby band, were appearing at the hall in November, 1963, when part way into their set the inevitable punch-up started. In trying to calm the melee the vicar of Winshill, the Rev E Edwards, managed to cop a few punches, and the trouble continued out into the street, watched by a sizeable proportion of *Janie's* audience. PC Hulme finally arrived on his motorbike to restore order, whereupon he himself was assaulted by one of the urban warriors. Other fights later broke out in Bearwood Hill, and the people who ran the club decided they had seen enough and shut the place down. One of the main instigators of the trouble was later sent to a detention centre for six months, and by the January of next year the club was up and running again, this time with at least one adult 'helper' (the genteel term for a bouncer) on the door, who allowed entry into the club at his or her discretion.

The hall at St. Chads in Hunter Street, Horninglow, while possibly not having the same reputation as the Winshill hall, still saw its share of activity. Drawing punters from varied walks of life, it witnessed one night a combination of a posse of well oiled Scottish soldiers, out for a bit of r'n'r while housed at the Branston Ordnance Depot, and a visit from a young lad, who was, at that time, a more than capable amateur boxer. He will have to remain nameless as he is still quite a formidable chap and more than capable of sorting out a little herbert like me!

Inevitably during a quieter stage of the proceedings the young chap decided he was going to find out just what a Scotsman wears under his kilt. The Scot took this as a bit of a liberty and decided to teach the youngster a lesson, and with flailing fists he made for the lad, although he didn't get very far. By this time the Scot's mates were in for a bit of action too, and each one in turn tried to level the young upstart with no success at all. Eye witness accounts all agree that the youngster won by a unanimous decision after a couple of knockouts.

By no means was every live music event accompanied by outbreaks of trouble; the majority were played out to a good natured audience intent on nothing more than a good night out and a chance for a bit of dancing and flirting. At the 76 on New Year's Eve a traditional fancy dress contest was held, and winning the first prize of a year's free admission to the club was Rosemary Bondon dressed as a *Mummy*, Harold Critchlow ran second (*Baby*), while Joyce Veal and Jim Preston took third and fourth (*Salome and Lord Sutch*). The night helped raise £16, which was presented by Gordon Band to the Mayor of Burton, who in turn donated it to *The Freedom From Hunger Campaign*.

Some efforts were more successful than others. *The Rifleman Inn* in Derby Street had, like many pubs, a room above that was opened up as a new club in 1962. The Cresta Club was set up in an attempt to rival the immensely popular 76, though in fairness it was never more than a passing side-show. It did, however, host some pretty tasty bands during its short existence. Its grand opening night was Thursday, February 8, with **The Keith Smith Climax Jazz Band** getting things underway.

The new club advertised in the Mail, claiming in one advert:

"If its life you're after, or just fun and laughter,
If you Rock and Jive, We'll give it five".

This was a reference to television's *Thank Your Lucky Stars* and Janice Nicholl who, if she liked a song, would say in a thick Birmingham accent, "Oill'll give it foive".

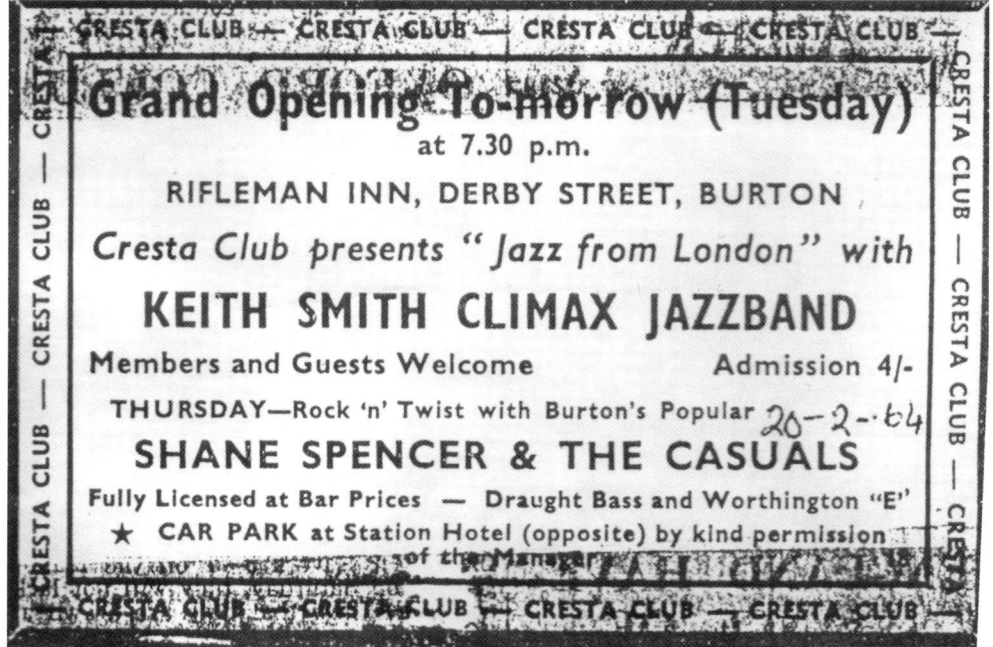

Many of the Burton bands played there, in addition to a number of Birmingham based bands including **The Renegades** and **Rockin Henry and the Hayseeds** (no really!), but probably with the benefit of hindsight we can safely say that the most prominent musician to appear there was Trevor Burton with **The Everglades**. Trevor subsequently returned both with Roy Wood's **Move** (Roy being another regular visitor to Burton), and with **The Steve Gibbons Band**. Trevor is also still out there and still doing it, and at the time of writing still appearing in Burton, a true rock and roller.

A couple of the Burton-based groups were beginning to get noticed by some of the bigger fish, both Shane Spencer and the Casuals and The Alpines (now with *Mike Everest*, aka Johnny Butler, handling vocals) attracting interest.

Impresario Reg Calvert took The Alpines under his wing, getting the lads gigs all over the country. Up to this time they had managed to take care of their own affairs, hunting around for venues, employing girlfriends and others to help out. They popped up all over town, including, amongst other places, another venue that many people remember fondly, the Co-op Hall in Byrkley Street, though many of the group members recall it for its 'echo chamber' acoustics.

Up to now the group had existed on a diet of covers, especially *The Shadows* stuff, but many in the audience, not to mention the group, were growing weary of the same songs time after time. Two of the original *Alpines*, Ken Ratcliffe and Tony Tipper, recall when it all changed for them. Reg Calvert was in the habit of phoning up Ken at extremely short notice, which meant that all the rest of the band would have to be contacted and the van would then tour round picking up everyone after they had finished work (the van was normally kept fully loaded with all their equipment because of this eventuality). "We had no time for a wash or shave, it was straight to the gig" - any member of a working band will recognise this scenario. This particular day Ken got the phone call "you're playing the BRS Club in Erdington, in Birmingham, tonight".

They had been through the routine many times: the van, packed to the gunnels with guitars, amps and drums, along with a few weary musicians, grabbing a bite to eat as best they could on the way. They travelled up the old A38 (no motorways or dual carriageways then) and eventually arrived at the club where they met the band they were to support outside. From out of an old Bedford van the other band, "a scruffy load of gits", emerged and disappeared into the hall to set up their gear. This particular night The Alpines were to open up proceedings, which they duly did. There was no time to check who they were on with so they just plugged in and did their stuff. After they had finished their set they were given polite applause from the Brummies and exited the stage to take up a position at the bar. This was the normal routine for the band, who would often would be required to do two or even three sets a night. They would have a drink at the bar, suss out the next band on and, if they were half decent, would hang around and perhaps pick up a few tips or check out the chord sequence for a song they were playing. If they were crap they would make for the nearest pub (alcohol and nicotine were by far the only drugs encountered by most bands at the time), and return in time for their next set.

The next band took the stage, they certainly looked very different from any other band The Alpines had backed, and instead of the usual 'one, two three, four..' intro, the rhythm guitarist "just looked at the others when he was ready and nodded his head, at which point the rest of the group started up, all in perfect time". This was something entirely different, they were not doing covers, this was their own stuff, it was new, it was original and it was exciting.

"The audience rushed towards the stage, nobody danced, nobody said a word".

The group at the bar were mesmerised: "we were astounded, our jaws dropped to the ground". They remained rooted to the spot for the whole set, only Tony leaving the bar, after noticing that the bass drum on the drummer's kit was working itself loose. Tony, knowing how to deal with the problem, leaned over the side of the stage and pushed it back into place. "Ta Whack" said the drummer, in a thick Liverpool accent, as his head swung from side to side in time with his steady beat. The group was from Liverpool, and they had gained a reputation around their home city from regular performances as well as honing their act to near perfection entertaining at a club in Germany. They had just cut their first single for *Parlaphone*, and this was a group who were going places; the place they were going was to be, as we now all know, to the very top "to the toppermost of the poppermost" as they themselves would say.

Burton's own Mike Everest and the Alpines, had just played support to a band that would change the face of popular music. They would be THE biggest band in the world, and even *Elvis Presley* would sit up and take notice. The headline band that night were Buddy Britten and the Regents, but it was to be the last time *The Beatles'* name would appear on adverts smaller than anyone else's, for The Beatles was indeed who they were!

This experience was put to good use by Mike Everest and the Alpines. They had just seen and heard the future, and became one of the first, if not *the* first, Burton band to cover 'Please, Please Me' on stage. They also set about writing some of their own material. The Beatles had provided the impetus for them - and others - to start thinking of their own way of doing things. It also paved the way for a million imitators, and suddenly everyone involved in bands was a Scouser.

AT THE

CORPORATION HOTEL
NEW STREET

The Fiesta

Present for your pleasure

TO-NIGHT—DANCE NIGHT with

THE ALPINES and the ROGERS
FROM NOTTINGHAM

From 7—10.30   Bar, Light refreshments   Admission 2/6

SUNDAY—STAR NIGHT

with STARS from all over the country

Bar   Light refreshments   Admission 2/6

(Gary Barnett)

*One night you're on stage with **The Rogers** in Burton....*

.... another you're with The Beatles in Brum!

B.R.S. Ballroom
BROMFORD LANE

Teen Beat
Thursday

TV and RECORDING STAR
BUDDY BRITTEN
and THE REGENTS

A Great New Recording Group
making their first appearance in
Birmingham

THE BEATLES

Also MIKE EVEREST and THE ALPINES
7.30 to 10.30 p.m.   4/-

(Birmingham Evening Mail)

Tomorrow belongs to us......

Promotional photo – **Shane Spencer and the Casuals**
(l-r): **Maurice Hall, Trevor Williams, Shane Spencer** *(Alan Thompson),*
Derek Bladon *and* **Tony McKerracher**.

(Trevor Williams)

Once the skiffle phase had passed by, and with it the loss of individuals who decided that this music thing was not for them, those who remained were starting to create a following, both locally and in some cases further a field. No group could have functioned at all without help from mates, girlfriends, boyfriends, parents and understanding bosses.

Among the bands plugging away there were starting to emerge in Burton some who would remain pretty much committed to the cause. As always with these things, personnel tended to flit between bands, either because of the perennial 'musical differences' (being pissed off to give it the correct terminology), perhaps because they were poached by another group, or simply because they saw a better chance for recognition of their talents with some more forward-looking chancers.

The Dolphins were one of the first of the burgeoning bands to establish themselves in Burton. Bernie Prince, one of the founder members, describing how they blossomed from an enthusiastic, if not particularly talented, skiffle group called The Rebels, recalls: "it was bloody awful!". Bernie knows full well that when you are young you had the nerve to do it, and get away with it.

Bernie had practised at school with a couple of others who would also be involved with the music scene, Derek Bladon and Tom Faulkner. **The Rebels** secured an afternoon spot at the *Technical College Students Union*, which was in Union Street at that time. One problem that arose was that it was to be an afternoon gig, meaning that Bernie would have to ask for the afternoon off school, which he duly asked for, and to his teacher's credit, was given. What he failed to tell the teacher was that he would be wearing the group's stage outfit, which consisted of a nifty little suit complete with lace tie, for the morning. Spending the morning self-consciously aware of the looks from both schoolmasters and pupils, but being far to excited to worry about it, he had his mind focused on the afternoon's performance, which apparently went down well.

Deciding to rename themselves as The Dolphins, the band set out securing gigs all over town, and in the surrounding villages, mainly at village halls. Their original line-up consisted of Bernie, Trevor Williams, Maurice Hall, Brian Allen, Harold Lord (who later left) and Johnny Wheelhouse, who himself would shortly be replaced by Alan Thompson later Shane Spencer of Casuals fame.

*The Dolphins at The Jubilee Hall: (l-r) **Maurice Hall, Bernie Prince, Brian Allen, Derek Bladon, Trevor Williams** and **Alan Thompson.***

(Bernie Prince)

While onstage at *Truman's* Sports Club at Shobnall, which later became *Robirch* club, the band were approached by a young fella who enquired if there was "any chance I could do a couple of numbers with you?" The answer was yes, why not? The lad got up and the band were impressed, and so started off Alan Thompson's (Shane Spencer's) singing career which would eventually find him on performing all over Europe.

It was during this period, 1961-62, that they shared 'house band' duties with The Casuals at the 76 Club as well as holding down regular performances with other Burton bands at the Jubilee Hall, which after being put to various other uses over the years is now a restaurant. Another outlet for the lads was the *Top Tune Time* at the Town Hall, where, as we have already heard, their Master of Ceremonies for the night would be Burton's own DJ (BODJ), Ivan Parker. Word of mouth was now getting them the majority of their bookings, any money the group made would be ploughed back in to the venture by the purchase of equipment and other stuff vital for any working band.

Some more additions to the line-up brought in female backing vocalists going by the name of **The Dreamers**.

The Dolphins and The Dreamers at Burton Town Hall

(Bernie Prince)

They were now beginning to back up some of the big names around the live circuit, including **Gerry Levene and the Avengers** at the 76, in 1963, complete with a young lad by the name of Roy Wood on guitar. This journey into the high life was not without incident, and when they appeared in Stoke some of the ladies in the audience managed to grab hold of Alan Thompson and drag him off the stage. What they then did with him is not recorded.

Bernie eventually left and formed **Bernie and the Raiders**, with Johnny Gosling taking over the vocals and Chris Knighton drums. Again, they were on regular support slots, including when **Peter Lee Stirling and the Bruisers** appeared at Burton Tech. Colleges Rag Rock event in 1964. Bernie was most impressed with their live renditions of songs utilising what he still remembers as "fantastic harmonies", belting out a spot on version of *Frankie Valli's* 'Rag Doll', hitting the high notes with perfection - even the *Four Seasons* themselves struggled to accomplish this on a live setting.

Following on from all this activity Bernie decided it was time to treat himself to a new instrument. Both Buddy Holly and Hank Marvin were established Fender Strat' users, and most of the Burton bands, including The Dolphins, were using some form of Strat copy, either German or Italian made, but no one had the real thing. After waiting 16 weeks for the guitar to arrive from the USA, Bernie parted with a hard earned £167 (this was the early 60s don't forget, that was a lot of money!) and took delivery of a brand spanking new Pink Fender Stratocaster, and the guitar soon became the talk of the town amongst other musicians. Bernie continued with *Bernie and the Raiders*, but life, as it always does, was deciding things. With the Fender his prized possession he had to do a great deal of soul searching when he was due to become a father for the first time. As many of us find out eventually, children are an expensive item; a new pram was needed and so it was that he had to sell off the Fender for the grand sum of £35. He knows if he had kept hold of it, it would now be worth an absolute fortune, but admirably he put his family first – he still thinks about it though!

Once Bernie had left the Dolphins, Maurice Hall ditched the bass and took over on lead guitar (being an accomplished musician he could also turn his hand to piano playing). The group also decided on a change of style and image, and with the basis of what was The Dolphins they changed their name to one that many local people will still recognise as one of Burton's most successful groups, Shane Spencer and the Casuals.

Probably holding the all comers record for appearances at the 76, the former Casuals, became known by their longer title due to Alan Thompson's name change to his stage name Shane Spencer. The group were prolific in the Burton area, popping up at every venue that was laying on live entertainment during the early 60s. They gathered admirers from all over town, from Winshill Church Hall to the Town Hall and St. Pauls Institute, and were regular performers at The Jubilee Hall supporting some very well known names.

One of their more memorable dates was with 'The Killer' himself, *Jerry Lee Lewis*, who they supported at Coventry, the lads still proudly possess the great mans autograph, as well as *Little Richard's*, who they also supported. Trevor Williams, or

Wilf as he was known, now occupied the drum stool for The Casuals following their metamorphosis from The Dolphins. Trevor, who recalls having to go 'rag and boning' to raise money for his first real drum kit from 'Normans' music shop, recalls some of the stars they supported, reeling off some of the most talented names of the 60s, some of whom still tread the boards today: **The Honeycombs**, **The Tornados**, *Johnny Kid and the Pirates*, and **Billie Davies**, who's 'Tell Him' (later covered by **Hello**) was riding high in the charts at the time. Billie turned up at the Jubilee Hall a full 5 minutes before she was due to go on stage, and the lads in the group, having no time at all to rehearse or run through any songs beforehand, had to play it by ear. They must have done a pretty good job, as they were taken on as her backing band and toured round the country with her for a fortnight.

***Billie Davies**, another autograph for the collection.*
(Trevor Williams)

Billie had appeared on *Thank Your Lucky Stars*, and was one of the protégés of Joe Meek, a man who would later on play his own part in the Casuals story.

One of the new additions to the group who had not been part of the Dolphins set up was Tony McKerracher who, being a music mad youth at the time of the skiffle boom, had taken guitar lessons from Eddie Wood, saving up to buy himself what he describes as "a great big Hofner, nearly as big as I was". He soon joined up with **The Atlantix**, reputedly one of the first skiffle groups in town, another member being Rob Smith, who later moved on to **The Skilletts**.

Tony saw an advert placed by The Casuals for a rhythm guitarist, passing the audition held at *St. Aidens Church Hall*, and became an enthusiastic player in the group. The group worked hard on their image; everyone at this time was looking for something different to present to their audience to make them stand out from the others. Shane Spencer was kitted out with a very attention grabbing bright red suit, with the other bandsmen donning fetching lime green numbers of a sort you certainly wouldn't miss in a crowd. Following on from Bernie's example they were kitted out with Fender guitars and Vox amps, a classic 1960s combination.

Their manager at the time was Michael Finley, from Stapenhill, who was responsible for securing gigs for the group. They are one of the only Burton groups to recall playing at the short lived Cresta Club, and Maurice Hall even remembers one of the songs they played; 'Pretend' (later a chart hit with Mansfield's own **Alvin Stardust** nee Shane Fenton). Trevor Williams remembers the club as being pretty basic, and the pub below did not have too good a reputation in some quarters. As many of their gigs were further a field than the Cresta, the band managed to procure the item that, if it could, would have some pretty good stories to tell by itself. I am referring to the van, which would come in all shapes and sizes, and somehow keep going despite all appearances, which would suggest that the thing shouldn't be able to move at all. It would normally be rammed full of equipment and bodies, often doubling up as the bands accommodation for the night, the nominated driver was often Shane, who got used to being stopped regular by the police, who would demand to know what were they up to driving round at that time of the night.

On one of the bands trips out, this time to Glasgow in the depth of winter, the lads got snowed in. They had travelled by train, loading all their gear on the train with them. In desperation to secure somewhere to bed down for the night, they approached the local constabulary and enquired if would be possible for them to put the group up for the night, the prospect of a night in the cells being more a more attractive than the thought of dying of hypothermia outside, and a damn site cheaper than a hotel or boarding house. Amazingly the boys in blue did indeed offer them accommodation in one of their cells for the night, just as soon as one became available. Now I don't want to get involved in any stereotyping here, but this was Glasgow, and our intrepid travellers sat in the police station reception area and watched a steady flow of drunks being hauled in. Eventually, at 2am, a 'room' became available and, getting themselves as comfortable as they could (police cells are generally not designed with comfort in mind), they quickly fell into the land of nod, only to be rudely awakened at 6am by the duty sergeant. It was time to go, so, bleary-eyed, they set off for their return to Burton.

Loaded up and ready to roll, The Casuals' transport/accommodation
(Trevor Williams)

The rehearsal rooms for the band were, at different times, Holy Trinity Sunday School Rooms and the *Derby Turn*, where the lads would run through their repertoire of songs, mainly covers of the top tunes of the day, which they would be expected to know when they were acting as a backing band.

When they appeared with crooner **Johnny Bev** at the Jubilee Hall in 1963 they were given the set list, which they copied out, complete with the key each song was to be in:

What I'd Say – E
Treat Her Right – A
One Night – E
Trying To Get To You – E
Cut Across Shorty – A
Old Apache Squaw – E
Some Of These Days – F
Twist and Shout – C

Though they perhaps sometimes got a little fed up with following instructions, as the little note one of the lads added to the back of the set list above may indicate:

Bbm + 6b9 +13 + 9#7o9 + 513, 1305 Millionth Fret, and good night Fred.

Johnny Bev   *(Trevor Williams)*

Though things could get mighty confusing for both band and audience alike, generally when they appeared as Johnny Bev's backing band they were called *The G Men*, and while belting out the songs behind *Garry Mills* they were *The Decades*. This was all well and good until the inevitable happened: appearing on the same bill as Garry, they were advertised as Shane Spencer and the Casuals, while Garry was, of course, appearing with The Decades. It must have been an especially bemused audience who, after witnessing The Casuals set, saw the same people walk back on to the stage as The Decades.

As their success grew they were taken on by the Stoke based *Terry Blood Agency*. Terry signed up the band after they had appeared at Hanley Town Hall, his mother having watched, and enjoyed, the group recommended them (was she one of the women who dragged Shane off stage? We shall never know!). This widened the extent of their travels and Tony McKerracher recalls playing at many seaside venues including Great Yarmouth and Bournemouth. In addition to this they were getting gigs in the place you had to play to be noticed, London.

It was at one of these London shows that a rep from the *King's Agency*, based in Denmark Street, London, right at the heart of 'Tin Pan Alley' as it was known, saw the group. The agency not only took the band on to their books, but also recommended that they audition for Joe Meek, who, following the success of The Tornados 'Telstar', was hot property as a record producer.

KING'S
7 DENMARK ST., LONDON, W.C.2
TEMple Bar 6303/4
Midlands Office:
54 CHEVERTON RD., BIRMINGHAM 31
PRIORY 6123

SCREAMIN LORD SUTCH
& THE SAVAGES
'I'M A HOG FOR YOU'

ROCKIN' BERRIES
★ BIRMINGHAM'S TOP AND MOST BOOKED GROUP

THE FORTUNES
★ SIX-PIECE VOCAL INSTRUMENTAL TEAM—GREAT ENTERTAINMENT

WAYNE GIBSON with
THE DYNAMIC SOUNDS
★ FILM & RECORDING STARS

DANNY STORM
& THE STROLLERS
Unrivalled Presentation & Performance

THE ZEPHYRS • JOHNNY BEV • GARRY MILLS • TANYA DAY
GULIVER & THE TRAVE~~~~SHANE SPENCER & THE CASUALS • etc.

Maurice Hall recalls the band making demo tapes at a studio in London Road, Derby, which were subsequently sent on to Joe in London. Joe had a reputation as being very unorthodox in his approach to recording techniques; this is what set him out apart from the rest. He was never frightened of experimentation, often using his home bathroom for recording because of its peculiar sonic reproduction. Maurice points out that Joe was very protective of his methods:

"He was fanatical about people taking recording stuff into his studios, he didn't want his ideas pinching".

This didn't deter Maurice, who managed to get some sound recordings and some extremely rare 8mm recordings of the studio. Although the quality is pretty poor Maurice holds out hope that the film will eventually find its way into the public domain. "The BBC have it now, working on it to try to lighten up the quality of the images, though it has still not been seen by the public".

A recording date was set for the band at Joe Meek's studios in October, 1963. In the studio at the same time were to be The Honeycombs, who the band became very friendly with. During their recording session The Casuals managed to get several tracks down on tape, and one in particular, 'I Believe', was singled out by Meek,.

"Joe Meek jumped up and down with excitement" recalls Tony McKerracher, "he told us we had a Number One!".

Joe decided that the song would be the best bet for the band's first release, and the recording was passed on to *Decca Records*, who arranged several release dates, each one heightening the lads excitement, only for the release to be continually postponed by Decca. This was especially irritating for the group, who were under strict instructions that they could not perform the song live until a release day was set (how times have changed, nowadays the song would be given airplay on every available medium to drum up sales). Then the bombshell was dropped. The band were out in Derby when manager Mick Finley informed them "I've got some bad news for you". Decca, in their wisdom, had decided that the song would be released, but not by Shane Spencer and the Casuals, but instead for the good, wholesome, clean living Irish band *The Bachelors* (*Westlife*'s prototypes?). The Casuals were gutted. This was their introduction to the cutthroat world of record companies, where morals, then as now, were generally left at home. Joe Meek shared their feeling of betrayal, though he was proved to be right in his professional judgement when the tune became a Number One hit.

Being in a band would obviously mean that eventually local people would recognise you out and about. Trevor Williams used to dread getting the bus into Burton: "There was always somebody who would recognise you, and give you flak, saying they had been to see a much better band at Swad Rink!". Maurice Hall, who had been introduced to the music of *Chet Atkins*, by band mate Tony and set out to emulate his style of playing, very successfully as many locals will vouch, enjoyed being recognised. Wearing the broadest of smiles Maurice thinks back to the time when a young musician by the name of Alan Price asked Maurice for **his** autograph.

Not all the band's followers would have been so pleased to see them though. Not long after Brian Hallam took over the rhythm guitar slot they were going through their *Shadows* routine when, during one number, Brian's shoe flew off his foot and arced gracefully into the audience!

Sadly, the inevitable happened, and the band, for various reasons, broke up in 1966. The times they were a changing someone sang. Trevor retired from the music scene, although Maurice stuck at it for a while, as did Shane Spencer, initially appearing locally still as Shane Spencer he eventually moved on to the next stage of his career, becoming *Jason Korde* on the way to a spell at Butlin's camps before moving to live in Belgium, amongst other places on the Continent.

Tony McKerracher meanwhile, after admittedly "feeling terrible" after his last performance with the group, was contacted by Chris Roe, the manager of another of Burton's semi-professional groups, **The Memphis Five**. Would he be interested in becoming one of the five?

The Alpines, practising at the 8 Bar Rest   (Gary Barnett)

The band that would evolve into the Memphis 5, The Alpines, were building up regular performances in the Burton clubs (and of course the Church Halls), *The Alpines* became one of the town's top draws during the late 50s and early 60s, appearing at the *8 Bar Rest* in late 1959, when their full title was The Alpines *Rhythm Group*; the rhythm part possibly being appended to avoid any misunderstanding with punters turning up expecting to see a jazz ensemble. The original line up had Gary Fletcher on drums – Fletcher later joined up with Pete Youngman's **Spidermen**, and was replaced by Tony Tipper - with Johnny Butler (later *Johnny Byrd* of The Falcons) on vocals, (Butler himself would be replaced by Sydney Street's Mike Banks *aka* Mike *Everest*, following on from Jim Oakley), Doug Perry, Bob Bishop and, of course, Ken Ratcliffe completing the line up. The eye catching stage attire, modelled above, would be matching checked shirts and black trousers, with matching Hofner guitars and Gene Vincent quiffs.

Rehearsing at New Street's *Green Man* pub, they were aware of the close proximity of the Working Men's Club's 'Jubilee Hall', the pub's next-door neighbour. Making enquiries at the club, they managed to help set up the regular *Rock Jamboree* nights there. This was a smart move; the Jubilee was a big venue and, along with the other Burton groups appearing on the opening night they attracted a crowd of 600 music fans. With girlfriends operating the between act entertainment, a record player hidden behind closed curtains and the forerunner of the modern disco, and friends Barry Wheeldon and Jim Preston, taking tickets on the door, the nights events passed more smoothly than the organisers dared dream. They did have to pay for the presence of a policeman at the door to provide the authoritarian figure it deemed wise to have at such events, but enough money was made by the group to enable them to purchase a van, which would see much work during the coming months.

They wasted no time seeking to widen their appeal, and an early approach to the ATV Studios, home of *Opportunity Knocks*, the game show with the technological wonder that was *The Clapometer*, in 1959, saw them initially turned down because of the timing of auditions in the company's Birmingham studios. They would, however, be given their chance for a TV audience at a later date.

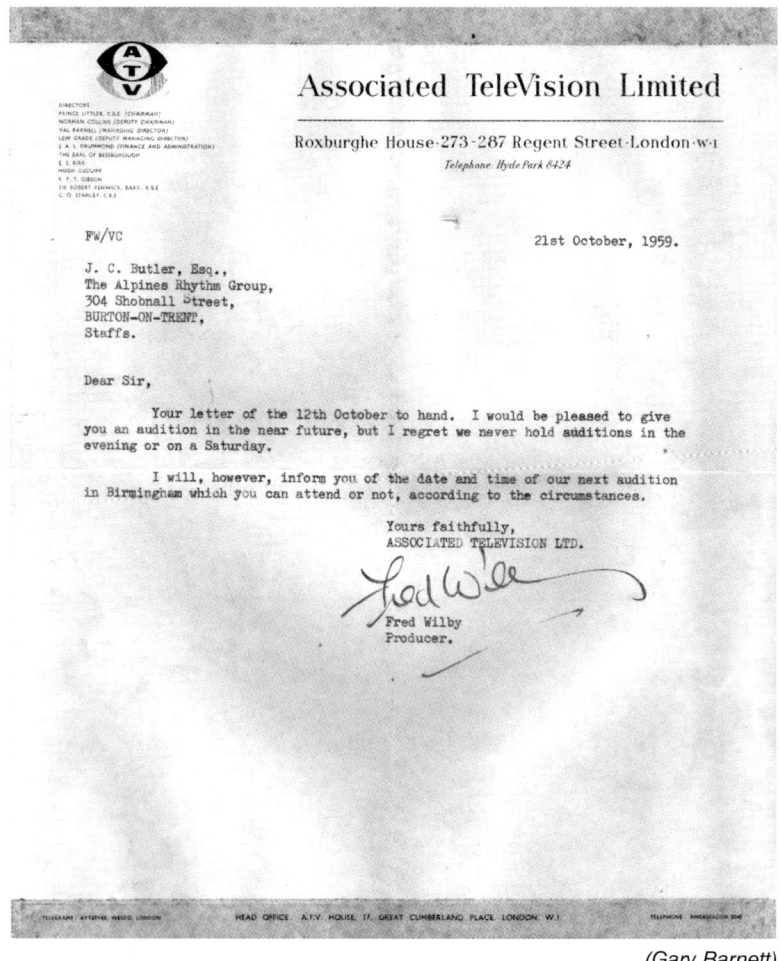

(Gary Barnett)

By July, 1962 the group were ready to turn professional and plans were put in place for the lads to become part of the British invasion of the Hamburg nightspots. They would no doubt have encountered The Beatles during that particular excursion, but as events turned out it was not to be.

The Jubilee gigs continued, with their success starting to create interest from others in the music industry. The lads were now starting to play support to some of the acts on Reg Calvert's roster, including the ever-young Joe Brown, who they were more than impressed with. Not so The Honeycombs whose gimmick was that they had a female drummer. The fact that, apparently, many of her comtempories didn't particularly rate her abilities with the skins didn't help endearing her to fellow musicians. When The Honeycombs turned up late for a Jubilee gig in 1964 she didn't have a set of drums with her, and Tony Tipper reluctantly agreed to allow her the use of his, pointing out that the one hit wonders "didn't go down too well' with the patient crowd.

Tony was slightly less reluctant to hand over the prized percussion instruments to our old friend Phil Seamen when the band appeared with him. Tony was handed back the drums stool after the maestro had completed his session to find that his skins were now adorned with cigarette burns from Phil's ever-present cigarette.

Reg Calvert's extrovert nature has been well documented elsewhere. As well as taking care of a number of the young groups doing the club circuit in the UK, he also personally housed a number of them at his *Clifton Hall Music Academy* in Rugby. Within the confines of the former stately home he would keep the lads and lasses, included occasional visitors such as *The Alpines*, entertained by holding 'gunfights', recalled by Ken Ratcliffe.

"He would drop fireworks into tubes and aim them at people".

None of the former group members have trouble recalling another one of his favourite routines: "He used to eat whole 'cards' of peanuts" the ones that hang up behind bars with perhaps a dozen, or more, packets on them. Each time another packet was removed more of a scantily clad female underneath would be revealed, remember?

"He would appear in the dressing room afterwards, and astound the group by dropping his kecks and lighting his farts!".

Reg's wife was always ready to become the centre attention due to her habit of attending gigs with her pet monkey, William, perched on her shoulder.

The Alpines' gimmick was their Swiss-style garb, and fresh from the snow covered slopes of the Alps they would bound on stage with green waistcoats covering brown shirts, shorts, climbing boots and thick socks, all topped off with nifty green titfers. The singer stood out from the others with red shorts and a white shirt and mauve waistcoat. A well-rehearsed comedy routine would be staged throughout the performance. The Alpines, along with other local groups, had their own fan club, complete with newsletter and membership cards, run by Carol Hudson from her home in Albert Village.

Their continued support of some of the more r'n'b-based groups was starting to influence individuals, with a call for more r'n'b numbers to be included in the group's set from some quarters, until the famed 'musical differences' started to have their effect. Doug Perry took his leave from the band to look at the bigger picture, moving to London and eventually landing a spot in one of *Joe Loss's* bands. This didn't work out and he took on a job writing for the 'teentastique' *Fabulous* magazine, later *FAB* and later still *FAB 208*. Further down the line he helped entertain on ocean liners, a long way away from his Burtonian roots.

By this stage it was obvious to all involved that The Alpines had now reached the end of their natural life, though it had been eventful and a fantastic experience for all involved. There aren't many round this town that can say they've appeared with *The Beatles*, although none of the former Alpines that I have spoken to would ever dream of actually boasting about it.

With Mike Everest now leaving the fold it was time for that new direction, and the lads took on a new vocalist in the shape of Jim Waddell, emerging, ready to entertain, as The Memphis Five.

***Memphis Five:** (l-r)* **Ken Ratcliffe, Bob Bishop, Tony Tipper, Jim Waddell and Bob Faulkner.** *Warming up film fans at Burton Odeon Cinema.* *(Chris Roe)*

The new look band went back to playing predominantly local gigs in 1964. and had dropped the semi-comic image (as the Alpines they were often billed as "The Crazy Gang Show"), for more sober, and obviously Beatle-influenced, suits and black ties. They fulfilled many hometown engagements, including a spot entertaining cinema-goers at the old *Burton Odeon* in Guild Street, as the picture shows, taking the 'stage' (from where go-go dancing young beauties would strut their stuff miming to pop hits at the *Saturday Morning Picture* shows) between the cheesy adverts for local jewellers and restaurants, and the main showing. Still ambitious, and channelled through Chris Roe's management, they later managed to secure recording time in *Pye Records'* London studio following an audition in a pub. Setting off for the big day they all clambered into the group's J2 van, which by now had seen more than its fair share of action along the roads and lanes of Britain. Chris Roe recalls the hair-raising adventure: "(the van) had virtually no brakes or steering, inevitably they couldn't find their way, so they stopped and asked a policeman". In a fashion that shows how far removed we now are from those days, the bobby offered to lead the way through the Metropolis.

"We followed him in the van, lurching precariously over the highway, trying to avoid using the brakes".

The subsequent session was overseen by top muso Tony Hatch, and The Memphis Five set up and played in front of him, dropping into the set one or two of their own, self-penned tunes. It was to be some time later that Chris and the lads heard a familiar chord progression over the start of *Petula Clarke's* 'Downtown', which they instantly recognised as one of their own compositions which had obviously been found another home!

This excursion to the capital resulted in the band often being advertised as "Burtons only professional recording group", which is how they were advertised for a Jubilee Hall appearance with **The Dimensions** in January, 1965. Things could get mighty confusing sometimes, as exactly one week later Shane Spencer and the Casuals were described in exactly the same words in a *Burton Daily Mail* advertisement for another Jubilee show.

Once they had re-established themselves, the group were found work further a field, very often having to put on two shows at two different venues on the same night, with two or even three appearances at each venue. This is where the wear and tear on the van, and the performers, began to build up. It was not unusual (as Tom Jones would have said), for them to appear at Willington Power Station Club, complete their set, load up the battle bus, and carry their sweaty bodies all the way over to Stafford's Top of the World for more of the same. At the end of the night they would then trek all the way back to Burton for a couple of hours kip before work. Bands doing the rounds all over the country at this time would have been more than familiar with this routine.

Supporting some of the top groups could bring its own problems; Chris recalls the time the group supported *The Hollies* at Coventry's Lanchester School of Technology. The hall had two dance areas, one which the main draw, The Hollies, were to appear in front of, and the other the support's area. As they were already part of their set, The Memphis Five belted out a few choice Hollies numbers by way of warming up the crowd for the main event, and were duly met with a robust round of booing and hissing. The Coventry fans obviously didn't take too kindly to what, they thought, were these upstarts trying to outdo the main event, although this was not the case with The Hollies themselves, "The Hollies liked them, they stopped and watched the whole set".

Horninglow Flower Show *– Kens new pink Fender bass, with new addition on a free transfer from The Casuals, Tony McKerracher (extreme right hand side).* *(Chris Roe)*

Every opportunity to display the band's talents was taken up, word of mouth being, by far, the best advert for any performing band. This included events like the *Horninglow Flower Show*, this type of show was common in 60s Burton, it would give the horticulturists the chance to display their green fingers and local bands an opportunity to liven up proceedings, the chance for local youngsters to let off a bit of steam (though the young chap at the front has just found out what a powerful combination a Gibson 335 and a Vox AC30 amplifier can be).

Amongst The Memphis Five's successes was third place in a national talent contest held in London. Once again they tried for a spot on *Opportunity Knocks*, as the fall out from a successful appearance on the show could prove very lucrative to all concerned. An audition was arranged for the band at the *Gaumont* in Nottingham, with the band travelling over in style via their latest acquisition, a Hillman Pullman. Arriving early with time to kill, they decide to pay a visit to the boozer (as you do). With the lunchtime seemingly well spent they set up in front the main man himself, Hughie Green, who, accompanied by a few others, was ready to give the thumbs up - or down. When they were ready to roll guitarist Bob Bishop counted them in: one, two, three, four…, the subsequent sound emanating from the bands rig was so loud that the shock waves almost toppled the table Hughie and Co. were sat behind.

They heard at a later date that they had been successful, possibly when Hughie Green was fully able to hear again, though sadly the band had to turn the programme down. During the interim period vocalist, Jim Waddell, had got married and had set off for a new life with his wife in New Zealand. They tried desperately for a replacement, but to no avail, so we shall never know whether they would have managed to get the *Clapometer* off the scale by audience reaction, or perhaps by turning everything up to 11.

For a short while drummer Tony Tipper, played for Pro band **Johnny Washington and the Congressmen** (not to be confused with **Johnny Congress and his Whitehousemen**), with Clive Johnson stepping up to do the business behind the kit. But after six months Tony decided to return to the fold. Meanwhile the support slots continued apace.

Memphis Five at Rolleston, (l-r): **Tony McKerracher, Bob Bishop, Jim Waddell, Clive Johnson** *and* **Ken Ratcliffe**. *The name of the little boy on the tractor in the stream is not known.* *(Ken Ratcliffe)*

The Memphis Five were due to warm up for **The Merseybeats** at the Co-op Hall in Nuneaton, as the main act had not yet shown up the band went on stage to get things going, on completion of the set there was still no sign of the Merseysider's, so on the Memphis Five went again.

With the crowd's patience now starting to wear a bit thin they went through the numbers again with as much enthusiasm as they could. When it eventually dawned on them that The Merseybeats weren't going to show up, the lads reluctantly went back onstage for a third time eventually retreating back to the dressing rooms amid growing disquiet amongst the gathered throng, The Merseybeats, for reasons now long forgotten, never did turn up.

Eventually, as often happens, the band lost its impetus, alhough they were active during 1966 with, amongst other things, an appearance as part of the *Tech. College Rag Procession*. However, the era of the Beatle inspired 'beat groups', and with it The Memphis Five and their contemporaries, was drawing to a close. With the *Summer of Love* and *Flower Power* just around the corner, the emphasis switched to an entirely different approach to music and lifestyle.

Somethin' Else.......

Top Tune Time for *The Falcons* at Burton Town Hall, back,
l-r): *Trevor Causer, Nigel Barnett, Gary Barnett* and *Mike Burman*.
Front: *Johnny Butler* (Johnny Byrd)   *(Gary Barnett)*

There were many more groups aligned to Burton's arsenal of "beat merchants" during this most prolific musical period. For the most part they were quite content to showcase their talents on the live circuit, combining a day job with the routine of going straight from their place of work to local clubs and pubs; The 76, Co-op Hall in Byrkley Street, Jubilee Hall, in addition to the church halls. **The Falcons** first gig was held round the corner from the West Street home of the Barnett brothers, Gary and Nigel, (lead and rhythm guitar respectively), at the Winshill Church Hall. Initially known as just the Falcons, they became **Johnny Byrd and the Falcons** when Johnny Butler joined the crew after parting with The Alpines. Almost every band in the land had a vocalist who went by the name of Johnny, be it Byrd, Carr, Dean, Peel, Tremayne or Washington. The list is endless, though often there appeared to be some historical connection, often some key figure in American history, perhaps hoping to give the group an air of colonial mystique. In Johnny Byrd's case he did insist on the spelling containing the 'y', later adopted by USA's 12-string favourites *The Byrds*.

The Falcons gained a well earned reputation around the town for their live shows, with a equal sprinkling of *Shadows* numbers such as 'FBI' and, once the word was out, The Beatles, who's 'Please, Please Me' was accompanied by some fine harmonica from Mr. Byrd. Following on from the Fab Fours' lead, they also penned, and played, their own songs including one called 'Slow Moving'. Gary Barnett points out "(Shadows and Beatles) covers were all well and good, but if you wanted to get them up and dancing Chuck Berry was the stuff". The *Burton Daily Mail* seemed to like The Falcons too. A review of one of their 76 performances saw them established as "firm favourites at the club…another brilliant performance by The Falcons."

They tried for an audition with the now defunct, Oriole Records, a prominent outlet for new and up and coming groups during the beat heyday, but were unsuccessful. Eventually the band's drummer, Mike Burman, left for pastures new amongst the jazz fraternity, though he also popped up amongst the folkies as we will hear later. Clive Johnson took his place before his own stint with the Memphis Five began.

Like any number of local bands, travelling was part of the normal routine, Twycross Country Club was often frequented by the Burton and South Derbyshire music men, though they often took second place to the main event, which was normally a full on punch up. Many Leicester lads used to like to frequent the place, and it wouldn't be long before they had found someone to fall out with. On one occasion the local Vicar was again caught up in the ruck - well they say He moves in mysterious ways.

After seeing Joe Brown performing complete with a Gibson 335 semi-acoustic (Chuck Berry's favoured weapon of choice), Johnny decided no other guitar would do. He approached Norman Willey, of *Normans Music Shop*, and arranged HP terms on the 150 Guinea beauty, by all accounts the first in Burton. This was such

Johnny Byrd receives his treasured possession from Norman Willey
(Gary Barnett)

a newsworthy event that *The Mail* went along and took a snap of the handover once the machine had arrived.

The band eventually went their separate ways, though, like many of their generation, they never quite left the music behind. Popping up here and there at one of the many 'get togethers' organised by one of the 60s 'band of brothers', it's safe to say that the majority of those involved liked nothing more than getting a good response from their audience, after all isn't this what its all supposed to be about, everybody having fun? The Falcons last performed (at the time of writing) as The Falcons in 1991, at one of a series of charity fund-raisers organised by Tony Mulcahy, alongside a number of their old contemporaries. Sadly Johnny Butler passed away a few years later, aged only 52.

Taking advantage of some early tuition in the form of rudimentary guitar chords from Judith Aldous at St. Aiden's church hall, a young Kevin Kent started to increase his prowess on the instrument via further help from Terry 'Maz' Mason.

It wasn't too long before Kevin was invited to become part of Terry's group, **Steve Conway and the Strangers**. One of the lads, David Clay, was moving on, so Kevin stepped up as rhythm guitarist, teaming up with Terry, Chris Webster, Ian Jackson and vocalist Mick Payne.

Home base for the band was to be the *Byrkley Arms* in Byrkley Street, for no other reason than that Ian Jackson, the group's bass player, lived there. From here they practiced and did the usual round of the town's venues, including one particular gig at the Drill Hall, which Kevin remembers well.

"We needed a pole to hang the curtain backdrop off", as the Drill Hall was spartan, to say the least, with no such provision supplied.

"We had a scaffold pole at St. Aidens, which was ideal for the job".

Having no transport to hand at that particular time they came up with a splendid idea.

"Two of us got on our pushbikes and grabbed each end of the 20 ft pole, then started cycling from Shobnall to the Drill Hall".

Inevitably they were stopped by a policeman, on the corner of Shobnall Street. Maybe the bobby was having a good day, or maybe he was just not very observant, but he overlooked the fact that the two intrepid cyclists were linked by 20 feet of steel trying to negotiate the towns busy roads, and let them on their way.

By the January of 1962 Kevin became part of the Overseal based **Dean Rivers and the Crusaders**. As well as performing around the town they, like many others, started to perform all over the midlands. *The Moors Arms* in Appleby Magna, was one venue, many Burton musicians recall playing there. Kevin is no exception, though his reason for having such a vivid memory of the place has nothing to do with music. Watching form the relative safety of the stage you were, in Kevin's words "guaranteed a good scrap - it used to resemble a cowboy free for all".

In quieter moments, one job that always seemed to become Kevin's responsibility would be the completion of the *Performing Rights* form after each live show. It may well have been a pain at the time, but the *Musicians' Union*, which held monthly meetings in Burton at *The Dog Inn*, insisted that each group received reasonable rates for their time.

Eventually becoming one of the, by now, large number of groups coming under the guidance of Reg Calvert through Liverpool-based agent Bill Tester, the lads turned on the style. With a choice of two stage outfits, one a turquoise jerkin, black trousers, white shirt and dickie bow, the other a silver lamé suit (gold for the singer), and again the dickie bow, they began to write some of their own stuff. The Grand Finale to any show would be Roger Anderson's blindfold drum solo, which never failed to bring the house down.

Playing for the last time with The Crusaders at Swadlincote Rink in December, 1963, Kevin left the group. They continued for a short while, though the last time Dean Rivers appeared in Burton under that name was probably at Winshill in 1964.

After seeing an advert placed by a group for a vocalist in a local paper, Tony Mulcahy replied and found himself invited for an audition. Along he went and gave them his best rendition of Joe Brown's 'Pictures of You', the rest of the band liked his style and he was in. His band mates were 'Maz' Mason, Ian Jackson, Tony Draycott, Brian Draycott and Chris Webster, which some among you will recognise as former Steve Conway and the Strangers. The band, who had since become **Karl Justice and the Jury**, were subsequently added to the roster of local acts on the bill of the 1962 *Pop Jamboree* at the Jubilee Hall. With no time to think about nerves, the young Tony, only six months out of school, found himself performing in front of the packed hall. This introduction to the heady world of pop did nothing to deter him; he thoroughly enjoyed himself, and all it did do was instil a lifelong love of performing live.

The group soon had themselves their own fan club; the numbers being boosted by combining hometown gigs with those further a field, including work in the two hotbeds of their respective beat scenes, London and Liverpool. The lads needed to set themselves apart from the sheer number of competitors around at the time and, as we have seen from The Alpines, a gimmick was seen to be the answer. To tie in with the name the lads devised a routine, normally done during the second half of the set, during which the musicians behind Karl would each don a Judges wig and ask him, dressed as a leather clad 'baddy', questions about various misdemeanours. The routine may well have been influenced by American comedian Dewey *"Pigmeat"* Markham, who's 'Here Comes the Judge' was later

Karl justice and the Jury   *(Tony Mulcahy)*

taken into the charts by *Shorty Long* in 1968. It could just as easily have been an influence on *The Specials* on-stage court routine in the early 80s.

Tony recalls playing at some of the local venues, backing up comments made by others about the Burton Town Hall as a venue for rock groups, the acoustics of the place were just not suited to amplified guitar music, and few of the groups who appeared there were too impressed by the sound quality. By all accounts the louder you tried to turn up your amp to be heard, the more the sonic quality got lost amongst the void below the roof space. The Drill Hall is another place that holds no place in the hearts of any of the musicians who have appeared there: the sound quality was dreadful and the hall itself "big and cold".

The band went through one name change to become **Karl and the Teddy Bears**, although this was fairly short lived. Some of the band went on to form **The Queue** (sorry about that one!), but Tony struck out on his own to become a cabaret artist, spending time in the US. Now returned to these shores, he still likes to be involved in the music scene.

Duke Demont and the Dominators appear to be the Burton band who hold the all comers record for the most miss-spellings of their name (I've probably just done it myself). *Dermont, Demant* and *Demart* are just a few examples, though, to confuse matters even further, they appeared as **The Detonators** in later life, whether through a genuine error by advertisers or, as may well be the case, deliberate mischief making, will perhaps never be known. Contained within their number, doubling up as driver and manager, was one of Burton's most naturally funny men, the late comedian *Al Rich*, now very much missed around the town. The Duke himself was none other than Graham McMurragh, with, allegedly, the Dominators part of the name being taken from the name of the old double decker Corporation buses that used to circulate the town, the *Dennis Dominator*.

When the Duke and the lads played the Norman Cochran Youth Club All those interested were invited, according to the advert, to 'see their fab get up', anybody remember what exactly the 'get up' was?

Tim Kennedy was a 12 year old pupil at Anglesey School when he first took up drumming. He was taken along to *Normans* - where else? - and as a result became the proud possessor of £12 worth of drum kit. I must confess that I never before realised that a drum kit had to be tuned, its just one of those things that never entered my head (and they reckon drummers are thick!). Tim's method of tuning was typical of the "do it yourself" attitude which prevailed at the time "I used to have to hold it in front of the fire to tighten it up!"

Tim took up his chance after replacing Graham Davidson, the drummer with **Ricky Topaz and the Diamonds**, whose guitarist was a South Derbyshire lad, Ken Jackson, the uncle of another South Derbyshire lad, (who is often wrongly said to be from Burton) *Joe Jackson*. Who would pen the late 70s classic 'Is She Really Going Out With Him'. "Pretty women going out with gorillas in my street?" They sure are Joe.

Ricky Topaz and The Diamonds

Tim recalls an incident with which most band members would be familiar. While on the road after a northern gig they decided to stop off at a Chinese takeaway for some grub. "One of the locals, a big lad, was in there. Recognising the band members he had just been watching he said "good gig lads". We continued talking to him, but soon one of the group, who was well known for it, disappeared outside and proceeded to chat up the big fella's missus". The local left the shop and within seconds our hero came steaming back in, leapt over the counter and ran off out the back, closely followed by the shop owner who was brandishing a meat cleaver. The local lad obviously took umbrage with his girlfriend being chatted up.

"Another member of the band who had been outside suddenly appeared with his nose now at 90 degrees to the rest of his face, bleeding profusely, followed by the big lad who was non too pleased."

Tim, thinking on his feet, decided to act quickly, and leapt up and got the man in a headlock. "Hit him somebody," he shouted, only to be met with silence and a total lack of action from his band mates. The man quickly recovered his advantage and proceeded to "sort the whole lot of 'em out". They all managed to make their escape, hastily boarded their van and fired her up ready for the getaway, enthusiastically sent on their travels by an extremely irate northener brandishing a piece of wood that he was now in the process of beating the van with.

The line-up of Ricky Topaz and the Diamonds included Reg Bloss, Brian Reed, Terry Jackson and Keyboardist Harold Lee Lord. The band, like most others, performed mainly covers, especially Screaming Lord Sutch stuff. Once the Beat explosion of the early 60s had died away, the band would diversify, take stock and emerge from the latter end of the 60s as, firstly, **The Expressions**, later still dropping the last 's'. To become just **The Expression**, now containing within their number the formidable talents of bass player Mick Dyche, another one of Burton's unsung musical sons, who has appeared with some of the finest exponents of popular music and is still much in demand as a London-based session musician. Harold Lord later teamed up with Moira's Steve Sharratt and performed on the popular *New Faces* Talent Show as comedy duo **Lewis and Lord**.

The three groups in the following advert were all regulars on the Burton circuit. The Coalville-based **Outlaws** were also regular performers at the 76, and supported **The Bachelors** at the Jubilee Hall in 1963. The Sapphires, as well as appearing at the 76, cropped up at just about every place it was possible to pop up in, including the regular Sunday afternoon events held 'al fresco' on Shobnall Fields during the summer. The Kavemen's drummer, Dave Hughes, recalls these Sunday afternoon outings. On one occasion, sitting behind his drums he looked up mid-song to see the gaunt figure of a certain Phil Seamen watching him, accompanied by his Alsatian dog. It's difficult to decide which one of the two onlookers would be the most unnerving for any percussionist.

Often being billed as The Sapphires featuring Ian Little, the band were described as "one of Burton's most promising groups", providing "modern rhythm music" for a 1962 gig with The Falcons at the Co-op Hall. The Sapphires' bass player, Brian Kite, would later pop up in The Expression, replacing Mick Dyche.

Burton Round Table

IN AID OF FREEDOM FROM HUNGER CAMPAIGN

ROCK 'N' TWIST
BARBECUE

THE BROADHOLME

Saturday, June 29th — 7.30 to 11.45

The Outlaws Rock Group   —   The Atlantix
The Saphires

Licensed Bars   Barbecued Food   Side Shows   Car Park

Tickets 2/6 . . . . Admission at Gate 4/-

Tickets from Round Table Members and Norman's, New Street

This space kindly donated by Messrs Ordish & Hall Ltd., Station Street, Burton

---

A full 22 years before Live Aid, Burton groups show they not only have talent, but also a conscience.

(Burton Mail)

Mick Woodward (1st left), with **The Unknown**

(Mick Woodward)

The obvious youthfulness of many of the groups around the town at this time meant that they were perhaps relying, especially in their earlier gigs, on enthusiasm more than ability.

Mick Woodward remembers his introduction to the wonderful world of pop. "My dad bought me a Beatles record in 1963, at the same time I got my first tatty acoustic guitar". Saving up his paper round money he would scour the second hand shops on the lookout for a suitable replacement.

Eventually linking up with buddies, Ken Gale, Phil Hughes and Eric Cox, all from Dovecliffe Grammar School, he formed **The Unknown**. Their first "gig" was a performance in front of the Saturday morning pictures crowd at the Odeon, a baptism of fire if ever there was one. Mick has remained with the live music fraternity in Burton, more of which later.

The Spidermen were a combination of some Burton-based musicians Pete Youngman, Gary Fletcher (who have both already had a mention), and bass player Andy Clarke and two Derby lads, Geoff Whittaker and Mike Grewcock. They were taken under Mick Finley's management and by Christmas, 1961, the lads had secured a spot at London's showcase *2 'I's Coffee Bar*, the ideal place for groups trying to catch the eye of the nearby Soho based talent scouts. Not forgetting to keep the hometown sweet before departing by wishing everyone, via the medium of the *Burton Mail*, 'A Happy New Year'. Pete, after doing the rounds as a musician at the Burton venues, would later live in London, where he became a vital scout for Gordon Band, checking live bands to recommend them to Gordon. Ever wondered just why so many quality bands later appeared at the 76?

'THE SPIDERMEN'
WITH
Pete Youngman

Personal Manager :—
MICHAEL A. FINLEY,
92 MALVERN STREET,
BURTON UPON TRENT,
Staffs.

While I was researching for this book I was constantly told that I must have a word with Pete, he has been involved in playing, and putting on, live music in this town for a long time. It was only when I finally got round to meet him that I realised that I had already encountered him many, many times in Burton - he crops up at just about every local gig, and is still performing all over the place.

Pete, quite rightly, points out that we don't seem to value just what talent we have produced here musically as much as we should, and I hope what I am doing here helps to redress that imbalance a little bit.

Small Club...Big Noise

76 *Stage area, and new extension, 1963*   (*Arthur Phillips*)

By May, 1963, the dominance of the pop charts by The Beatles, and *Beatlemania*, was in full swing. 'From Me To' *You* was the number one UK single in April, followed up with the Merseysiders' declaration of intent LP, 'Please, Please Me', with its mixture of original songs and covers, and Ringo looking down on us from the cover, still resplendent with his pre *Mop Top* rocker's quiff. Most groups, if they were not to be left behind, took note, and changed their act, and their image accordingly.

Always ahead of the game, Gordon Band had given the *76* a facelift, informing the town's music fans with the following broadcast:

"Special Announcement – The management of the club takes great pleasure in announcing the opening of their extension, which will provide more dancing and seating space, together with, a little later on, another bar."

Thus signalling the onset of the club's heyday. It would become part of the circuit for touring groups from far and wide, with some mighty players appearing within the building's small confines. In a definite move away from being just a local club putting on local bands, the 76 was now presenting predominantly Midlands-based acts, although Gordon Band was also establishing connections with agents countrywide, and they were sending him down some of the top acts, the popularity of which was reflected in the full membership books. Being a Licensed club, strict membership rules applied, and a 76 membership card was a prized possession, giving the owner access to some fine entertainment in addition to the opportunity for forming life long friendships - not to mention the chance for amorous encounters with the opposite sex. The card still has such prominence that it has, in many cases, survived all sorts of life's upheavals, and become a memento of times past. The production of such a card in a crowded Burton pub can still, to this day, draw a sizeable crowd of admirers, each having their own particular memories of the place.

The Kavemen at the *76*   (John Bisbrown)

The new look club quickly became a favourite with the touring bands, and most got a welcome reception. Although in many cases, they were playing exactly the same stuff as the local bands, but they came from more exotic places like Birmingham or Mansfield and that added to their fascination.

Gary Levene and the Avengers, were a Birmingham band who managed to put in a total of four appearances at the club during this ground breaking year. Being asked back was a sure sign that they had been well received.

Within their ranks was one *Roy Wood*, a man who has the undoubted ability to turn out classic pop tunes. Wood moved on to **Mike Sheridan and the Nightriders**, another Birmingham based bunch, who also put in a few performances in Burton during their time. Later, of course, Roy was one of the lead members of The Move, who were showman in every sense of the word, and would also play in Burton. Maybe Roy likes the place, and now living near the town he is often spotted round and about, still every bit the Rock'n'Roller.

Another son of the second city, **Denny Laine**, turned up with his **Diplomats**, giving the lucky lads and lasses present on the night a taste of things to come, when he would team up with a Mr & Mrs Paul McCartney to form the post-Beatles *Wings*. The bloke behind the drums that night would also go on to provide the percussion that would back up the string arrangements for *ELO, Bev Bevan*.

The *Fab Four's* home town seemed to be an endless source of beat groups, only to happy to supply the nation with as much of that fabulous *Merseybeat* as they could handle, even if one or two of them were stretching the geographical limits of the city beyond the bounds of credibility. Definitely Scouse were **The Big Three**, described at the time as 'loud, aggressive and visually appealing", everything *The Beatles* were before they were drowned out by their fans screams.

The *Big Three* had a pretty raucous stage act, with the *Guinness* music guide 'Who's Who of Sixties Music' pointing out that "their characteristic unruliness proved their undoing". Their first time at the 76, September 63, was as one of Mr. Epstein's protégé's, Epstein also tried to smarten them up and get them to sing "pop ditties" which they were obviously not too comfortable with.

Bass player, Johnny Gustafson jumped ship in 1964 for fellow Liverpudlians The Merseybeats, returning with them to the club a couple of times before heading off for duties with many other bands, including one version of *Roxy Music*. By the time of their last appearance in the club, in 1965, the game was almost up for them.

The Mojo's were another Liverpool group who had regular personnel changes throughout their career. The picture of the group shows the original line up, and this would be the one that played the club in 1963. The band returned in 1966 with new personnel. Taking over on drums was Ansley Dunbar, who later enjoyed a stint with *John Mayall's Blues Breakers* and, after that, the Mother of Invention himself, Frank Zappa. The ladies (and possibly some of the men) who were in the audience that night in 1966 would have been unaware that they were also watching the future star of macho 70s TV nonsense *The Professionals*, Lewis Collins, on bass, his dad being manager of the group.

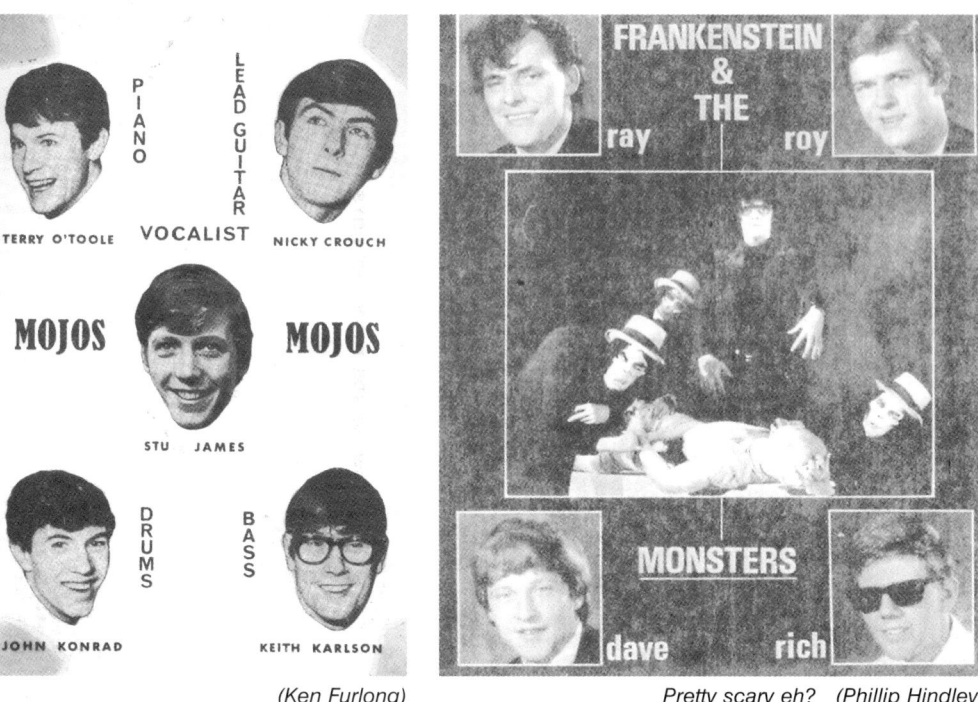

PIANO

LEAD GUITAR

VOCALIST

TERRY O'TOOLE   NICKY CROUCH

MOJOS   MOJOS

STU   JAMES

DRUMS

BASS

JOHN KONRAD   KEITH KARLSON

FRANKENSTEIN
&
THE
ray   roy

MONSTERS
dave   rich

(Ken Furlong)   *Pretty scary eh?   (Phillip Hindley)*

Taking a quick cross section of some of the acts who also played the club this year, we find Beatles connections all over the place. **Johnny Gentle** had the distinction of taking The Beatles on the road with *him* as his backing band in 1960, while **Rory Storm and the Hurricanes** had a fantastic reputation in their own right. Now minus their most illustrious performer, they were just, well, Rory Storm and the Hurricanes, another Merseyside Beat group.

A pre–Dozy, Beaky, Mick and Tich **Dave Dee**, brought his **Bostons** down with him, while 'out Sutching' Lord Sutch in the theatrical department were Manchester's **Frankenstein and his Monsters**.

Our neighbours up the road in Derby were able to send us down a constant supply of bands, among them The Vibrons. They had built up a steady reputation from performances all over town, and played support in Burton, and elsewhere, for some of the bigger name bands. They managed to establish a fan club from Burton, principally through their 76 Club appearances. They were regulars on stage at the club throughout 1963,64 and 65.

Guitarist Paul Henman recalls their visits, and remembers the period with great affection. "We had nothing but great receptions whenever we played in Burton". Paul still has his original 1952 Fender Telecaster guitar, and recollects the fee paid to the band, "around £8 to £10 for a pub gig - I think the 76 Club paid about £15". The extra would help cover the expense of travelling from Derby, though Paul reflects, "In those days Burton seemed a hell of a long way from Derby".

He also recollects the rudimentary electrics that were utilised in their cheap - often home made - equipment, which provided some amusing "side shows" during performances.

"On our very first large gig at the (old) Derby Assembly Rooms, we were using amps with huge magnetised speakers and valve driven units. Deep into our first number we were mortified to hear our amps distort and screech, and the sound of two way communications between a police Panda patrol, being taken on a fools' chase around the streets by some blokes in a stolen car, and the police headquarters." This tended to have the effect of shattering the confidence of the already nervous band members, but Paul has to admit: "The police conversations were hilarious. Our audience thought it was hilarious - we were decidedly unimpressed. Some urgent re-wiring was called for before we could resume our performance".

*Lipstick traces – **The Vibrons'** van*   *(Paul Henman)*

The Vibrons had just returned from a tour of Scotland with **The Applejacks**, and the group's van was covered in lipstick messages from adoring Scots lasses, although I'm assured by Paul that the Burton girls managed to find space for a few more!

Later the Vibrons would play support to **The Kinks** at the Jubilee Hall in Burton, one of the town's biggest gigs (more of that later).

By 1964 the *Mods and Rockers* seaside encounters were whipping up the nation into a storm of indignation, stoked by ample media coverage. What was little more than a few testosteroned teenagers letting off a bit of steam was transformed, mainly through newspapers, into a headlong slide by this once great land into the morass.

Locally it didn't seem to be quite so cut and dried (possibly blow dried in the case of the mods). Where once rows of motorbikes lined the pavement outside the Mocambo Café, now stood rows of gleaming scooters, though *The Wimpey Bar* in Station Street was the preferred meeting point for the faces before heading on down to the 76 Club.

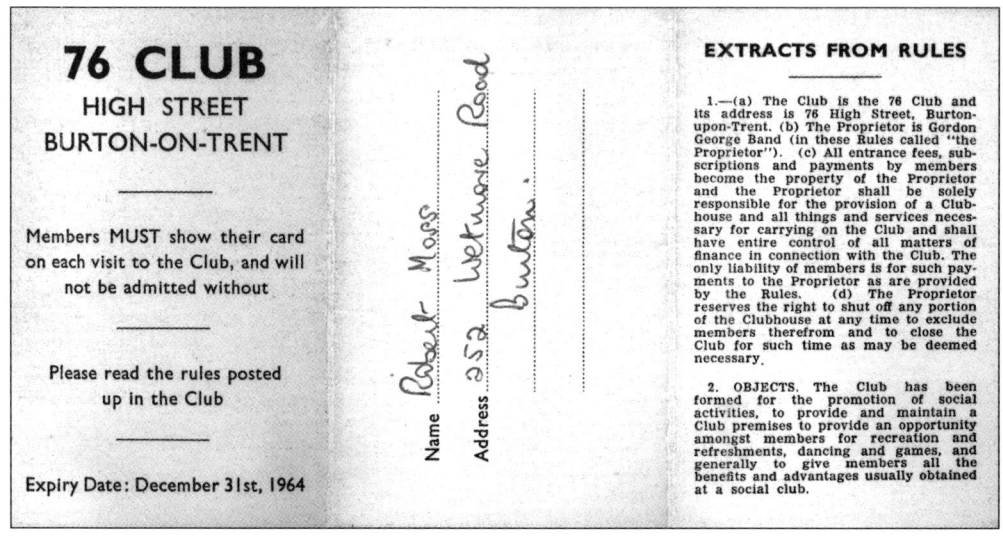

1964 vintage 76 Membership Card. (Bob Moss)

Many of the, would be, combatants were often in reality good friends. Tim Emmerson, one of the old Mocambo regulars, points out that, if you were out and about and you spotted someone broken down by the roadside, be it scooter boy or biker, you would stop to help them out, and expect them to do likewise. Both gangs found an unlikely supporter in the form of Burton's police chief, Superintendent Edwards, who, you may recall, was not so keen on the rock and rollers earlier on. In 1964, he had this to say in *The Burton Mail*: "There are so many of them and no one will do anything for them."

Not quite so sympathetic was an Army spokesman. In response to the expected outcry to call them all up and nail some sense into 'em, he pointed out that: "the Army didn't want mods or rockers, it wanted intelligent and dependable types."

The steady stream, week in week out, of quality live acts continued at the club, like Shane Fenton and the Fentones, the pre-*glam* rock vehicle for Bernard Jewry's vocal talents, before he found a black leather glove somewhere and re-invented himself as moody Alvin Stardust.

Some special talents were on display, a school teacher at Yardley's Whittingham Oval Primary, one Spencer Davis, travelled with his group **The Saints** to play the club twice in 1964. Within the year he would be discovering the twin talents of Muff Winwood and his majestically voiced brother Steve, and forming up the powerful *Spencer Davis Group*.

Fellow Brummies **Keith Powell and the Valets**, were also, like *Spencer Davis*, experimenting with an organ-based sound, and meeting up with two of the group, I found they still have the infectious enthusiasm that was very much part of the make up of 60s musicians. Mal Ritter, The Valets' former drummer, still lives in Birmingham, although guitarist Colin Wood took up the Governments "£10 to Australia" scheme in 1966 - swapping the prospect of a life spent in cold, damp, miserable Britain for the sunshine of Oz must have been a hard decision. Mal's major influence was jazz, he would watch other drummers to see what they did to get their sound and rhythms, thus teaching himself to play.

Colin had witnessed shows by both *Eddie Cochran* and **Gene Vincent** and decided that some of that was for him. After witnessing *Keith Powell and the Vikings* at a youth club, they decided to form up a group themselves, later teaming up with Keith and progressing up to the point where they had within their ranks an organ player, Mal Ford, and a saxophonist, John Gainer. The inclusion of these instruments was very innovative for those days, and provided a rare treat for the 76 Club regulars with covers of *Smokey Robinson* stuff and provided, I would imagine, a welcome distraction from the usual beat stuff.

Keith Powell and the Valets
– (l-r): Mal Ritter, Keith Powell, Mal Ford, Colin Wood, John Richards and Phil Gainer.
(Mal Ritter)

The group, and this is a common thing amongst bands at that time, had a very professional outlook: "No drinks on stage, all onstage on time, no noise from the band before the start and all turning up regularly, and on time, for practice".

This was a common thread amongst the Burton bands also; they were all most professional in their outlook and approach, even though, by necessity, they had to be semi-pro, although I suspect that sometimes the 'no drinks' ruling may have been transgressed – come on we're Burtonians, we were put on this Earth to drink beer!

The *Valets* came under the wing of Norrie Paramour, playing all over with the likes of *The Rolling Stones* and *Helen Sapphiro*, though not always in the most luxurious venues. Colin distinctly recalls appearing at one club and having to perform with his overcoat on indoors! They broke up in 1966, which seems to have been a key point in the changing of the musical atmosphere in Burton, as well as everywhere else.

Birmingham and the Black Country were still well represented at the 76, and Denny Laine was again in attendance with the Diplomats. His last visit with them before he became part of the original **Moody Blues**, who would also pay the town a visit, as we shall hear later. *The Diplomats*, as we have already heard, now included latter day *Saga Radio* DJ Bev Bevan, who would, after a short stint with Roy Wood and The Move, become a member of Jeff Lynne's ELO. It could be argued that, individually, all members of the original ELO had, at some time, performed in Burton, either in these earlier *Brum Beat* combo's or, in Jeff Lynne's case, as part of **The Idle Race**, performing at the *Newton Park Hotel* in Newton Solney – not strictly in Burton. Bev himself, cannot recall his appearance in Burton pointing out: "40 years of gigs and they all merge into one!"

Mike Sheridan's Night Riders were here again, though this time without Roy Wood, so the Burton fans would not be treated to Roy's donning of a blonde wig and, by most accounts, a most impressive, if not too convincing, *Dusty Springfield* impersonation.

Manchester was represented in the form of **Hermans Hermits**, playing the 76 in October, 1964. They were extremely popular at the time having just topped the charts with 'I'm Into Something Good', which itself had just knocked The Kinks off the top of the tree. Two chart toppers performing live in the town in two months - these were heady days for the town's pop music fans! The *Hermits* were later to tour the USA with *The Who*, a puzzling combination. One group had a maniac for a drummer, a guitarist who beat the crap out of his equipment and abused fellow group members and audience alike, the other was led by a bloke who had a lovely smile and nice teeth. Even more bizarrely, the Yanks initially went for the bloke with the teeth in a big way, and it was to be some time later before *The Who* really established themselves over the water.

Perhaps pointing towards what was looming over the horizon on the British music scene, Southend group, **The Paramounts**, advertised, as were many others, as *'Stars of Stage, Screen and TV'*, had among their number both Robin Trower and Gary Brooker, the latter being (allegedly) the composer of Procul Harem's 'Whiter Shade of Pale', Progressive Music – *Prog Rock* - was on the way.

1965, the middle year of the decade that we now know as The Swinging Sixties, seems to have been the natural pivot, in musical terms, for a change in direction. We were still getting the tail end of Merseybeat and a steady flow of beat groups, but their time was almost up. The Merseybeats were here again, but first timers, and fellow Merseysider's, The Dennisons, held an ace up their sleeves. Performing for them that night on the drums was future Emmerdale heartthrob (?!) and top pretend angst-ridden farmer Jack Sugden, aka Clive Hornby.

A major scoop for the club was to secure a visit, in June, from up and coming Belfast lads **Them**, billed as 'The Sensational Hit Parade Stars from Ireland', and led by Van Morrison, who himself was described as "a Ray Charles fan, and apprentice fitter." I think I'm correct in saying that the Ray Charles influence had a bigger effect on Van than being an apprentice fitter. The 76 was now fully operational under the guidance of the Band Enterprises organisation, complete with a man who became part of the legend of the little club, Mr. Tom Broster.

Tom Broster

Many will recall Tom Broster. He was a big tough man, an ex–Liverpool policeman, and on club nights he would be responsible not only for the running of the club but also in dealing with any outbreaks of trouble. He was more than capable of doing this, although its fair to say that there was relatively few problems at this time. However should anybody start getting punchy, big Tom would always deal with them in the same manner: each would be combatant would be placed in a headlock by the big fella, and frog marched unceremoniously to the door. They would not return until the following week, whereupon Tom would inform them that if they stepped out of line again they would receive similar treatment. They very rarely did.

Gordon Band was now dealing with a Nottingham Agency, *Banner Productions*, which was furnishing him with some of the best of the talent that part of the Midlands had to offer, **The Jaybirds** were rebooked after their first appearance, no doubt the mercurial talents of their lead guitarist Alvin Lee, having impressed the Burton audience. Alvin would later become part of *Ten Years After*, appearing at the Woodstock festival in the US. He still lives in the land of the free.

Others on the books of the agency included **The Mansfields** (can you guess where they are from?), who evolved into the aforementioned *Ten Years After*. Their drummer, Keith (Nip) Woodcock, was a salesman for Mansfield's *Carlsboro* music shop, later becoming the managing director of the firm, now known as *Academy of Sound*.

As was the case with most Burton groups, *Buddy Holly* and *The Shadows* were a major influence on many of the visiting bands, and another Mansfield-based outfit, **The Dalesmen**, were no exception.

Tony Dayne and the Dalesmen
– Jeff Coulson, Tony Dayne, Mac Mills, Ken Horner and Geoff Walker.

(Geoff Walker)

However, by the time of their visit to the 76 they had progressed, both in their image and their instruments. Geoff Walker recalls: "We didn't start off with the equipment we really wanted and had to work up to that late. At that time you couldn't just walk into a shop and buy a Fender Stratocaster, it had to come from California". He waited seven weeks for the arrival of his Fender, but he was not disappointed. "Sunburst was the colour - GREAT!"

Adding to the steady stream of beat groups arriving from around the Nottingham/Mansfield area were **The Defiants**, who provide a good example of the change that groups went through to accommodate the "progression" in popular music after the mid–60s. Initially fully paid up members of the beat explosion (check out the sign at the foot of the bass drum), they appeared at the 76 in 1965 and 1966. However, by 1967 they had changed personnel, and name, and embraced the hippy ideal, returning to the club as **The Watermelon Men** (returning even later, in 1971, in another guise, **Emery Chase**).

Rob Woodward joined the new look Watermelon Men as a keyboard player, along with Keith Woodcock on drums. The group toured extensively, picking up elements of the growing hippy movement at 'happenings' along the way. Rob recalls the Summer of Love itself. "In August, 1967 we had a "holiday," kipping in the van on Hampstead Heath, London. We all bought flower power gear and (on our return) wore it at Lincoln Co-op Hall and created a storm! I had green flowered flares, a brown kaftan and a cowbell." It was probably the first time many of the Lincoln crowd had actually seen first hand real hippy "threads."

The Defiants, pre – Watermelon 'Hippy Chic'
– (l-r): Steve Hawkes, Tony Vickerstaff, Ian Robinson, Bob Watton and Brian Hopley.
(Rob Woodward)

Some other Midlands groups' influences were obviously from a different place altogether, though still firmly American in origin. When **The Vigilantes**, appeared at the 76 in 1965, their style of dress indicated, perhaps, a leaning towards a *Beach Boys/surfing* mode of dress and playing. They would soon fall into line with the new way of thinking and playing once the new fashions had reached these shores with its flowing, colourful robes, and little bells ringing.

The Vigilantes *(Alan Dobb)*

During the Summer of 1965 a major pre-occupation with the press, and therefore the population, was still the mods/rockers business. This story has nothing to do with Burton or the 76, though it was probably repeated many times in encounters with the boys in blue. While the beaches of Brighton, and even Skegness and Yarmouth, became the venue for a spot of fisticuffs, some of the less lucky pugilists - or maybe the slowest runners - became the scapegoats for the wrath of the chattering classes.

Up before the courts in Brighton after the Bank Holiday ruck in April, 1965, one young rocker was questioned about his possession of an 'offensive weapon' - a studded leather belt. The arresting officer was trying to convince the court that the belt was going to be put to violent use, and the magistrates asked the young fella why he needed to carry such an offensive item. With as much dignity as the occasion deserved (none), he replied: "I need it to keep my trousers up."

One advert for the 76 from August, 1965 is very intriguing, announcing the visit of a group going by the name of **The High Numbers**. *The Who* had only just changed their name from this - were they due to appear at the club, or was this some other group? We will probably never know.

Many groups from further away were touring the country at the time, trying to establish a foothold in the UK, which was, at this time, the grooviest place on Earth. Australia's **Easybeats** were no exception, and the future recorders of 'Friday on my Mind' put on a show at the club in October. Guitarist George Young possibly took mental notes to pass on to kid brother, Angus, who would himself show us all what a Scottish/Australian hybrid group could do to a tiny rock 'n' roll club a decade later, with *his* group, **AC/DC**.

Towards the end of 1965 *Band Catering Enterprises* announced the closure of The Mocambo Café, to be re-opened as *The Jolly Fryer*, fish and chip shop, restaurant and snack bar. Not mentioned in the advert is its other function, vital to the nearby 76 Club - changing rooms. It was to the dining room extension of the chip shop that the - often bemused - visiting bands were led when they asked: 'Where's the changing rooms?'

1966 is rightly remembered as the year when, to the musical backdrop of some of the finest bands and music this land has ever produced, an East End lad, who could out-football some of today's players in his sleep, complete with a fearsome hangover and, on some occasions, whilst actually being partially inebriated from the usual pre-match snifter, would take on, and beat, the world's best. Bobby Moore epitomised the English 60s mindset, and with it the whole *Swinging 60s* era. It was the period when this country, officially, shook off the drab post war epoch. We were looking forward, not back. With the benefit of hindsight, we can now pinpoint this period musically, as the transition from home grown, wholesome beat/pop groups, on the way to another, altogether different, place.

The burgeoning cultural movement across the Atlantic would have a tremendous influence on popular culture and music. London would no longer be the centre of the universe, the *uber-beatnick* community in California would soon be dictating to the rest of the planet the mantra of peace, love and understanding, and for a short while they convinced us all that they meant it… man!

If we take a glance at the groups appearing in this town in 1966 we can see that many were already ahead of the game. A number of bands visiting Burton had already indulged in that endless shuffle of personnel that is necessary to take on, and - like Bobby's England team - beat the world. New people brought new ideas, and some would eventually emerge, a little later on, as leaders of the pack in the early 70s.

According to the advert in the *Burton Mail* *'an exciting recording group'* were about to hit the 76 stage, going by the name of **The Spectres**. Already fairly well established as a resident *Butlins* band, they were now out on the road, courtesy of the guitarist's dad's ice cream van which ferried them between gigs. However, shortly after their appearance in Burton they felt the need for a change, sensing the shift in emphasis from mere beat music, to a more sophisticated, and drug assisted form: *psychedelia*. They decided to start calling themselves *Traffic*. Unfortunately Steve Winwood and company had already stolen the march on them with that one, letting them know in no uncertain terms that they would regret continuing under that name, so they simply lengthened it to *Traffic Jam*. That was a very short-lived affair, and soon they changed their title again. From now on they would be known simply as Status Quo, who would come in for some serious flack during the ensuing years for, allegedly, churning out the same three chords in various orders. I think they have stood the test of time. How many people in that 76 audience in 1966 realised that they were watching Francis Rossi, Alan Lancaster and John Coughlan in action, the only Quo element missing was the blond haired *riff-meister*, Woking's Mr Rick Parfitt?

The remnants of the more innocent, swinging 60s bands, playing out the last of that era before the big bad world of hippydom and its accompanying drugs came along and blew everybody's minds, played out their own coda's down the club. Including **Bobby Shafto and the Cyclones** - surely one of the best, and daftest, named bands of all time - another visit from The Mojo's and **Brian Poole and his Tremeloes**, who would defy the cull and remain successful for some time to come.

Rugby's **Pinkerton's Assorted Colours** were riding high following a Top Ten hit with 'Mirror Mirror', which charted in January, though they soon would be no more. From the hip world of the London club scene we got the **Graham Bond Organisation**. Bond was in the unfortunate position of being 'too rocky' for his jazz contempories, and 'too jazzy' for the rock fans. He would visit the club again later.

Liverpool's sinister sounding **The Fix** also showed up. They were later forced to change their name due to its drug reference, which led to many club's refusal to book them.

Again, with his eye clearly on what was occurring, both in terms of the music scene, and the youth culture that went with it, Gordon Band decided that it was time for another re-fit. Not long before this he had tried to introduce another element to the town's entertainment, announcing the arrival in September 1966 of *'The 76 Club Dancers'*, basically go-go dancers who were to be found in just about every London Club. He had first tried this out in 1962. There has recently been some discussion in the local press about this, some feeling that Gordon's memory was perhaps not what it was. Not so: they were advertised as *'The Dancing Gordonettes'* in 1962. The Gordonettes were very short lived, as were the 1966 versions, Burton obviously not being ready for that kind of er..sophistication.

Would you believe we are in the 21st Century and arguments are still raging in the town about the acceptability of erotic dancers in this town. Apparently there are people out there who think they are here to enjoy themselves, and we can't have that can we!

The facelift down the club brought it right up to date, Gordon stating his intentions in the local press: "It is our intention to give the members the best entertainment possible...". Not many who found themselves down the club after this date could argue with that. The membership now averaged 1500 people, the place was open five nights a week, with resident 'disc jockey' Ray Phillips providing the soundtrack with his *'Sounds on Location'* on nights when the music wasn't live.

A cabaret evening was introduced on a Sunday night, but again this sort of sophistication proved too much for the Burton audience, it was a very brief enterprise, how many of this town's inhabitants were ready for **Markus** the comedian/conjuror? Not many obviously.

The punters were now able to enjoy "new thermostatically controlled heating and ventilation". Anyone who has ever spent any time in that lovely little club will smile at that one, the only thermostat you ever needed was the one on your own body, the one that made you sweat like a pig whenever you found yourself in the middle of the heaving mass of bodies that made up the audience on a good night. Not only that, apparently the beer was now a product of that delightful 60s concept, 'temperature controlled tank beer'. By the time many people got down the club the quality of the ale really didn't matter, how many you could throw down your neck before last orders was the only item on the agenda.

*The **76 Bar Area** in the early/mid 1960s. With a couple of well dressed gents swapping banter with 76 staff - Frank and Margaret.* *(Frank Thomas)*

Not all the members of the club were happy with their lot, a petition was got together by like-minded individuals in 1966, who were very dissatisfied with the "complete lack, in Burton, of somewhere where youngish people could go" - all 401 of them. They were trying to influence the council in allowing the conversion of the old *Electric Cinema* into a cabaret/night club, which would be known as the *Bamba Social Club*, and, as the petitioners pointed out, would cater for the 'slightly older people'. The occupants of the neighbouring YMCA premises were not too happy; they sent a letter to the council objecting to the scheme. How pleased they must now be that the place is now an amusement arcade.

They would, of course, have welcomed the members of the Burton and District Engineering Society, who had organised a 'Ladies Night' to help warm up a cold November night, with open arms. Those of you who would take this as an invite to a drunken evening watching some oiled up psuedo 'fireman', prancing round and dipping his todger into your vodka and coke would have been sadly disappointed, the entertainment laid on was a film show 'Exploration in the Sahara'. How times change.

Other distractions at the time were a reported sighting in the town of Harry Roberts, on the run from the police for the cold-blooded murder of a some 'Bobbies'. The rumour mill had it that he was seen at Burnaston's Derby Airport, and subsequently given a lift to Burton Railway Station. A huge search was underway, but this eventually proved fruitless.

1966 and all that, possibly Liverpool's **Tiffany and the Thoughts**, *or is it* **Tanya Day**, *or how about* **Miar Davis**? *Answers on a postcard please to: 'It was that long ago nobody cares anymore'. According to Gordon Band it's 'that girl off the telly'. The thermostatically controlled* **76 Club**, *with a packed house.*
(Gordon Band)

One constant rumour that has flourished over the years is that *The Beatles* themselves appeared at the 76 club, not so I'm afraid, though there is a Beatles story to be told. In the early 60s Gordon Band was offered the services of the, then, fairly obscure Liverpool group, *The Beatles* for £25. He turned them down. Gordon, being the businessman that he is, doesn't lose any sleep over the decision, as he pointed out: "I already had enough bands booked".

To round off our look into this year of transition we can place ourselves in front of a band that were, at the time, already deemed as one of the loudest outfits around. **The N'Betweens** (wrongly advertised locally as The In Betweens) were a Wolverhampton based group, caught up on the endless round of touring that sets any group, lucky breaks permitting, on the road to becoming a *supergroup*. When they appeared at the 76 they were a tight unit, having completed the usual stint in the seedy Hamburg nightclubs.

They were shortly to add the vital element that would see them, via a few transitions, take on the known world. Eventually the band acquired the decibel shattering talents of the former **Steve Brett and the Mavericks** guitarist, and human foghorn that is Mr. Neville "Noddy" Holder. The group were guided along their way to success by *Svengali*, Chas Chandler. For many people Christmas would never be the same again – it would have less to do with a beardy, long haired bloke being born and forever be remembered for a bloke with mutton chop sideburns, platform soled brogues, Prince of Wales chequered *Oxford Bags* and a home made top hat covered in glued on mirrors, all accompanied by the former N'Betweenies guitarist - and self styled crappy haired *Superyob* - Dave Hill, electric violin maestro Jimmy Lea and drummer Don Powell. Yes sensation seekers, they went on to become Slade.

For those of you watching in
black and white...
...this one's in Technicolor.

Karl and the Teddy Bears on stage at **Swadlincote Rink**.

(Tony Mulcahy)

Being so close to the boundaries of Burton, places like Swadlincote are often assumed by outsiders to be part of the town, much to the annoyance of the Swaddies! After all we don't even share the same language do we?! Similarly, in the case of the historic village of Tutbury, sitting on the outskirts of the town, its easy, possibly due to the modern use of postcodes, to think that it is just a small outpost of Burton. Again, any Tutbury native will be only too happy to put you right on this!!

However, both these places were culturally linked to Burton on Trent during the 50s and 60s heyday of rock and pop, both through the younger elements love of the 'new' music, and through the presence in both these places of superb live music venues.

Swadlincote Rink gained its name through its use early in the 20th Century, as a roller skating rink. By 1910, Benjamin Robinson had a stage installed and the venue became a 'Palace of Varieties', laying on all sorts of entertainment, not only for the South Derbyshire folk, but also for those from Burton.

It soon acquired a reputation locally for providing some of the best entertainment around, with many of the top big bands from Burton, South Derbyshire and beyond appearing there. Wednesday night was the designated time for these bands, Victor Sylvestor being a very popular draw just before the explosion of rock 'n' roll in 1956. Not only that, by all accounts the dance floor was a dream for those who were nimble of foot. Many recall the floor being kept in meticulous condition under the watchful gaze of the Rink's manager during this period, Ernie Hall.

Initially the new 'Jitterbug' craze, which had first arrived on these shores during the 'overpaid, oversexed, and over here' presence of the American GIs during World War Two, and which was now evolving into 'the Jive', was outlawed by the ever present Ernie, who only later gave in to the inevitable and allowed the new, 'lewd' form of dance behind a specially roped off area of the floor. The Red Rockers' Tony Leech recalls: "you were only allowed to Jive on a Tuesday night!" One of the reasons for this was possibly to prevent the other dancers receiving injuries from the flailing limbs of the jivers.

Tuesday night at the club was originally known locally as 'The Tanner Hop', the tanner being the slang name for the sixpenny bit, the cost of your admission on the night. On this night, according to the *Burton Mail*, the 'hoofers' could receive a dancing lesson, *'Free Ballroom lessons for all, then dancing to Bill Haley'*. How useful this would have been when put into practice to the kiss curled one's grooves is open to question.

ROCK AT THE RINK!

NEW TUESDAY PROGRAMME

FREE BALLROOM LESSONS FOR ALL – THEN!!

ROCKIN' TO BILL HALEY

Complete new Record Programme—Hear the Finest, Best of Bill Haley, Earl Bostick, etc.

FREE NIGHT—TO-NIGHT

(Burton Mail)

What is not in question is the undoubted quality of the floor at the Rink, which was of such a high calibre that many thought taking up the offer of the free lessons worth the effort. (Those who would like to read more on this period of The Rink in its prime should check out both Graham Nutt's *'Tuppenny Rush'* and *'Out of the Dark – Swadlincote Stories'* produced by the South Derbyshire Writers' Group).

By 1957, recognising, as all good places should, that there was a market for it, the Rink started putting on 'Teens and Twenty nights' to cater for the new fad. **Sydney Roy** and the **Ripchords** were to provide the musical accompaniment, but were later to be replaced by some of the new, up and coming home grown youngsters like The Red Rockers and Alpines, both groups regularly taking to the big stage during 1958, 1959 and 1960. In 1959, with the venue still being advertised as the *Alexandra Rink*, a Whit 'Rock Party' was the place to be seen, where you could catch both the previous mentioned groups as well as 'all the Top Twenty Pops', for as little as two shillings (10p).

ALEXANDRA RINK, SWADLINCOTE — NEXT WEDNESDAY

"GET IN THE MOOD" with Britain's Premier Band

JOE LOSS

and his Full Orchestra with Singing Stars - Rose Brennan. Larry Gretton and Ross McManus

Supported by RONNIE McCREA

Admission 5'- by Ticket only   Strictly limited   Late Transport

Joe Loss appeared with Elvis Costello's dad, **Ross McManus**

(Burton Mail)

By 1958, Thursday night was now set aside as the rock night, while the main attraction on Saturdays was still primarily the big bands, such as **Ted Taylor's**, with musical ambience during the intervals generally provided by one of the local rock ensembles, to cater for all tastes. The Rink had a capacity of 1,200, making it much more capacious than the majority of local venues, which meant that from an early stage it was able to put on some of the more nationally well-known artists, including **Wee Willie Harris** (described by the local press as 'a Scottish Teddy Boy'), in 1958.

The owners of the Rink, in an attempt to improve the sound quality from the stage, installed a curved backdrop, which was, by all accounts, most effective.

Taking advantage of this through the ensuing years were some of the biggest crowd pullers of the 60s, including **The Checkmates**, mean moody and magnificent **Dave Berry** and his **Cruisers, The Hollies**, and **The Four Seasons** (their only Ballroom appearance that year in the UK according to the press), not forgetting the bloke with the name that was light years ahead of its time in 1960, **Eddie Sex**!

As with other local venues, 1963 was *the* year, if you were a regular at the Rink you would have witnessed the formative talents of a certain Mr Ritchie Blackmore on guitar with **The Outlaws** (this was the London version, not to be confused with the Coalville group of the same name), along with Chas Hodges, later to find fame providing the Cockney pub singalong style with Chas and Dave (the London Outlaws would amuse themselves between gigs by driving round the locality throwing flour bombs at innocent passers by - rock and roll !!), **The Rockin' Berries, The Searchers** and our old friend Roy Wood with the **Nite-Riders**, not forgetting the teddy boys' favourite rocker, **Gene Vincent**.

One such regular at the Rink was Burton lad Don Jones, who remembers that particular venue as probably the best place around for seeing bands. "When we went to see The Hollies the queue was the length of the passageway up to the building".

A trip on a Midland Red bus up to Swad was not the preferred mode of transport for Don and his buddies: "we used to get driven to Swad by Graham Fearn in his white Jaguar - we would swan around the town in it".

Don also recalls that the place had other attractions, including *Barmy Barry* the DJ, and the pinball machines at the rear where you could occupy time between watching the acts.

Tony Leech was himself a Rink regular, though generally as a performer rather than a punter. The Red Rockers appeared there many times, and he recalls it as "a fantastic time". They were South Derbyshire lads, so that was their home base, and they would commute between the Rink and other local venues such as the *Moores Arms* in Appleby, on many occasions they would utilise their Austin 7 van for the transport of some of their fans as well as equipment.

"There were twelve of use crammed in there - the wheel arches were rubbing on the wheels as we went along!" The local bobbies witnessing such events would give a knowing look that would be an indication that, perhaps, they wouldn't turn a blind eye next time. They later traded the van in for an upgrade, an American Buick, don't know how many they managed to cram in there, though.

Another Rink regular at the time, Maria Chambers, recalls that the place held no alcohol Licence and that no booze was available at the venue. "Lads used to go down to the pub during the interval, so there was no time really to get drunk". Maria also recalls some of the acts she saw down The Rink: The **4 Penny's, Dave Dee Dozy Beaky Mick and Tich, The Zombies** and the evergreen **Lu-Lu**.

The Rink eventually went they way of all old venues, conversion into a Bingo Hall.

"That was in the 60s, though they still ran dance nights".

Many of those old regulars were in attendance for the Rink's final bow. Long since past its glory days, or its usefulness, the site was earmarked for demolition. The *Burton Mail* ran a story on the 21st of October 1991, highlighting the impending demolition, and that very same night the place caught fire, possibly the result of some rubble left smouldering by the wrecking crew. At the height of the blaze word got round and a large crowd soon gathered, many of the old regulars saying goodbye to the old gel, a good many had taken the opportunity to help themselves to a bit of the old dance floor as a memento - or anything else they liked the look of! Over the years many memorable nights had been had at the Rink and fond memories remain. It could certainly compete with any other venue in the country in its heyday, many more were to comment that the place still had the ability to entertain with its final gesture.

*"Witnessed by its last large attendance." The remains of the **Rink**, 1991*
(Neil Barker/Burton Mail)

Travel back down the old Ashby Road, keep on going through Horninglow, and eventually you would have dropped down the hill into Tutbury (this is the time before the bypass). Just before you hit the tight right-hander into the High Street, look to your right and there sits what was the **Tutbury Palladium**. These days, of course, it is a restaurant, but for a time, albeit very briefly, it was another good live music venue. It seems to have hit its peak during 1964, when the whole country was bristling with live entertainment, and places to see it.

A chap by the name of Peter Gamble used to organise the groups for the Palladium, booking round the other attractions such as Thursday nights *Discagogo* record night and, but of course, Friday nights Bingo!!

THE PALLADIUM - TUTBURY

GRAND OPENING — TO-NIGHT

TWO GROUPS FOR YOUR FIRST ROCK AND TWIST NIGHT

TELEVISION STARS —

JOHNNY WASHINGTON & THE CONGRESSMEN

— STARS OF "FOR TEENAGERS ONLY"

Birmingham's Most Popular Group—and

IAN & THE SAPHIRES

One of Burton's Most Promising Groups

LATE TRANSPORT   5/-   7-45 — 11-30

Watch for further announcements concerning Grand Opening Nights for Ballroom Dancing and Bingo

---

The *Grand Opening Night* was on February 1, 1964, and kicking off proceedings were Brummies **Johnny Washington and the Congressman** supported by Burton's own **Sapphires**. The majority of the bands booked were from around the Midlands, with Stoke in particular providing a steady supply. **The Orbeats** were from the Potteries, appearing in a support slot for the **Brumbeats**. The Bradwell youngsters were probably one of the youngest groups around at the time, and were initially thrilled to bits when they were told by their manager, Alan Hollis, that he had secured them a gig on stage at The Palladium.

"We later found out it was not the London Palladium, as we imagined, but up the road in Tutbury" recalls guitarist Terry Probyn. Terry recalls it was a good night although he has one thing to add: "we didn't get paid enough!"

Terry formed up the group from among his school friends, including Stan Bayliss, who was taught the bass guitar by his brother. The lads remain firm friends, and have recently reformed the group for the occasional gig. Though it seems unlikely they will be repeating their performance from The Palladium's stage!

The youthful **Orbeats** *at Trentham Gardens:*
(l-r) **Phil Johnson, Terry Probyn, Stan Bayliss** *and* **Tony Chatterley**.

(Stan Bayliss)

In order to drum up support for the club an advertisement was placed in the *Burton Daily Mail*:

"Wanted – Prancing Pensioners, Sober Squares, Jazz Juveniles"

In the May, 1964 Burton's Mr Music, Pete Youngman, appeared at the club along with **Brian Gulliver and the Travellers**, though obviously there is no way I'm suggesting that there is any connection with this event and the aforementioned advert!

Bernie and the Dolphins were support for the visit of one of the bigger draws at the time, **Screaming Lord Sutch**, and the Dolphins' Bernie Prince recalls the night "Lord Sutch and his group managed to fuse the electrics for the whole place. While they were being repaired the band's drummer kept the punters entertained with a 15 minute drum solo!"

Prog rock was definitely on the way. The visit of the *Lord* was to celebrate the grand re-opening of the venue, though the reasons for its shut down in the first place remain a mystery, unless it was down to dodgy electrics!

Eventually the provision of live music nights at the Palladium came to a halt, the reason for this, at the time of writing, is unknown, though I suspect lack of support - as ever - may have been a factor.

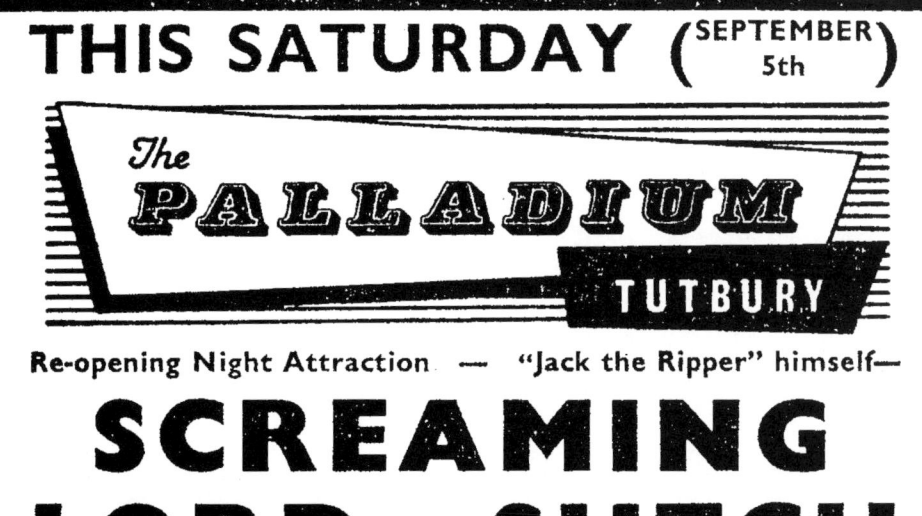

THIS SATURDAY (SEPTEMBER 5th)

The PALLADIUM TUTBURY

Re-opening Night Attraction — "Jack the Ripper" himself—

SCREAMING LORD SUTCH

and THE SAVAGES

Oriole Record—"She Fell in Love with a Monster"

Horror, Thrills and Suspense   Support Show—

THE RAIDERS

8—11.30 p.m.   Refreshments   Late Transport

And all of the night...

BAND CATERING ENTERPRISES LTD.

present

BIG BEAT NIGHT

JUBILEE HALL :: BURTON ON TRENT

NEXT MONDAY
7-45—10.45

Presenting fabulous Hit Makers
of "You Really Got Me"

THE

KINKS

Plus—Top Derby vocal and
instrumental group

THE VIBRONS

Admission 6/6   Late Transport

Monday, October 5th—CLOSED

Monday, October 12th—Hit Paraders
THE HONEYCOMBS

Burton got its first taste of something approaching the well-publicised *Beatlemania* histrionics in September 1964. Gordon Band had managed to organise a visit of The Kinks, as part of his 'Big Beat Nights', at the Jubilee Hall. The London based lads, including the forever-squabbling Davies brothers, were just hitting big with 'You Really Got Me', a belting rocker, which still sounds as good as ever today. Anticipating, perhaps, a livelier night than was normal as far as audience behaviour, both inside and out, was concerned, Gordon and his crew had to organise a police presence outside the venue. This didn't deter some of the more determined female admirers of the band attempting to reach the group. "They managed to batter the Fire doors in!" remembers Gordon.

Word had got round town about the groups impending visit beforehand and Maria Chambers, then a student at Burton's Technical College, travelled down with a group of friends from Donisthorpe to see them, "They were up on stage and it seemed sort of small compared to the (Swadlincote) Rink". Making her way through the crowd she joined in with the crescendo of screaming that was a normal accompaniment for the top bands of the day. After the gig she also indulged in the new fan adulation of their hero pop stars. "Once we got outside we stormed the car that was ferrying the band to their next destination. I managed to get hold of Dave's (Davies) jacket!"

The Kavemen's drummer, Dave Hughes, remembers witnessing similar scenes of *Fan Mania*. "People were fainting, it was packed out". Others recall the occasion for different reasons. Don Jones: "It was the first time I'd seen people dancing on their own (up to this time you were expected to perform the function holding onto a partner), I thought "What bloody idiots!" Don, treading that fine line that distinguished a mod from a rocker, travelled down to the Jubilee on his moped, and was well impressed with the group. "It was the first big group I had seen, I thought they were great".

For a splendid first hand account of a local lad attending The Kinks' gig, check out this reminiscence by Reggie Hawker:

"I'd seen my first big group, The Rolling Stones, at the Odeon in Weston Super Mare in the previous July, so I was eager to see The Kinks and add them to my list. I was in the fourth year at The Technical High School in Bond Street...(myself) and a school mate, Keith (Hoofy) Cooper, decided, on the Monday afternoon during a Woodwork lesson, to go to the gig. Keith lived in Ash Street and I in Uxbridge Street, so we walked down to the Jubilee Hall with a little bit of trepidation, being that we were only 14! We paid on the door (cannot remember how much), and we bought half of cider each to look grown up, and stood over by a wall out of the way of the big lads. I don't think (they) played more than 30 or 40 minutes, but they did look the business in their red riding jackets and frilly dress shirts. In those days there were no mixing desks, monitors or fancy light shows, so the sound balance was performed by the group adjusting the volume on their Vox AC30 amps. We both enjoyed their performance, they did 'You Really Got Me' and the crowd went mad, a bit too mad in my opinion as a fight ensued at the back of the hall near the bar. All in all a great night out!"

Reggie cannot recall whether there was a support group on that night, though there most certainly was. The support, as the advert points out, was to be Derby's The Vibrons. Group member Paul Henman harks back to that night (though he himself recalls it as taking place at the Town Hall!), and gives us a different angle on events, confirming, though, what others recall.

"...the gig with The kinks was manic as Beatlemania had taught the girls that it was okay to scream". The sight of the aforementioned girls passing out with the hysteria is still a fresh memory. "The Security guys were carrying fainting girls over our heads and piling them into our dressing room, and that was just for our set! When we returned backstage we were literally stepping over comatose bodies to get to our room".

The *Burton Daily Mail*, probably sending out one of its younger hacks to report on the nights events, managed to get in a mention for the Derby lads, enthusing that The Vibrons 'more than satisfied as the supporting bill'.

Gordon Bands' plan with the *Big Beat* nights was, quite simply, to put on some of the bigger acts doing the rounds. Those groups that would be too popular for the capacity of the 76 Club. The acts seen by the crowd below at the inaugural event were **Mike Berry**, with support from **Jimmy Powell and the Five Dimensions**, the latter group in their early days often being accompanied by a very young harmonica player and vocalist, one Rodney Stewart, the worlds greatest living Scotsman (born in England). Though I don't think he was there on this night.

When **The Brooks Brothers**, Britain's answer to the Everly Brothers, took the stage in 1963, the support act was a Birmingham group, the **Rhythm and Blues Quartet**, which was, in effect, the nucleus of the *Spencer Davis Group*, including the youthful genius of Stevie Winwood. The Brooks Brothers were, to quote a well known phrase, very popular with the ladies, so much so that Gordon Band remembers having to rescue them from a mauling by waiting for the lads outside the club afterwards. "They were chased out of the club by girls, I sat in the car with the motor running and sped off a soon as they were onboard, followed by their female admirers!".

The Big Beat Crowd, opening night Monday, February 4, 1963.
Recognise yourself?   (Burton Mail)

One of the most notable visitors to the club was Gene Vincent, it could be said that by the time of his first visit to the town (he passed this way a number of times, including stints at the 76 and Swad Rink) his *15 minutes* was already up: he was on the decline most notably due to his headfirst rock'n'roll lifestyle. However, to many of his fans, and there were many there to see him that night, he was still the personification of rock and roll.

Many a budding rocker based their whole appearance on the man: the greased up quiff, strands hanging lankly across the forehead, black leather, moody looking. Gene also had that tragic element that we like to see in our hero's, his leg shattered in a motorbike accident (what else?), dragged around stage with him, adding some theatrical tragedy to some of his more heart rending vocal outings.

Like many others tended to do, Gene stopped off at the *Green Man*, next door to the Jubilee, for a couple of liveners before the show, and it was here, I can reveal at last, that one of Burton's most celebrated - if less well known - rock and roll moments took place. Gene, having downed a couple, needed to partake of the

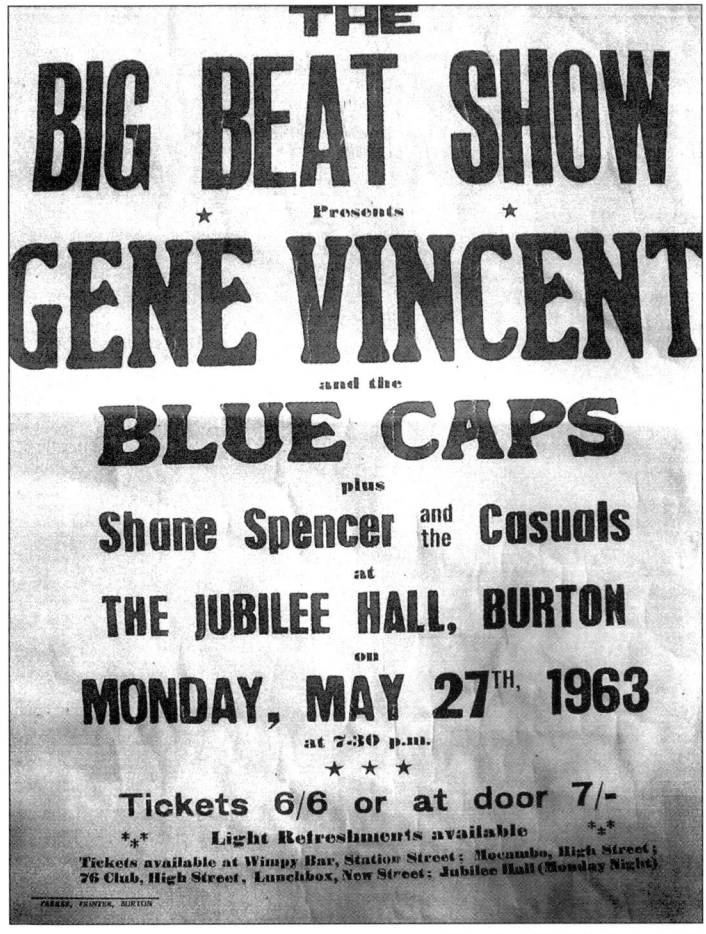

(Maurice Hall/Graham Nutt)

facilities in the pub's gentleman's toilet and was followed in to the 'little boys' room' by one of this town's more well known 'characters'. No record exists of what actually took place in there, but after Gene's exit our local hero held aloft a bundle of soggy toilet paper and announced to all assembled: "I've got one of Gene Vincent's turds!" Some recoiled in horror, others looked on with disgust, while one or two, quite disturbingly, wanted a closer inspection. As it turned out the whole thing was a cruel hoax, drawing nervous laughter from those around him, although those who knew the instigator would have had no trouble believing that he would actually fish out the results of Gene's toiletry effort.

Another good crowd turned up to see Eire's favourite sons, The Bachelors, supported by Coaville's Outlaws. It seems that the majority of events at the Jubilee were well supported. Liverpool's second most favourite group, **Gerry and the Pacemakers**, entertained there, as did Screaming Lord Sutch and his Savages (I get the sneaking feeling this bloke liked it around here, he put in many appearances over the years, always going down a bomb with the punters, both before, during and after the show). There was no problem with the electrics at the venue this time, though a good example of how things were done at live shows in those days is highlighted by Gordon Bands right hand man Arthur Phillips.

"For his entrance Lord Sutch suddenly appeared at the fire exits at the rear of the hall, he walked through the crowd to the stage". Arthur, being a versatile sort of person had agreed to operate the lighting for the band during the show, though he points out: "no one told me what I was actually supposed to do!"

One visiting group were destined for great things, The Honeycombs were a massive draw at the time, down in some part to the 'novelty' female drummer.

The Honeycombs – *right group, wrong venue, the backdrop is the early 60s 76 Club.* **Ann 'Honey' Lantree**, *the female drumming attraction.*
(Don Pikitt)

As events have turned out they became just another group in the long list of 'One Hit Wonders'. At the time of their show at the Jubilee they were riding high in the charts with that one hit 'Have I The Right'. Packing out the house, a great many of the punters that evening were kids, including Don Pikitt, who now resides in Stretton.

"I remember queuing outside with the other kids, once inside, to be able to actually see the band over the heads of the grown ups I had to stand on a chair. I thought they were very good live".

A steady stream of the era's popular hit makers passed through the Jubilee's doors: **The Barron Nights**, **The Fortunes**, and **Cliff Bennett and the Rebel Rousers**. The stream slowly dried up by 1966, with Liverpool's' **Fabulous Koobas** and **The Expressions** being that years final visitors.

The pace picked up again by the mid-seventies, *DB Promotions* (former 76 Doorman Dave Butler) started to reel in a few good live acts for the locals, kicking off in 1974 with **The Heartbreakers** (not Johnny Thunders LA mob or Tom Petty's group I suspect). In 1975 super loud noise merchants **The Groundhogs** were due to appear, I have been told, by more than one person, that these were one of the loudest bands around, a friend of mine went to see them once and during the gig bits of plaster and concrete were falling off the ceiling on to his head, dislodged by the wave of noise coming off the stage! Unfortunately they failed to show up, their van (allegedly) broke down, (rumour has it that strings were pulled to ensure they didn't appear), a replacement was quickly found in the form of London lads **The Winkies**, publicised as 'London's New York Dolls' in the music press. They more than impressed, and gave some of the 700 or so locals a bit of a taster of what was also fermenting amongst the younger groups in the nations capital. Also on the same bill were **The Spangled Mob** and **The Isotape Band**.

GALAXY PROMOTIONS present
at the JUBILEE HALL, BURTON
TO-NIGHT

ROCK RAVE

with JILL SAWARDS FUSION ORCHESTRA

plus OAKDALE and P.T.L. ROCK DISCO

7.30 — 12.00.   Licensed Bar

TICKETS £1 EACH from Abbey Music, Market Place

Jill Saward at the Jubilee, and *Oakdale's* chance to shine

(Burton Mail)

That same year, a band who always drew plenty of observers were at the Jubilee. **Jill Sawards Fusion Orchestra**, an extremely talented band, had the added attraction of being fronted by vocalist Jill. The gig was promoted by Burtons favourite (and surely by now longest serving) DJ, Pete Lawrence, with local favourites **Oakdale** as support. Both bands went down well with the punters. Jill and the band returned to the town many times and were always well received. There is no link between the band's popularity and the fact that, according to Oakdale keyboardist Geoff Noble, Jill "would do the most obscene things with the microphone stand". He was not so impressed with the way Oakdale appeared to have been set up by the main act's sound engineer. "We think we may have been set up to make us sound bad" - a tried and tested method of making sure no one outshines you musically.

FUSION ORCHESTRA.

They may have been attired in psuedo teddy boy rigouts, but the lads in **Showaddy Waddy** were no novices, many of them had plied their trade in a number of bands through the 60s (yep, they were no youngsters either). A seasoned, professional outfit, they treated their fans to a run through of their greatest hits at the hall in 1975.

By this time of course heavy metal was starting to make its mark on the music scene. **Judas Priest** were lined up for a gig at the venue, though the plug was pulled after the local magistrates refused to give the place a Public Performance Licence. The reasons why were not fully explained - surely the bench was not discriminating against local rock fans?!!

Due to introduce the band and spin the discs was everybody's favourite, the late great **John Peel**. Luckily he did appear in Burton later.

JUBILEE ROCK

JUBILEE HALL, BURTON
FRIDAY, 14th MARCH

JOHN PEEL

plus JUDAS PRIEST plus LOCAL SUPPORT
Advance Tickets from ABBEY MUSIC £1.20

The gig that never was.   *(Burton Mail)*

A bonus as a result of the no licence business was the cancellation of a visit by *'Smashy and Nicey'* type DJ Dave Lee Travers. *Cozy Powell's Hammer* also cancelled and the incidence of gigs at the venue seemed to slow down. In 1976 only one took place, **The Dodgers** pairing up with Jerseys' **'O'** (not The O Band – just O!).

*At least if they had turned it into a bingo hall it would have still been serving it's purpose - to allow humans to be entertained. Here the **Jubilee** is converted into a distinctly non-human bed shop.*

Although there is still a club based in the old Working Men's Club on the corner of Orchard Street the site of the Jubilee Hall itself is now a restaurant. If you look up while you are eating you can still see the remnants of the arched ceiling of the old hall, and if you listen closely enough you could perhaps still hear the echo of the screams of those girls watching The Kinks.

8 Beats to the bar...

Brian Fennell Quartet *at the* **8 Bar Rest Jazz Club**
(l-r): **Dave Smith, Les Bloor, Brian Fennell** *and* **Dave Brown**, *c.1959/60*

(Brian Fennell)

Jazz and folk music have both been, and still are, tremendously popular in Burton, and both genres of music still retain a loyal following with thriving clubs still drawing fans weekly at various venues. Folk carries on the tradition of story telling through song, itself going back through British history, often being the only outlet to vent your feelings on what is going on accompanied by a few pints and some like minded individuals. While jazz does tend to have many more worldwide influences, it still retains a Britishness through the constant stream of home grown talent that has contributed to the sound, and still does of course.

Perhaps of the two, jazz has that element of being different, by its very nature; it has a free form, though not free enough for some during the early 60s. The music is split into two camps, *traditional* or *trad*, as it is better known, and *modern*, which was a style welcomed by some of the younger element, which made it "out on a limb". It is possibly for that reason that it was the staple for most teenagers and youngsters before the dirty sound of rock 'n' roll led some of Burton's youth astray.

The **8 Bar Rest Club** convened in a room at the rear of the *Market Hotel* in High Street (occupied now by solicitors' offices). The room was actually called *The Rodney Room*, but it became the *8 Bar* in the late 50s as the club was being run initially, among other things, as a folk club by Colin 'Nogger' Norris ably assisted by Ken Harris.

At this time jazz bands would entertain during the interval between the main acts, which was very often the Sydney Roy Band, or one of the number of dance bands around at that time. Many of these bands contained musicians who would form the core of the jazz groups during this period.

Brian Fennell was an alto sax player in both the Ted Taylor Band and Sydney Roy's outfit. He had always gone down to the Central Club in Derby Street to catch the **Dixieland Jazz Band**, in turn becoming aware of the *8 Bar* and, once he had been demobbed from the army, started to appear down there regularly.

Dave Brown, another dance band stalwart on the drums, started out performing at works functions and village halls. This was in the era before guitar bands and the drummer very often sat prominently stage front, in front of all the rest of the band, unlike modern times when they are generally tucked away at the back somewhere (and are also the target for drummer jokes). Dave heard about the 8 Bar and decided to go down and see what it had to offer. Before long he was asked if he would form a band which, along with Les Bloor, Trevor Mears and Dave Smith, and later of course Brian Fennell, he promptly did.

A Merry Xmas

and a

Happy New Year

from

Burton's Eight Bar Rest Jazz Club

(Brian Fennell)

The club was run by the members, for the members, and they would decorate the club themselves, giving it its distinctive identity with LP sleeves adorning the walls and ceilings. A stage was purpose built by Arthur Sherratt costing a mighty £79.10s. This was a wise move, for there are many stories of less than adequate 'stages' (anything from planks of wood to wooden crates) giving way under the combined weight of the performers, resulting in one of the members legs noisily disappearing earthwards mid song!

The friendly and light-hearted atmosphere at the club was often reflected in the advertising, in December 1960 you had *'Four Bands, Free Buffet, Four Bob'*, by the following May it had become *'Alcoholic Music – Swingin' Beer'*. The gentleman that passed by one Saturday night and decided to help himself to the Burton Jazz Club sign outside the club had no doubt been checking out the *'swingin' beer'*. He was up before the magistrates the following Monday, and fined £3. His reason for helping himself? "I collect them" - a perfectly reasonable excuse I think. (I myself am the proud owner of a roadworks sign, it appeared one Sunday morning in my back yard. Where it came from, or indeed why I felt I needed it, is a total mystery).

The calibre of the musicians appearing at the club was very high. A cross section of the local music scene included Joe Fearn's band, the **Norman Willey Group** and of course **The Brian Fennell Quartet**, while often a combination of the bands would occur under the collective title **The 8 Bar Rest Big Band**.

Sunday nights were generally guest nights, with the likes of **Georgie Watt** the sax player, **Johnny Patrick** and **Ken Ingerfield** all gracing with their presence. The year for the club was split into seasons. During the cold dark winter nights the place would provide a welcome nights dancing, but during the summer season it shut down. This puzzled me for a while, then I realised that possibly many people would look for their kicks outdoors in the sun somewhere, or they would simply be away on holidays. The answer was so much simpler than that, as Brian pointed out the obvious to me: "the sun used to stream in through the windows". Hardly the right atmosphere for the beatnicks!

The constant round of travelling and gigging would eventually take its toll on the musicians (this applies for all musicians, not just jazz), it was common for 'dog-tired' band members to actually fall asleep during some of the slower numbers, much to the amusement of fellow bandsmen and the audience. This leads us on very nicely to Burton's most famous musical son, for you cannot mention the 8 Bar Rest and jazz without including one Phillip Seamen.

Phil Seamen was, without doubt, one of the most talented drummers the world has ever known. The fact that he could be a pain in the arse and a total embarrassment to those around him is far outweighed by the entertainment factor of the man. It has often been recalled that he would sometimes appear to be asleep while seated behind the kit, and very often this was because he actually was! But he would still manage to bring the house down, while unconscious.

His story is worth a book on its own, of which I believe plans for one are already afoot. He could "out-Keith Moon" Keith Moon, but still had the talent to be recognised as 'a superb British jazz drummer' by the *Penguin Encyclopedia of Popular Music*.

He learned his trade playing along to records in the Seamen family's Outwoods Street home, leaving the windows open to give the neighbours a treat, an early indication that the man just didn't give a shit. He would regularly guest with the bands at the 8 Bar Rest, and in between sets he would retreat to the *Locomotive* pub for more refreshments with a man who he quickly recognised as a kindred spirit.

Paddy Moran ran the record department at *W T Parkers* by day, but by night he played lead alto saxophone, and was by all accounts "a brilliant musician". He also rivalled Phil in his fondness for a tipple and accompanied him on their constant forays to the *Loco*.

*"I have much more to tell you, though I must keep it short,
otherwise you will have no hole in the middle of the record"*
(Decibel Records/Brian Peters)

Phil Seamen, *quoted from the Phil Seamen Story. (Decibel Records)*

The genius of Paddy can be found in the fact that his wife insisted that they leave their native Ireland because of the constant availability of the drink, so where did Paddy manage to persuade his wife to set up their new home? Why, Burton of course, the capital of the British brewing industry!

Phil would often return to the town in between bookings in London, where he was later based, and inevitably he would gather up some pals and 'do the town', though nobody would be actually daft enough to try and keep up with him. (*"he drank and smoked in quantities that would have levelled anybody else"* – Charles Fox). Passing a pub where some band were giving it what they'd got, he would lean into the doorway and, with reference to the efforts of the drummer, announce: "sounds like they're building a shed in there!"

By the end of the night, a little peckish he would join others from the 8 Bar in the *Lee Yen Chinese Restaurant*, whereupon he would demolish two meals at once, all served up on one plate, though invariably most of the meals would end up on his jumper and trousers. Occasionally they would all retire to Dave Browns flat, where Phil would top up with a few more whiskies, throwing the dregs left in the bottom of the glass on to Dave's coal fire for effect - more effect sometimes than he bargained for, in one instance, "there was more left in the glass than he thought" recalls Dave. "The whole fireplace went up in flame, licking up the front of the hearth, engulfing Phil and burning off his eyebrows and eyelashes". It was all part of the fun for Phil.

He succumbed in the end, Heroin did for him and he died the pathetic death that that stuff affords its users, but he left us with timeless memories, not to mention the talents of *Ginger Baker*, who he taught. We will leave the last words on the subject to the man himself.

"If that guy can do it so can I," he commented to Charles Fox after studiously listening to an African drumming LP (a type of music he had a great fondness for). He duly taught himself to play the piece, only realising later that it was an African drumming *band*.

By 1962 the trad crowd were looking for their own venue, they were duly provided with a jazz night on Thursdays at Gordon Bands' 76 Club thanks to the efforts of Glynn Williams, who many will remember not only as a big jazz enthusiast, but also for his work initially in picture houses and as a travelling cinema operator, but also for his electrical shop in Bargates where, in later years, in conjunction with Alf 'Burtonian' Moss, he produced a number of videos about 'Old Burton'.

The opening act for the new jazz nights at the 76 was to be **Cyril Preston's Jazz Band**, who went down well with the trad fans from Burton and beyond, the *Burton Mail* later reporting that it was "a great success and members were unanimous in their approval". Sadly both Glynn Williams and Ken Harris have now passed away: I hope this section of the book does justice to two stalwarts of the Burton jazz scene.

By this time the *Market Hotel*, no doubt looking out for a way to pull in more punters, latched on to another 'craze' - a *'New Nyles Twistys Twisting Competition'* as well as offering *'Rock at The Rodney'*. It continued with the 8 Bar as the jazz venue, though obviously some of the regulars were now given the choice of trying out the 76.

Robert Morris was a jazz club regular who tended to follow the trad crowd down to the club further down the High Street. He was perhaps typical of the young jazz enthusiast of the era (and still is!), following the tried and tested ritual of going down to record shops to not only catch up on some of the latest sounds but also keep one eye on the girls behind the counter. (Very common at the time amongst the young set, I would say the 1960s equivalent of modern youth downloading – or 'ripping' – as I believe its termed, music off the Internet for their *iPod's*. Though probably a great deal more fun).

The Harris-Moran Quartet
*(l-r): **David Smith, Ken Harris, Ivan Parker, Paddy Moran***

(Burton Mail)

On one of his visits to the record shop in Swadlincote, Robert Morris heard a tune that he was very taken with. "Whats that?" he enquired. "That's **Humphrey Lyttleton**, that's jazz" said his mate, informatively. Following this, and intrigued by what he had heard, he made a point of catching the Humphrey Lyttleton show as often as he could on the radio. Now, in this age where we can switch on our computer and not only listen to, but suck whatever sound we choose down the phone lines and into our little electronic boxes, it is perhaps difficult to comprehend that, in the 50s, 60s and 70s, to find out what was hot musically we had to tune our tiny little transistor radios to a station that was continually drifting away, particularly at night (remember Luxembourg?), making for very frustrating listening, and you could guarantee that after the one sound you were especially fond of had faded out, the DJ would fail to mention either the title, or the artists, or both during his or her self opinionated drivel afterwards. (Unless, of course, it was John Peel whom we all loved like a kindly father).

Though Robert would often attend other nights at the 76, his main night was a Thursday, catching some of the top Jazz bands of the time such as **Kenny Ball and his Jazzmen**, **Acker Bilk**, **3 Spires Jazzmen** and **The Gloryland Jazz Band**. Though quality wasn't just confined to the 76, the 8 Bar could offer the best as well, including **The Johnny Patrick Quintet**, and in April 63, **The Riverside Jazzmen**, among whose number were Tubby Hayes, Ronnie Scott and Joe Harriot.

"On Sunday nights the 8 Bar Rest would be absolutely rammed" smiles Burton musician Brian Fennell, who would be in an ideal position to know.

In February, 1963 The Brian Fennell Quartet had guesting for them, behind the drums, one Phil Seamen, and this would pack in both sets of fans. It was possibly this very night that Robert Morris got to personally meet the man. "Do you want to meet Phil Seamen?" he was asked. Of course he did, who wouldn't? He was led towards a figure lying prostrate on his back on the floor of the 8 Bar. Suddenly, as he neared, an arm shot up in the air, and a huge hand offered a formal greeting. They shook hands, the extended limb returned back to side of the owners' body and that was that.

(I realise that some time ago I said that the final word had been said on Mr. Seamen but the bloke is just irresistible aint he?).

THIS SUNDAY AT

THE EIGHT BAR REST   7-30 — 10-30 p.m.

SPECIAL GUEST APPEARANCE OF EUROPE'S GREATEST DRUMMER
PHIL SEAMAN
with THE BRIAN FENNELL QUARTET

The Drummer Man's in town – Burton Daily Mail, February 8, 1963.

(Burton Mail)

The Burton crowd were used to seeing Phil drop in every now and again. When he was in town he couldn't resist sitting in, and some of the visiting groups had the shock of their lives when he turned up. On one occasion during a heavy fall of snow the visiting group, **The Tony Lee Trio**, found themselves reduced to a duo. Their drummer, Alec Gold, had been snowed in and was not going to make the gig. "No problem" said Dave Brown, "I'll get Phil Seamen here to fill in, what do you want him to play?" The looks on their faces told their own story, this blokes havin' a laugh right?

"No seriously, what do you want him to play?".

By the mid 60s the 8 Bar was feeling the pinch, attendances had dwindled and there was competition for the attention of the jazz followers. Dave Brown, who was now running the club, had decided it was no longer viable. The fact that the Market Hotel was reaching the end of its useful life must also have played a part.

There are many people in this town, and beyond, who will fondly remember those balmy nights down the 8 Bar, an extremely popular little club, with enthusiasm for the music being a unifying force, that has helped build friendships that have stood the test of time.

The 76 became the main venue for the jazz club from 1965 to 1970, under the guidance of Glynn Williams, but they were also suffering dwindling attendance figures by this time so the venue was moved to the room above the *British Oak* in Byrkley Street. It then seemed to do a couple of circuits of the town via Stapenhill's Redhill Lodge, (this building has just disappeared off the skyline) before coming back full circle after an invite from Gordon Band, to return to the 76 again in the late 70s.

The Town Hall was also a popular place for visiting jazzmen. Humphrey Lyttleton, with support from Joe Fearn, appeared there in 1966, and the following year Acker Bilk made a welcome return to our town, bringing his **Paramounts** with him, this event being organised by the *Burton Abbey Round Table*. (Footnote for trivia fans: Acker Bilk's big hit 'Stranger on the Shore', reputedly has Phil Seamen playing the - barely audible to the human ear - brush stroked accompaniment).

Following the closure of the 8 Bar, many of the musicians went their separate ways, taking up with other bands around the midlands. Brian Fennell joined up with the **Tony Lee Band**, who were now exponents of the jazz/rock hybrid that was gaining momentum around the country. Eventually they formulated an idea which was to provide a platform for musicians and performers from the many acts doing the rounds or, to use the terminology of the times 'allow them to do their thing'.

The band members, now calling themselves **Concept**, organised events in early 1976, at Burton Rugby Club and other places, under the banner *'Platform'*, which was just that, giving an outlet for various talents, which would perhaps otherwise not have had the opportunity.

The opening night of the enterprising event proved to be a 'storming success'. One hundred and thirty packed in to the club to witness the inaugural musical extravaganza, with the *Burton Mail* later reporting that this showcase for budding talent 'amazed everyone'. Among those given a means of an outlet for their talents over the coming weeks were **The Graham Hair Band**, **Phaetons Funeral** (Neil Hancox, Graham Foster and Martin Brown), **Amphioxus** and the debut gig for one of the most successful and well supported Burton groups, **The Hi-Ballers**. The latter containing personnel who, together, would provide the nucleus of the local rock scene for some years to come.

These days we get used to hearing about what special requirements artists have for performing at any particular venue, or *'The Rider'* as it is quaintly termed. This can range from something as diverse as computer games, certain brands of drink or cigarettes and food to the insane, I'm so important, 'everything has to be white' Mariah Carey approach. During the 60s and 70s things were so much easier, and so much more basic and functional, Brian Fennell: "Worthington 'E' to spit down my alto sax to soften the pads up".

*The expensively produced **Platform** poster, hand drawn and autographed by 'Charlie Parker'*

(Brian Fennell)

In 1976 the Burton Jazz Club celebrated its 15th Birthday, with Humphrey Lyttleton providing another 'storming show' at the 76 (maybe the use of this particular superlative was, perhaps, outstaying its welcome). It was Lyttletons's second visit in four months, for which he was backed up by the popular, and seemingly indestructible, **Zenith Hot Stompers**.

Here we are in 2007, and jazz remains as popular as it ever was in Burton. The club is still thriving, now in its 45th year. It has had its ups and downs, with attendances varying from 'house full' to 'is anybody out there?' but the club and its supporters remain. Lets raise a glass to that, though preferably something that's a little bit more palatable nowadays than Worthington 'E', please.

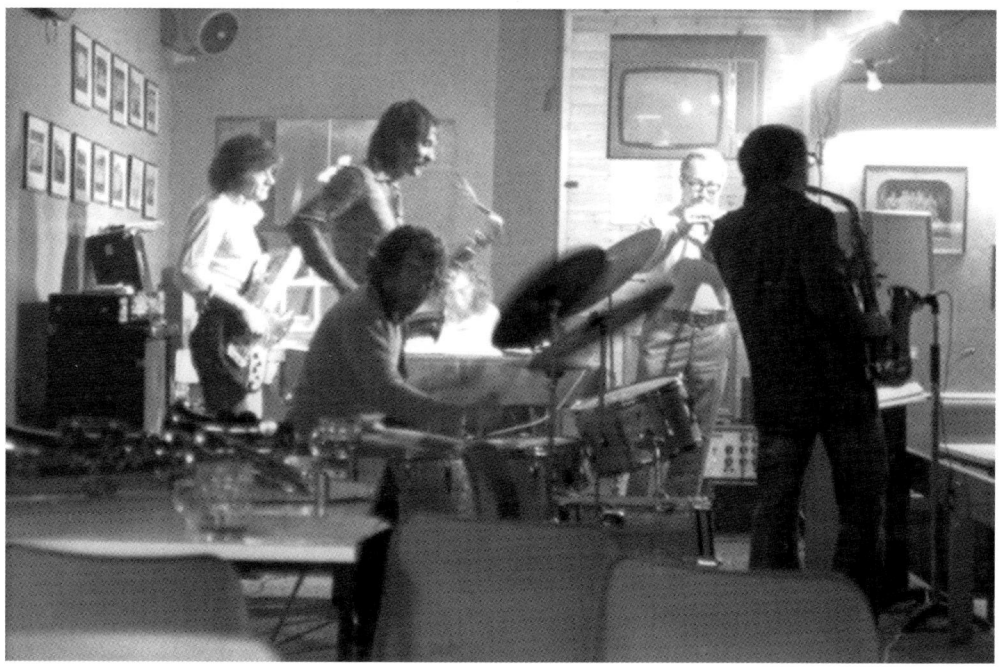

Concept at Burton Rugby Club, c1970
(l-r): **Vernon Wygrove** (bass), **Kip Wilkes** (sax), **Tony Lee** (keyboards),
Dave Brown (drums), **Dicky Hawden** (trumpet) and **Brian Fennell** (sax).

(Brian Fennell)

The singing Englishmen, (and Scotsmen)... (and Women)...

The Barley Mow, *the setting for **The Burton Folk Club**, before it was turned into 'a posh lounge'.*

(Roy Mason)

Like the jazz club, Burtons folk club had a tendency to roam around a bit and on occasions still does. But for many years it was based at the *Barley Mow* in Main Street, Stapenhill, conveniently at the end of a pleasant stroll over the picturesque Ferry Bridge. Music fads come and go, but folk music has seen them all, and outlived them all. The fact that the club is still going strong is testament to that.

Roy Mason took over the running of the club in 1967, although running is probably a bit too lightweight a term for the time and effort that Roy, and others, put into the project. Looking back now he recalls, with obvious pleasure, some of the entertainers, and the good times had at the club.

Before Roy took over the folk club was being handled by Dave Bull, who many will remember by his stage name of **'Hollerin' Dave Bull**. Dave was involved with the forerunner of the club, held initially on Thursday nights at the 76, later changing to a Monday when the Jazz Club was reinstated. Other venues in Burton were holding regular folk nights, and one in particular, The Leander Club, was showcasing some of the top acts around during 1966, including Solihull-based **The Sandlewoods** and local band **The Skilletts**, promoted as "Burton's leading group."

However by November, 1966 the *Burton Daily Mail* was heralding the arrival of a 'new entertainment venue', namely the *Barley Mow*, with the Leander now catering more for the 'beat' groups. The Barley's opening night saw **Godfreys Grit n' Soul Band** livening up the punters. Though very soon it was to become the home of the folk club.

It very quickly established itself as one of the 'finest folk clubs in England', one year being voted 'most popular club' by the readers of *Sing About*, the Midlands' own folk magazine. Membership was to include people from all over the Midlands, 318 card-carrying affiliates - that's a lot of people trying to get into a smallish room at the back of a pub. But try they did, The Skillets were always a sound bet for filling the place, while another favourite was a bloke by the name of Bob Davies, better known by his stage moniker **Jasper Carrott**. When he was on those unlucky enough not to get there early enough to be allowed in had to make do with "watching through the window while lying on the flat roof outside!".

Roy recalls Jasper's set, which generally consisted of an average of two songs - "the rest of the time he was talking". He would have the audience in fits of laughter with his tales of life's more absurd aspects, with the Brummy lad himself often being the butt of the joke. This he transferred most successfully in later years to television, and as we all now know, his daughter inherited her dad's comic timing to produce some fine performances as Dawn in *The Office*, also utilising Jasper's technique of facial expressions, which negated the need for words.

Roy Mason's involvement in running the club didn't just mean booking the acts and making sure they were paid, he also housed and fed many of them - "Jasper used to bring along his wife and three kids" - putting them all up at his Saxon Street, Stapenhill, home. "Jasper's kids would be in my house watching telly while their dad was on" (at the *Barley Mow*). Initially his fee was £18 although, understandably, this was increased due to his popularity.

One of the long standing traditions at the club is the floor spot, with members of the audience invited up to do a number or two. This was and remains today a very popular element and one which emphasised the convivial atmosphere encountered and welcomed by all comers.

Though some acts could be a bit more picky than others. **Ewan MacColl**, one of this country's folk greats, was a very politically motivated, headstrong veteran of the *Hunger Marches*. The father of the very sadly missed *Kirsty MacColl* was once arrested for 'disturbance of the peace', for here was a man who walked it like he talked it. For his first appearance at the Barley he had some simple requests: £48 for the gig, a high backed chair and NO floor singers. Roy treated him the same as everyone else: the money and chair? No problem. Floor singers? "You'll have two like everyone else" - and he did.

We cannot mention the floor singers at the club without referring to one very popular local lad. For those that were regular attendees the name **Mike Burman** will be most familiar.

Mike Burman, '*The Singing Barber*'

(Roy Mason)

Mike, who ran a barbers shop in Swadlincote, soon became known as *'The Singing Barber'*. He would often pick up on popular songs of the day, and give them the singing barber treatment, converting them, via use of the South Derbyshire vernacular, into a format that the locals would be familiar with. *Peter Starstedt's* 'Where Did You Go To My Lovely,' for example, became 'Where Did Yer Goo To Me Duck?' Though he was also capable of writing his own stuff, most notably the 'Swaddies' Lament', which detailed the finer (and not so finer) elements of everyday life for the occupants of a small mining town. Mike would often team up with others, most notably Kath Talbot, a teacher from the nearby Robert Sutton school.

From just up the road, Derby's **'Big' Jack Hudson**, would always be guaranteed a good reception that would secure him a regular spot on the *Barley* stage.

'Big' Jack Hudson
(Roy Mason)

Other local favourites were often found among the diverse talents in the clubs audience. These included the likes of Ziggy Patras, who would 'guest from the floor' running through 'Ballad of Geraldine' or maybe the instrumental 'Slowhands'. Ziggy is well remembered for his guitar technique, admired by many of his comtempories, often treating his neighbours to a free rendition of a guitar classic. In fact there were - by all accounts - two things that would let the good residents of Horninglow know that it was a Sunday: the sound of the church bells of St. John's calling the faithful to worship, and the sound of Ziggy's well amplified guitar drowning out the sound.

Another regular, taking time out from his duties drumming with local rock outfits, was Pete 'Dolly' Dolman, who would showcase his talents on the guitar for the benefit of the folk club audience.

John Squire, a teacher from Rolleston, was a self-taught fiddle player who initially agreed to appear at the *Barley* to raise some much needed funds for the club. As Roy points out, "the club often overstretched itself financially, needing to keep costs down to a minimum while at the same time trying to book acts that would draw in the punters". That cost money. Roy was most impressed, not only with John's talents, but also his commitment to the cause. "He used to knock 'em dead". John would later duet on stage with John Leonard, later to become a Radio 1 producer.

Due to the increased interest in the folk scene during the 60s and 70s, it was decided to expand into different venues across town. The Panjandrum Room at the *Royal Oak* in the Market Place (now back as the *Old Royal Oak*) was set up as a Sunday night venue, being run by Roy and Irishman Brendan Doyle, who worked at the, now gone, Burton General Hospital in New Street. Working in tandem with Mike Burman, Roy also opened up the George Street Club for fortnightly Wednesday night sessions, with Pete Clyde occupying the resident slot. The opening night of the club, was to end in disaster for the visiting band **Agincourt**. Although their appearance went down well, they were involved in a car accident on their way home from the gig, resulting in a stay in hospital.

Agincourt, with Mike Burman, at the opening night of
the **George Street Folk Club**. *October 29, 1971*.

Unfortunately neither outlet lasted for too long due to dwindling attendances. The *Royal Oak Folk Club* closed through 'lack of support', shutting its doors for the last time on the night of Sunday, February 15, 1970, with George Street shutting its doors to the folkies in 1972. Others tried to set up folk venues, one of these being held at *The Builders Arms* in Moor Street under the title *'The Staircase Folk Club'*. Most were fairly short lived, with the Barley remaining as the main player.

Your four shillings (20p) entrance fee bought you access to the top folk musicians of the era. Ewan MacColl, obviously not fazed by the floor singer ruling, appeared several times, along with his partner, **Peggy Segar**, plus there were return visits from local lads and lasses made good The Skilletts, who were under the management of one *Lonnie Donegan*, appearing on television with him on occasions. One regular visitor, not only at the *Barley*, but also the *Royal Oak*, was Mancunian **Pete Ryder**, (as far as I am aware no relation to that other Mancunian of note Shaun 'sell the furniture for crack' Ryder). Pete would revel in the atmosphere at the club, describing it as 'one of the friendliest clubs I've ever played in'. Pete's repertoire would range from 'blues and long hair' one week, to 'Irish rebellion' the next.

All that was great and good in folk music in this country paid a visit to the little room at the back of the pub. Mention the name **Alex Campbell** to any gathering of folk music fans and you would instantly be regaled with numerous 'on the road' stories concerning his 'hell raising' adventures. He had learned his trade the hard way, busking on the streets of Paris and London. By the time of his first visit to the club, in August 1969, he was billed as 'the incomparable' Alex Campbell, and no one was going to argue with that. The gig was, of course, a sell out, with those unable to get in reduced to listening in from the perimeter of the nearby bowling green - must have been a good weather that year. How many performers would get that sort of respect from their following?

Despite his hard-living reputation, Alex did, especially in his later years, insist on a little luxury. He would often stop over at some of the best hotels (why shouldn't he?), telling those who questioned his supposed extravagance: "we may not be millionaires, but we can live like them sometimes". He finally succumbed to throat cancer in 1987, maybe as a result of his lifestyle, with the title of one of his best known songs perhaps summed it all up: 'Been On The Road Too Long'.

Other names that are familiar with music fans of all genres appeared at the club, **Richard Digance** supplied his own particular brand of observational humour, and once recorded a TV special at the *Bass Museum* (that's what it was called then, and as far as I'm concerned that's what it's called now). **Tony Capstick**, another popular artist who combined folk with humour, was a favourite of Roy's. "He was a nutter, but a bloody good singer!". **Jake Thackerey** appeared there twice as well.

Barbara Dickson was another guest who would take up the kind invitation to stop the night in Stapenhill. The singer who went on to become very successful on the London stage, thrilling people with her "beautiful voice", would receive the full hospitality afforded many artists during the clubs time at the *Barley*. Did Roy's neighbours take advantage of the opportunity to catch a glimpse of the songstress sunbathing in Roy's back garden? I'd suspect some did.

The stopovers were always offered to anyone who would have too far to travel after appearing, although they did have a downside. After a hectic night organising the club and making sure everything was ready for entertainer and punter alike, Roy would find his house guests heading back to his home and tucking into the food and drink on hand. "They never wanted to go to bed" he recalls.

Sometimes it paid to put on some of the acts at a larger venue, normally the Burton Town Hall. Alex Campbell's name sake, **Ian Campbell**, another in a long line of Scotsman who plied their trade as travelling musicians (though Ian would find himself growing up deep in the heart of Sassenach territory, Birmingham), appeared at the venue in 1977. Ian had formed the *Clarion Skiffle Group* with his sister Lorna in the mid-50s, and she stayed on with him as part of the *Ian Campbell group*, scoring a hit single in 1965 with a cover of Dylan's 'The Times They are a Changin'. Ian's two sons, Robin and Ali, now carry on the songs for the people tradition as the mainstays of the world conquering ethnic and cultural mix that is *UB40*.

Probably one of the most successful folk groups to grace these lands, **The Settlers**, headlined at the Town Hall in October, 1971, with the 720-ticket allocation selling out within one week. Before they set foot on the ample stage the group were in need of a couple of liveners to get them in the mood. Enquiring of their genial host, "is there anywhere we could go for a quiet drink?", they were told: "why yes, there's a little pub over the water that will see to your needs". So we can say without fear of contradiction that The Settlers appeared at the *Barley Mow Folk Club*, albeit only for refreshments?

Also during 1977, with typical defiance in the face of the mainstream musical climate of the period, which was by now a *punk/new wave* crossover, a folk festival was organised at the BTR Club off Horninglow Road North. Among those turning out were local stalwart 'Hollerin' Dave Bull, **Miriams Backhouse** and **The Allcock Brothers**. Reports in the *Burton Daily Mail* anticipated a good turn out, which proved the case in what was seen as a successful event.

Though there are many crossover artists, who mix the acoustic traditional folk with a more modern amplified approach, it still remains one of the most elementary, yet popular forms of music, both locally and nationally. On one occasion a visiting group took a great deal of time setting up their equipment, some of which was electric. When it came to performance time the band took the 'stage' and played the full set oblivious to the fact that they had actually forgotten to power up their stuff, by all accounts no one, in either band or audience, had noticed!

The last night at the Barley was to be October 19, 1979, with **Strawhead** providing the swansong for the small backroom club, though Roy's running of the club would continue at various venues up until Christmas 1995, subsequent homes including the *Punch Bowl*, the *Meadowside* leisure centre and the *Bridge Brewery*, the latter being particularly successful.

*Strawhead at the Barley Mow on the last night
the folk club was held there.*

(Roy Mason)

In 1967 the club had a team that turned out in the Burton and District Sunday League Division One, they never lost a match, winning 12 and drawing 2 - not bad when you consider that games were played on the Sunday morning following a full on, no holds barred night out at the club the night before.

The mainstay of the club was still the live music, and maybe some of the football team decided to have a night out down there on Sunday, December 29, 1967. If they did they witnessed in action a man who within a few short years would be elevated to 'rock god' status, though its generally well known that he was also one of the nicest men in the whole business.

A group from Hull had been gigging for some time under the name *The Rats*; they had become quite well known and had appeared in London a few times. Their vocalist, Benny Marshall, takes up the story: "We had a manager at the time who, for reasons known to himself, decided we needed a name change. So we became, on his instruction, **Treacle**".

The name change was very short lived, though in that time they managed to put in an appearance down at the 76. Benny thinks he recalls the night: "If I remember right there was a barman there, an Irish fella, who indicated that we would be alright for a few late ones after we performed for the punters".

So the band took the stage, Benny on vocals and a lad by the name of Jim Simpson behind the drum kit and Geoff Appleby on bass. Maybe I should also mention the guitarist as he did rather well for himself some time later with another band. His name? **Mick Ronson**, one of the main players as David Bowie's *'Spiders from Mars'*. Mick went on to become a much respected producer, arranger, and contributor to any number of top names requiring his uncanny knack of putting together the right combination of notes and chords on his stripped down Les Paul.

If you were among the audience that night you got an early glimpse of the future star. The Rats reverted to their original name and still have re-unions, but now sadly without the talents of Mick, he passed away in 1993 at only 46 years old.

The majority of the groups taking to the little stage in the club were becoming deeply embroiled in the musical atmosphere at the time, as were many of the punters. Many of the bands who played there between 1967 and 1969 gave themselves names reflecting the new open attitude to life and music: **The Art Gallery, The Candy Bus, Cherry Blossom Clinic, The Inner Mind, Middle Earth** and **Sun Trolley**, with art, flowers, the Sun and the Earth reflecting the attitude of the new era by getting a name check.

Many, of course, had simply progressed from earlier 'Swinging 60s' groups. Dudley lad Roy (Dripper) Kent had already appeared down the 76 with the Birmingham outfit **The Strangers** in the early 60s, eventually turning out as vocalist for **Light Fantastic** (via a stint with Finders Keepers alongside Cannock lad Ian 'Sludge' Lees). This group would soon count amongst their number heavy metal pioneers Glenn Hughes and Mel Galley.

Light Fantastic were due to appear at the 76 in March, 1969, they were duly advertised in the local press as *'The Light featuring DIPPER [!] Kent'*. Dripper can recall the occasion of the visit: "We set off from Wolverhampton at about 5pm, we hadn't gone a mile down the road when we were stopped by the Old Bill for a check on our old Post Office van".

This was a normal enough event which most working groups regarded as just part of the experience. However, as the driving seat of the said vehicle was - at the time - being supported by house bricks Dripper wound down the window to talk with the officer with a certain amount of trepidation. "He ordered us to take the van off the road, so we phoned the lead guitar player's dad, who promptly came along with his Transit van. We eventually got to the gig (and had) a great night, but - sting in the tail! - I got six months driving ban for driving an un-roadworthy van! Well done Burton-on-Trent, the price of fame!"

One of the things that drew the attention of the forces of the law towards the van was that, in accordance with the times, it was painted with flower power symbols, although Dipper points out that at the time they themselves were just really a pop band - not that that would have made any difference to the representatives of Her Majesty's constabulary.

A very highly regarded group at this time were Tamworth's **Bakerloo Line**, (later becoming *Bakerloo Blues* Band), a polished blues trio often compared to *Cream* in the 'Power Blues Trio' genre, a very high compliment indeed. They went down very well at the club in 1968, so they should have - they were the support act for *Led Zeppelin's* opening night at their *Marquee Club* stint in London.

With the mention of *Cream* and therefore by association the man who was often termed 'God' by his fans, Eric Clapton, I would like to share with you a little anecdote passed on to me by Burton's Paul Dennis, it concerns a friend of his by the name of Terry:

"He (Terry) was in the Roebuck Pub (in Station Street) one night when three extravagantly dressed blokes came in. They ordered a round of drinks, then one came over to Terry - the pub was far from packed - and asked him which was the best road to take to get to Derby. Terry gave the guy the info, then asked if they were in a band. They said they were and that they had a gig in Derby. Terry asked "Is this

all of you then?" "Yes," replied the guy, "just the three of us, guitar, bass and drums." "Well" said Terry, "I think you'll struggle unless you get another guitarist." "Well, Eric can play a bit!" said the guy before finishing off his drink and leaving with the others."

A week or two later Terry thought he spotted the man he had been talking to performing with his group on a television show, playing bass alongside the group's drummer, Phil Seamen protégé *Ginger Baker* and guitarist *Eric Clapton*. Terry firmly believes that he had been offering some free, and it has to be said, well intentioned commercial advice to non other than Jack Bruce.

The aforementioned Jack and Ginger had not long left the **Graham Bond Organisation**, Ginger being the most recent departee shortly before that groups first visit to the 76 in 1968 - they re-visited again in 69. Bond was one of the main exponents of British R & B during this period, and is widely regarded as being the first person in the UK to play the organ using the distinctive rotating Hammond speaker.

What any of these visitors made of their changing facilities at the venue is anyone's guess: it would have been interesting to have seen the look on some of their faces when they were ushered towards the rear of the chip shop next door!

Don't know if any of them down the chip shop actually thought they were Elvis, what I do know is that some of the finest rock musicians in the land have removed their clothes in the back of this place.

Other frequent visitors to the town in their earlier days were Birmingham's **Moody Blues**, and their gigs here during 1967 would, I think, have made interesting listening to say the least. This was not only the year of *Sergeant Pepper*, but also the Moodys' 'Days of Future Passed' opus, a collaboration between the group and *The London Festival Orchestra*. I have recently come into possession of the said LP, which was greeted by some as the template for prog rock. To me being a follower of, first glam rock, and then punk during my teenage years, it just sounds, well, odd! I suppose you had to be there at the time.

Whether it did lay the groundwork for the next musical chapter in this nations life is open to debate. What is not in question, though, is the steady conversion of clubs into disco's. Still causing as much controversy as it ever did, the Bargates development sprung up over the road from the 76 in High Street, and with it came a place that would eventually become the antithesis of all the old 76 stood for.

Starting out as The Top Rank Bowling Club, it would eventually transform into the full-on flared trouser, glitter ball cheesy 70s disco madness that was *Adam's* or was it *Eve's*? No was it both.

Initially it was, what it has now become again, a tenpin bowling club, but in those early days it did provide another source of live entertainment for the youngsters of Burton. The club opened on March 21, 1964, (Maurice Hall recalls appearing there with local sporting personality Jack Bodell at the opening event), trying, straight away, to gather in the younger elements, advertising 'Teen and Twenty Nights' for a special price of three bob (15p) a game.

The Top Rank Club, January, 1968.

Soon the venue was putting on groups, and while the majority of them were covers bands, they were still a good draw for those who wanted to combine a night's bowling with a spot of boogie, if not to the band then at least to *'Mad' Mike Ryder*, the clubs resident DJ. Bands often performed while games were still in play, with the tables in the bar having to be unscrewed by maintenance men beforehand. Among the first to take the stage in the Top Rank were Brummies **The Boll Weevils** and **The Seven Eight Set**, along with Liverpool's **Escorts**.

The acts came and went, though perhaps the notion of going for a game of tenpin and trying to watch a group at the same time proved a bit to distracting for some folk. By the time Stoke's **Story Book** were in the spotlight the curtain was already beginning to fall, with Freedom Suite providing the finale for the live music nights in 1970, for the time being at least.

Live music did return, with some enterprising souls providing a steady stream of groups during the mid 70s era, although again a lack of support may have been a contributory factor to the halting of those.

Gordon Band, again sensing a gap in the market, attempted to set up an altogether more sophisticated night out for those who were, perhaps, no longer teenagers. Taking over a property in the middle of the High Street, which at various times in its history had been an armoury for the town's Rifle Volunteers and, in 1842, a private museum, owned by Sir Oswald Mosley for the newly formed Burton Natural History Society. The premises were converted into what were described at the time as a 'dancing club and restaurant', and were opened on Friday, November 8, 1968, as **The Tudor Club**.

The Tudor Club in High Street, 1968

There does seem to have been a need to provide a venue to which the slightly older age group would feel at home. This had been attempted in 1964 with the conversion of part of Cauldwell Hall near Swadlincote into a *Country Club*. By 1966, according to Dave Hughes "it was THE place to go.

They club was equipped with a Casino, and while Dave's group played in one room (Dave was now with **The Riddle**) a dance quartet performed in another, obviously catering for those used to a more traditional form of dance.

The Tudor Club possibly failed to take off because of the very need to ensure, shall we say, a more genteel type of clientele for the venue meant that a membership fee was charged. This didn't go down too well with prospective punters as they were then asked to pay an entrance fee at the door, at which many became a bit disgruntled. The Tudor Club folded fairly quickly. The place where it used to stand is now just an empty space, why was it knocked down? Who knows, this is Burton, we just do those sort of things.

We can round off the 60s in Burton, and welcome in the 70s, by paying a visit to the newly refurbished *Stable Bar* at *The Queens Hotel*, where the mainstay of those who frequented the 76 would form up. The dimmed room would often be packed to the rafters, there would be a hell of a lot of big hair about the place, both on the males and the females, the atmosphere would be sweetened up by the smell of *patchouli oil*, and, more than occasionally, there would be the faint whiff off an 'exotic' cigarette! (This particular form of relaxation was, apparently, introduced to the town by visiting American soldiers in World War Two).

The place was the meeting point for the lads and lasses before setting off on a Friday night to catch the latest band at the 76 Club or, if it was a Saturday, The Paradise Club above *The Star* in the High Street. They can be considered a lucky lot, whether they were in any condition to know it or not, they would, these nights, particularly at the 76, witness some of the best rock music to be had anywhere in the world.

And they didn't teach me
that in school....

burton students union presents:

rag
from 8 till midnite with

rock

fabulous value at only four bob per body !!!

WHIT SATURDAY, JUNE 1st
COLLEGE LAWNS
Abbey Street
★★ Big Stars and Big Beat ★★

JOHNNY GENTLE
JOHNNY BEV

The Astonaires
The Saphires

Bar
Buffet

Students are a good audience. They are (usually) young enough to have their fingers firmly on the pulse of the contemporary music scene, and, as they still retain the remnants of the gang mentality that helped them out in the school yard, when they attend an event its normally with a crowd.

The Burton Students Union (SU) was formed in 1941, at the same time as the *Burton Junior Technical and Commercial School* was established.

Events were organised by the union, including an annual dance usually held at the Town Hall, with the likes of Joe Fearn and Ted Taylor providing the sounds.

By 1963 the college authorities were persuaded (amid a fair amount of trepidation) by the union to allow the staging of the college's first 'rag' event, initially going out under the *'Rag Rock'* title. The students 'rag' became an annual event in the town, with much preparation going into the organisation of a weeks activities, culminating in a parade through the town centre on the Saturday, complete with live music performed from the back of a lorry.

Come night time, operations would move to either the college lawns or indoors if wet. The chief purpose (officially) of the event was to raise money for charity, which the students did very enthusiastically, and very successfully. The other vital ingredient was fun, and lots of it - be it trying to drown each other in the raft race along the Trent or dancing themselves to a standstill to one of the top local groups or one of the frequent visiting acts.

In that inaugural year the week's activities were to include a rag ball, the aforementioned raft race, a 'bedstead derby', a talent contest and piano smashing, for which would be contestants were given some useful advice: *'bring yer own 'ommer'*.

For jazz fans there was to be a jazz festival on the Friday night, followed the next evening by the rag rock event on the college lawns with **Johnny Dean and the Crestas**, Johnny Gentle, Johnny Bev, **The Astonaires** and Burton's Sapphires.

Birmingham's Lee Stirling and the Bruisers topped the bill in 1964. A very classy group, many recall them as having particularly well honed vocal talents. Also that year the jazz night was livened up by the appearance of Phil Seamen. Some of this performance was captured on cine film, albeit very briefly, and the clip can be found on video tape montage of the college rag activities during 63/64.

Phil Seamen in classic 'looks like he's asleep' drumming action

Organisers were given use of the staff common room, which also doubled up as the bands' changing rooms. Imagine how the lecturers must have laughed when, arriving for work after that weekend, the first sight they were met with, on opening the common room door, was that of a rather large helping of 'pavement pizza' left there by one of the 'artistes'. Although no one can be certain which one (you can't dust for vomit), all fingers pointed to the most likely. In fairness it was always easy to blame Phil for his excesses, and nobody would doubt you if you said it was him, although I imagine on more than one occasion he may have simply have been the most likely.

Initially, before the completion of the existing college, the SU clubroom was housed in an old corrugated tin building behind the old public library in Union Street, the building itself being part of the Technical High School engineering annexe. By 1962 members could make full use of the facilities; it was open each night from 7pm to 9.55pm, with what was described in an advert as *a Jukebox for the more energetic members.'* Clubroom dances were organised by the students committee and, of course, there was the annual ball. Some of the students were even more energetic than the advert imagined, Maria Chambers being one of them. "We used to have records on at dinner time, and we all used to get up and dance to them".

One man who many will remember from their student days is Andy Starbuck, Andy played a big part in the running of the SU, having been approached by the principle of the college, Eric White, who intended to increase the amount of youth work being carried out. Andy had already become a part-time youth leader in 1967, and was moved up to full-time the following year. He describes his old boss, Mr White, as very pro-youth, and with this in mind the committee decided to start putting on regular live bands as well as a Thursday night disco provided by PT Lawrence: "7.30 start, every Thursday after *Top of the Pops*".

The college lawns were the usual venue for the rock events. **Danny King and the Mayfair Set** brought affairs to a close in 1966, *"8 'til Midnight, 6/- or 7/- on the night"*. In 1967, Andy and the rest of the committee cranked things up somewhat by introducing more bands to Burton, on occasions at other venues. Though many local music fans will recall 1967 as the year The Moody Blues provided the musical full stop to Burton Rag, there was also events at the Drill Hall, with the SU annual dance taking place on Saturday October 14. Topping the bill, and advertised in the local press, were **The Traffic** - hold on a minute THE Traffic!? Steve Winwood and his psychedelia influenced companions? Er....no actually, this was The Traffic, a Leicester based band. One or two people who hadn't bothered to check the facts beforehand were a mite disappointed that night!

The Burton crowd nearly didn't get to see the Moodys either.

"We were intending to book the **Nashville Teens** for £100 but realised we could get hold of the Moody Blues for £90, leaving us £10 better off, so we booked them instead". Being 'right on', politically correct student types they now had a dilemma on their hands: £10 to the good, what could they use that for? Maybe a donation to charity, buy some needy folks a dinner? No, they thought, we worked hard, lets give us all a treat. So they booked, what in those days would be termed an 'exotic dancer', that's right, they booked a stripper, who, by all accounts, made good use of the local backing band's saxophone as an impromptu clothes peg.

(both illustrations - Burton Mail)

Meanwhile demolition work was taking place on the site of the - as yet - uncompleted Burton Technical College by Manor Croft. Old cottages were being demolished to make way for the building which we are now familiar with, and it was during this work that a long forgotten part of the old Soho Wharf was re-discovered, an underground brick-built vault, with an arched low-level ceiling.

BURTON OBSERVER & CHRONICLE, THURSDAY, OCTOBER 5th, 1967

OLD VAULT UNCOVERED ON BURTON COLLEGE SITE

126

It was probably an old storage area for commodities such as wine, which would remain naturally cool in all weathers. In a rare instance of foresight the authorities recognised that it would provide an ideal meeting place for the SU. Not only that, it would make a bloody good little club for putting on bands, with an atmosphere and feel to the place not too dissimilar to Liverpool's famous *Cavern*. Once the building inspectors had declared it safe for use it was incorporated in to the framework of the new building. What are the chances of something happening like that today?

With preparations going full steam ahead for the move to the plush new college building, the old Union Street facility was being slowly run down. Helping to say farewell to the old place were **Caravan**, who visited as part of the rag celebrations on the evening of the solstice, mid-summers day 1969. The Canterbury prog rockers, who had already performed at the 76 as their last incarnation - **The Wilde Flowers**, had Robert Wyatt on drums. You may remember Robert's superb version of *Elvis Costello's* anti Falklands War epic, 'Ship Building'. You may also recall that when he appeared on the nations favourite *poptastic* programme, *Top of the Pops*, the producers tried to dissuade him from appearing in his wheelchair. Couldn't he perform sitting on a chair instead? That way the nations youth wouldn't be offended by the sight of a crippled man singing his song, from a wheelchair. Could you think of anything more offensive to a human being than treatment like that?

With the new college officially opening up in a blaze of publicity in 1969, the SU people were ready to embark on a very successful programme of events, both at the newly opened **Vaults**, and also in organised trips to see quality bands elsewhere. A steady stream of trips was organised by the SU, with members getting the opportunity to see the likes of *Led Zeppelin, Genesis, Steely Span* and *Hawkind*, complete with pre-**Motorhead** Lemmy and, of course 'dancer' Stacy - (wonder if it was her performing at the Moody Blues after-gig bash?).

The group who 'christened' the Vaults appears to be, as far as I can tell, **Grizelda**, (no more information than that I'm afraid), though you can bet your life someone will come along and prove me wrong on that one. We'll say that they were the first to be advertised as appearing at the Vault in January, 1970. They were quickly followed in March by 'the progressive rock sound' of Londoners **Titus Groan**.

Though many of those who were in the audience soon found out that once the place was packed out the cooling effect, essential for storing inanimate objects, failed to work on sweating, breathing humans. If the place was rammed full the heat inside could get pretty intense. Air circulating fans were installed in the rear doors to alleviate the problem, but they were only partially successful. If you were one of the late comers to a gig you would find yourself pressed up against the curved walls and ceiling with the added discomfort of your head acting as a conductor for the condensation formed up on the ceiling.

Medicine Head, also signed up for the Vaults in 1970, always managing to pack the place out and leave those in the audience going home happy. The idea for the duo initiated by guitarist John Fiddler, who was courting a Stapenhill girl at the time, and often, by messing around on her family's piano he would form the basis of the future songs. With Fiddler on guitar, vocals and bass drum and Peter Hope-Evans providing accompanying harmonica or Jews harp, often taking a stroll through the audience at the same time, the duo soon had a powerful and entertaining stage presence, which the Burton crowd took to their hearts. They were asked back to the town many times, and by the time we had moved on a year they were booked as the main act at the rag revelry at the Town Hall.

The Mighty **Medicine Head**, *from their 'Two Man Band' LP*

(Barn Records)

Andy Starbuck, along with others including Yvonne Minham and Pete Anson (it was Pete who used to lead the rag parade through the town), used to try and pick some of the more well known bands for the student rag functions, using agent Jake Elcock from Wolverhampton's Lafayette Club. This meant bigger venues would be needed, such as the Town Hall and occasionally the Drill Hall. One of their most successful events featured the **Average White Band – Roy Young Band** combination, at the Town Hall in 1973. They managed to pack the place out, no mean feat in a place the size of the Town Hall.

Andy remembers the crowd outside getting a bit impatient and storming the doors to get in. Others were not so keen, and the staff on duty that night threatened to cut the power on a number of occasions. They objected to the noise levels being pumped out by the bands, and, in the case of Roy Young, decided that the show had gone on long enough. The cause of the time over-run was down to the fact that Roy, former Beatles cohort and Rebel Rouser, encored for nearly 30 minutes, with the crowd - or the 'hysterical audience' as the *Burton Mail* described them - still roaring for more when he eventually left the stage.

Chris Spedding's **Sharks** were the headliners in 1974, (Did he play on the **Sex Pistols** recordings? Who cares, at least that would have been cool. Appearing on TOTP in a Wombles suit? Oh dear!). Chris was backed by local lads Oakdale, of whom we will hear more later. The Sharks would turn up in a big American car, the *Sharkmobile*, with a big flashy winged rear, Chris himself would dye his hair - not much out of the ordinary today, but in them days, very rare, very daring, very rock and roll!

Other bands would sometimes be housed in the college refectory (that's a canteen to the rest of us), which was larger in capacity than the Vaults. Here Scotland's **Sutherland Brothers** gave Burtonians their first taste of 'Sailing', a song written by them which would later be turned into a lighter waving, set closing, *tour de force* by sometime leggy blonde molester Rod Stewart.

*Members of the Students Union, in the **Vaults**, with food parcels which they distributed to local, OAPs at Christmas, 1971.*   *(Burton Mail)*

Some visiting bands were more at home in the cramped surroundings of the Vaults, the Fusion Orchestra being one of them, they were quoted as saying the place reminded them of the *Cavern Club*. The band, fronted by Jill Saward, would make their way to the stage, picking their way through the assembled throng, who were more often than not sitting on the floor. Musician, and *Burton Daily Mail* reporter Brian Harrigan, was in attendance at their Vaults gig. Brian, who on occasion was less than complimentary about the town he now found himself in, and the quality of music therein, gave us his opinion of the night:

"(the band) *went down very well with connoisseurs of Heavy music, Jill Saward writhed around the stage, with the drummer playing percussion on everything as he wandered around the room*"

Harrigan then, I think, let himself and the rest of us down a bit, by proclaiming that the band were *"the biggest bunch of weirdoes to invade Burton for some time"* - or maybe that was meant to be a compliment?

Rag Parade *1973 – forming up outside Eatoughs*

(Burton Mail)

In 1973 Eric 'Chalky' or 'Dabber' White (depending on what era we're in) had retired as principal of the college but he had set in motion an enthusiastic and very well supported Students Union, encouraged by the presence and drive of Andy Starbuck. Andy himself finished with the SU in 1979, but during the intervening years after Eric left, Andy and his colleagues had introduced bands as diverse as **Greenslade**, **Sassafras**, **Mean Street Dealers** and the - very popular round these parts - **Trapeze** to the students and general public of Burton.

By the late 70s things had changed somewhat; rag rock still took place but now the rag ball was held at Eve's Disco and the weeks proceedings were kicked off with the *'Froth'* disco in the college refectory. *Froth* you may recall was the name of the *rag mag*, a fanzine type booklet sold around the town and pubs and clubs to raise money for charity and containing risqué jokes, all lavishly illustrated with pictures of women in various states of undress. It was a big favourite with us impressionable young lads I can tell you.

The key word with all the SU activities was fun, be it the rag stuff, the raft race (re-instated in 1972 after three years lay off due to fears of health issues), the flour bomb fest that was the rag parade, or simply the pleasure of organising a gig down the Vaults and seeing the place packed out with happy, sweating youngsters - even if they were watching weirdoes!

(Michael Badcock – Buevelands)

Rolleston Youth Club was housed in the Forest of Needwood School, only recently demolished, and like all youth clubs it was run to give youngsters the chance to do something constructive after school hours, an attempt to stave of the dreaded teenage boredom. The difference with Rolleston was that, as well as having superb facilities within the school, it also possessed a hall that was, acoustically, as good as you can get.

The club was started by John Redfern in 1965, but it was when Michael Badcock–Beuvelands took the helm in 1969 that things really took off. Being gifted with the ideal setting to put on live bands, with a capacity of around 600, it was soon realised that not only could they put on regular gigs but they could also, by use of the fully booked up membership subscriptions, afford some of the bigger acts doing the rounds. Initially they started off with a couple of local bands, **Six Across** and the **Which What** (formerly the **John Smith Affair**). Often bands were booked on the recommendation of a couple of the club regulars who also went to see bands at *The Hardinge Arms* in Kings Newton. Soon they were able to entice members of the Radio 1 DJ elite to perform at the club, with **Emperor Rosko** starting the ball rolling, gravely voiced **Tommy Vance** rocked 'em out and **DLT** also did a turn.

All members received a programme of events for the year ahead, with bands often booked a year in advance, with the hope that they stopped together for at least another year before the 'musical differences' set in and denied their audience the chance to see them.

plus Disco from 9-0—10-0 p.m. Cover charge 5p.
Committee meeting 8-0 p.m. in library

Thursday, September 20th
Outing to Whittington Youth Club. Leave club 7-0 p.m. Cost only 5p, collected on coach.

Saturday, September 22nd
The Burton and South Derbyshire Netball Association annual general meeting and tournament. The club are hosts.

Monday, September 23rd
Youth Club 7-30—9-30 p.m.

Wednesday, September 26th
"It's a knock-out" 7-0—10-30 p.m. with guest celebrities, comedianTony Lee, lots of games, loads of fun, disco from 9-30 to 10-30 p.m. Visiting youth clubs include Rocester, Uttoxeter, Tutbury and Mayfield Cost 5p (10p non-members)

Saturday, September 29th
Progressive Concert with "Super Tramp" 7-30—11-0 p.m. Admission 50p. Licensed bar for those over the age of 18.

Monday October 1st.
Youth Club 7-30—9-30 p.m.

Wednesday, October 3rd
Youth Club 7-30—9-30 p.m.
A netball tournament will take place.
Committee meeting 8-0 p.m. in library.

*See **Supertramp** for 50p! September 1973.*
(Michael Badcock – Buevelands)

Supertramp would, in all probability, not be described as a progressive group, they turned out to be leaning towards the poppier side of things, but they were a tremendous coup for the Rolleston team. On nights when they had groups appearing, the steps outside the school would have maybe 200 to 300 people waiting eagerly for entry, by 8pm the place would be full. The membership was drawn from around the Rolleston, Stretton, Tutbury and Horninglow areas, though sometimes they received visits from further away:

"We had a visit from the 444 gang one night (a group of bikers based at the old 444 café by St Peters and Main Street junction in Stapenhill) though for some reason the bikers all arrived in a Transit van!".

Radio 1 DJ **Tony Prince** *signs autographs on his Rolleston visit.*
(Burton Mail)

Club organisers had a novel way of reducing the prospect of tribal warfare breaking out. This being the 70s you could take your pick of any number of youth cults; *boot boys, grebos, hippies* (still) and *glam rockers*, but leather jackets and outdoor wear had to be left in the cloakroom, as did football scarves. "It broke down barriers and tribal gatherings". They would also try to encourage as many 'gang members' as they could on to the committee and get them involved in the decision-making process. Those caught causing trouble could find themselves banned, not only from the Rolleston club, but also any number of other clubs, reducing their social life to virtually zero. For the bigger events a local bobby, (and occasional 76 doorman), Byron Davies, was hired for the night. His presence would deter would be trouble causers, though as Michael points out: "hiring the police was often more expensive than hiring the band!"

For its Hallowe'en nights the club would always re-book a band going by the title of **Nightmare**, who would set the tone for the evening with their Lord Sutch style cavortings, making their entrance in coffins and employing liberal use of blood capsules.

In 1975 they had another visit from Radio 1, this time the rather likeable, smooth talking anti-*smashy and nicey* - **Stuart Henry**. Also that year Liverpool pop/funksters, and survivors from Merseybeat **The Real Thing** played at the club, another sell out night.

Enter 1977, a big, BIG year. The big man from Tupelo passed away in a very non-rock and roll style, the Pistols managed not to get to Number 1 in the charts, despite outselling everyone else and, and there was another coup by the club: top boy band **Slik** were on, marking Midge Ure's first foot on the ladder to global fame and *Band Aid*. The previous year the youngsters had topped the charts with 'Forever and Ever'. They were in with the big boys, but events in the music industry were passing them by.

The punk explosion was in full swing and Midge Ure, in particular, wanted to be part of it. He changed the name of the band and then very nearly became a teenage Sex Pistol, eventually teaming up with Glenn Matlock, who was a teenage Sex Pistol, forming the *Rich Kids*, later still joining up with 'techno rockers' **Ultravox**, who by co-incidence played at the 76 Club that very same year.

Very often support for the night's main act would be by one of the local bands, they would generally be required to do a 45-minute set to warm up the audience before the headliners came on. **Cargo** played as support for Supertramp's visit, while **Fingertricks** backed up **Wild Turkey** in 1972, both bands containing a fair sprinkling of Burton musicians.

Cargo**'s saxophonist, Alan 'Nala' Wright, on stage at **Rolleston Youth Club.

(Trina Barnes)

Stroll On were frequently used as support. The band contained the Horninglow based Poxon brothers, Stuart and Dick, the band had also appeared here beforehand as **Food For Thought**, a much travelled – and respected - group. The visit of **Principle Edwards Magic Theatre** in 1974 saw Nick Pallett, another native son and former *Kaveman*, returning (almost) to his Stapenhill roots. *Pub Quiz Fact*: This group were the first to be signed to John Peel's doomed *Dandelion* Record Label.

*An early line-up of **Stroll On**:*
Stuart Poxon, Dick Poxon, Keith Durkin, Brian Harrigan and Kev Spiers.

(Burton Mail)

Rolleston Youth Club was run very successfully up to 1985, but was then forced to close its doors, not because it failed in its aspirations, either from the leadership or the membership in any way, but simply because Staffordshire County Council decided it was to close. The irony of the situation was that they (the county council) had decided the Forest of Needwood was no longer required, and it was opened up as an annexe to Burton Technical College. Demolished some time later despite protests it is now a housing estate (how utterly predictable).

The youth club was probably about as close as you could possibly get to a professionally run club run for the youth of the area. The majority of the youth clubs around Burton were run by well intentioned people, restricted by a very limited budget, though not by limited enthusiasm or imagination. Up the road and over the border into Derbyshire, we encounter another effort to bring quality live music to the youth of the area, and for a short while during the early 70s, pretty successful it was too.

In 1971 a group of former members of Hatton Youth Club had outgrown the place, and moved on to the *18+ group*, all housed within the Hatton Secondary School. The school at the time doubled up as a community centre for the Village, offering various activities and a coffee bar for when the pubs were shut.

The youth leader at this time was Bob Cherry, who became increasingly exasperated by the older kids (ie, over 18s) hanging around the place, so he threw down a challenge to them; if you're fed up with the lack of activities for those of your age group, how about organising something yourselves more appropriate to an adult audience?

Taking up the gauntlet thrown down by their leader, a like-minded bunch of individuals set about supplying some of their own entertainment. Included in the group (though I must point out that these mentioned were not the only ones involved), were Chris Newton, Ian Redpath, Mick Bell, Steve Noon, Mick Underwood, Mick Spendlove and Dave Noon.

The best thing to do, I think, is to let Ian Redpath take up the story:

*"(Being as) sex and drugs were in short supply in Hatton at the time, we decided on rock and roll. It was Chris Newton who got the ball rolling by booking a then unknown band called **Genesis** for the rather large sum (at the time anyway) of £70.*

Unfortunately, we didn't have that sort of cash available (the modern equivalent would probably be about £1000) so Bob Cherry, possibly not wanting to discourage us at our first attempt, lent us the money. So on the 19th of December 1970 history was made with the appearance of Genesis at Hatton Centre!"

Obviously, at the time, the group were not the world-wide superstars they later went on to become, but it just shows what you can do with a bit of youthful audacity – and somebody else's money!

Ian again: *"The concert took place in the school hall, which had a good size stage and room enough for 200 people. The line up of the band at that time was Phil Collins, drums; Steve Hackett, guitar; Mike Rutherford, bass; Tony Banks, organ; and Peter Gabriel on vocals. All of them, except Gabriel, remained seated throughout the performance, something I'd never seen before, or since."*

Following the success of the evening the band were re-booked for a return visit the following year. By the time of that next performance they had become somewhat more successful, their LP 'Trespass' had become a hit, and the resultant booking fee had risen accordingly – to £700. Though the lads were canny operators, no contract had been signed by the group, and to their eternal credit, they agreed to perform for the original pre-arranged fee. The second visit was every bit as successful as the first; according to the Burton Mail the "delirious crowd wouldn't let them leave the stage."

There followed a steady stream of up and coming groups at the centre. Around two each month were laid on over the next six months including **Lindasfarne, Uriah Heep, Van der Graaf Generator, Medicine Head** and **Trapeze**. Starting to get the hang of this rock promoter lark, the lads decided to hunt down some of the bigger fish, though they were possibly getting a little bit too ambitious as the following story from Ian testifies.

"Chris tried to book The Who over the telephone, only to be told that they charged £1000 (1971 money) per hour!! Needless to say they never appeared at Hatton!"

This being the early 70s, many of the stage props and lighting effects in use were extremely primitive by modern standards.

Bob Whetton: "There were some very good shows at Hatton. Uriah Heep were superb. It was probably the first time I had ever seen anyone using a strobe light, though it was soon outlawed because of its effect on epileptics."

Technical problems, then as now, were frequent for the groups' sound engineers. In the audience for the Van der Graaf show was Ian Dyke, who recalls Dave Jackson having constant feedback problems with his electric saxophone. A resultant write up of the gig in music weekly Sounds cleared up the problem.

"...the octave divider creates the sound of a full sax section, and on Friday night at the Hatton Centre, Derby this was missing with Dave's equipment breaking down after the first number.....the situation was helped by an understanding audience."

Sadly opposition to the live band nights at the club was slowly mounting. The headmaster of the school pointed out that his permission for the concerts to be staged in the first place had never been sought, and that organisers had failed to put up notices that property left by visitors anywhere within the complex was at the owners risk. So when a coat was stolen from the cloakroom, compensation had to be paid to the owner, resulting in a serious shortfall of cash, and consequently no reserve left to book further bands.

So it was that the nights came to a bit of an abrupt end, though Ian is very philosophical about the whole thing: *"those concerts were some of the highlights of our lives"*. Though memories are now a bit vague for all concerned, Ian does recall some of the bizarre modes of transport employed by hard up groups. *"Most turned up in the usual beat up old Transit van except for Medicine Head who turned up in a beat up Morris Minor, and* **Tir Na Nog** *who completed the last leg of their journey by Trent Bus."*

Rock'n'Roll – you've gotta live the dream, ain't yer?!

Keep on steppin' -
never looking back...

Burton Soul Club - *76 Badge*

(Neil Turner)

Billy Butler's words were probably never less appropriate than within the context of this book, the whole concept being to take a backward glance at the wealth of great live music the people of this town were once offered. However exception can be made, especially in the case of the still fantastically popular *Northern Soul* scene in this town. Having passed through the Beat era and the Beatles, many of those who loved their music sought out sounds from further away than Liverpool or London, many who leaned over the mod side of the (imagined) great divide were starting to dig out their aural pleasures from the US, in particular Detroit's *Motown* label, others tuning their ears to some relatively obscure rhythm and blues acts - in fact, the more obscure – the better.

Though the bulk of the soul audience were specifically involved with the vinyl efforts of these entertainers, over a period of time they were able to enjoy live performances of some of their favourite dance tracks thanks to the efforts of individuals within Burton's soul community. This section is in no way meant to be a concise history of their endeavours (though there is a story there worth telling, surely time for someone to take on that job!?), more an overview of the live acts that were offered for the faithful to pay homage.

There was a great deal of interest in black r 'n' b music before the soul movement took off. Many of the groups involved in beat music, had, by the mid-sixties, turned towards the US for their inspiration, and this co-incided with the fermenting soul scene, with both Burton Rugby Club and the 76 offering suitable venues to put on live acts delivering soul and funk tinged sets. It was pretty sharp thinking by those involved at the rugby club. The ground needed new floodlights, and realising that laying on quality groups would not only raise the money needed, but also provide some good live entertainment, they went ahead with a series of events, both indoor and out.

Always in the vanguard where music was concerned Gordon Band's 76 was soon the - at this stage - unofficial HQ of Burton Soul Club. Stapenhill's Leander Club was also heavily involved, though we can visit them later.

Shaping up in 1967 for the soul grooves up ahead the 76 brought on **Souls a Go-Go** and the **Soul Movers** (I think the clue was in the name here). Later on they would import direct from the States **The Pitiful Souls**, the group being asked back again a few months later, by which time they had dropped the genre-identifying tag and became simply **The Pitifuls**. Moving up a notch or two in 1968, the club presented 'Mr. Barefootin' himself, **Robert Parker**, 'Sensational US R'n'B Stars' **James and Bobby Purify** and, direct from the USA, futuristic soul diva's **Patti Labelle and the Belles**.

Quite justifiably the 76 could boast in its adverts 'Soul – Beat – R'n'B – Tamla Motown – Jazz', although the rugby club was no slouch, initially putting on a steady stream of Midlands-based soul acts, such as **Fearns Brass Foundry**, who's version of 'Don't Change It' appears on a number of Northern Soul compilation CD's (though on one Decca item filed under 'Northern Soul' they share the billing with Tom Jones and David Essex, not exactly staples of the Northern circuit!), the club was, however, gearing up for altogether bigger affairs.

Making use of a large area of open space that was adjacent to the clubhouse (I think they call it a rugby pitch), the club realised they could tempt down to their Peel Croft home some mighty fine acts and draw in some big crowds. Adverts appeared for a Barbeque dance (they used to use the full word in those more staid times, even if it was spelt wrong), taking place on the club grounds on Saturday, August 24, 1968. Tickets sold well for the event, with organisers covering for the possibility of good old British bad weather mucking things up by erecting a marquee on the pitch. Headlining was to be Leicester's **Pesky Gee!** (the exclamation mark was important, as we shall hear), with support being from the more than capable figures of **Jethro Tull**, who, co-incidentally, were at that time resident at London's famous Marquee club (former home of psuedo mod rockers The Who).

The pairing of the nine-piece soul band (albeit with growing psychedelic tendencies) with madcap "Elizabethan" folk/proggies Tull seemed a strange combination, but as it turned out, it seemed to work. Pesky Gee!'s Chris Dredge recalls his time spent with the group. "We started out as a three piece, by the time we played at Burton's Rugby Club there were nine of us. We were paid about £200, which didn't amount to a lot when shared out. The marquee outside wasn't really suited for music; as a result the sound was crap!"

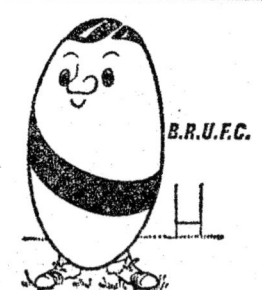

FRIDAYS . . 7-30 p.m.

PEEL CROFT

B.R.U.F.C.

THIS WEEK
THE FANTASTIC

BREED

BARBEQUE DANCE

SATURDAY, 24th AUG. 7-30—midnight
PEEL CROFT, Branston Road, Burton

PESKY GEE

(9 PIECE SOUL SHOW)

JETHRO TULL

(STARS OF BLUES NIGHT, 'MARQUEE' LONDON)

— in support DECOYS —

Food available   Side Shows   Licensed Bar

TICKETS 7/6   PAY AT DOOR 10/- (available from
Norman's, New Street or Burton Rugby Club)

(Burton Mail)

Pesky Gee! always insisted on the exclamation mark being included as part of the title, though as we can see it didn't appear in the *Mails'* advert. For their first LP they wanted to make sure that the symbol was included, and got in touch with the record company to insist that the exclamation mark had to be on the LP cover. Miss-interpreting this (allegedly) the LP made its appearance, the title? *Exclamation Mark!*

Chris Dredge also remembers the appearance of *Tull's* front man Ian Anderson (many people thought that *Jethro Tull* was his name), "He came to the ground wearing a suit. By the time he appeared on stage he was in his trademark scruffy mac and jeans, complete with his carrier bag which housed his harmonica". This carrier bag would also include on occasion other vital vocal accoutrements such as a flute, an alarm clock and, of course, a hot water bottle! His peculiarity of standing on one leg while playing said flute (and possibly even the hot water bottle) became his trademark.

Pesky Gee! returned the following January, though this time they were indoors in the clubhouse. Not ones to blow their own trumpets, an advert was placed in the press announcing that they were to appear at the club and that they were, quote: *'The best group ever to play in Burton!'* Really?

The 76 was supplying a steady supply of soul bands, both UK-based and from abroad, not just America either. **The Ebonies** came along and gave us some of that sweet soul music all the way from…Denmark! However the US was still a prime source. Within the space of a few weeks we were host to 'America's King of Soul,' **Garnet Mimms**, who's version of 'Looking for You' is a Northern favourite.

Meanwhile there was a new gang in town, very much on the other end of the scale from the flowered up hippies, the *skinhead* cult was starting to gain ground amongst the nation's youth. With a deliberately aggressive image, they managed to pick up on the sound of Britain's growing West Indian population amongst our industrial towns and cities, reggae based *blue beat*. The heavy, heavy sound being almost impossible to resist when you've got your dancing boots on. One of the chief pioneers of the sound, **The Skatalites** played down the 76 in March 1969, though most of Burton's recently arrived émigrés preferred to continue to arrange their own blues parties in the relative comfort of their front rooms, as a visit to the club was still somewhat frowned upon among their community.

By now the rugby club's barbecues were eagerly anticipated, and could be relied upon to host a big name from the soul circuit. Next time round it was to be **Johnny Johnson and his Bandwagon**, crossover pop/soul artists from America. They had already achieved chart success in the UK with 'Breaking Down the Walls of Heartache' (covered later by the young soul rebels *Dexy's Midnight Runners*) the year before their visit, and were due for further success later.

Although were they all here for the visit? South Derbyshire's Tony Middleton, who was in the audience that day recalls: "I went down the rugby club to see Johnny Johnson, though when they came on stage it was just The Bandwagon, the backing band. On the same bill was **Gene Latter**, who recorded 'Sign On the Dotted Line'. He used these same musicians as his backing band, all were dressed in similar, burgundy coloured suits."

Presumably the money was raised for the floodlights, for the summer events at the club seemed to tail off a bit through the early 70s, although a factor may well have been the threat of power cuts, which was ever present during this period. Things were relatively quiet until November, 1974, which saw the formation of *Burton Soul Club*. Rather than ad hoc events being organised by individuals, resources and ideas were all pooled together under the club's banner.

Led by the efforts of Kev Machin, Steve Summers and Michael Heath, a series of regular club nights, live events, all-dayers and all-nighters were lined up. Initially the *Galaxy* in the High Street was the base for the regular club nights on Mondays and Fridays, though just about every venue in the town was utilised in some form or other for get togethers for the faithful. The Burton Soul Club even had its own office in Bridge Street.

The club kicked off with **Chairmen of the Board** at the Jubilee Hall, followed the next month with **Afro** at the Paradise Rooms, then returning to the rugby club for **True Expression**. If you care to check out the Chairmen of the Board website you will encounter a message that informs you that 'General Johnson and Chairmen of the Board play beach music to shag to'. Now are they talking about the dance of that name or something entirely different?! If anyone in Burton remembers 'shagging' to Chairmen of the Board at the Jubilee can they get in touch?

The group's pedigree was beyond reproach, though. A series of early 70s chart busters saw them right at the top of their game; 'Finders Keepers', 'Everything's Tuesday' and the Classic 'Give Me Just a Little More Time' were proof that they were more than capable of sending the audience home happy.

By the time of the Burton Souls Clubs formation there appeared to be an almost religious following for the music around the town. Bags were packed with the essentials for an *all-nighter* - best leather soled shoes, talcum powder, records to sell, money to buy records and perhaps some small little blue round things to help stave of tiredness and keep energy levels up for the dancing. Membership of the *Northern Club* was made readily apparent by the T-shirts adorned with club badges, the ever constant sports bag (again covered in the relevant badges), not forgetting the baggy white *skinners*, which would flap around the legs of the most athletic (and therefore most admired) dancers, who would be given plenty of room to perform their gymnastics.

The 76 came to the fore again as one of the best known artists on the Northern scene, **Major Lance**, brought the house down with a string of well known tunes - so well known that the audience were often allowed to take over vocal duties on the songs completely.

Major Lance

Major Lance was, at this time, a British based artist, continuously working his way round the Northern circuit. A taste of how the man sounded live, and of how the audience enjoyed him, can be found on his live recording done at Stoke's *Torch Club* for the famous *Okeh* label. He did return to his native land in the 1980s, but fell from grace quite rapidly. Arrested and subsequently imprisoned for cocaine dealing, he passed away in 1995 - a bit of a sordid end for one with so much talent.

The week before, Detroit's **J.J. Barnes** had given live renditions of his hits 'Real Humdinger' and 'Our Love is in the Pocket' ably assisted by the vocal talents of some of Burton's youth, and youth is the correct word, as many in the audience were well below 18 years old. This was no attempt to get in early on the delights of alcohol, simply a will to see - and hear - some of the best sounds around. Some even had aspirations of playing their part in bringing the sounds to the Burton crew, and had the youthful audacity to bring it off. All clubs had their resident DJs for the soul events including Bill Baker and Neil Rushton, Carl Dene and Jason Hunt, P T Lawrence, Phil and Brian Clarke and Kev Orton. Kev started out in the early days at the rugby club, though at the time both P T and Jason worked the decks there. He eventually moved in on the 76 Club after the then resident DJ, Mel Adams, failed to appear one night.

***Kev Orton** at the **76** about 1977*

(Kev Orton)

143

Neil Rushton used to organise the *all dayers* at both the 76 and the Paradise Rooms, and was able to entice other DJs from around the Midlands, including, in 1978, Pete Allsopp and Steve Rogers. Live groups were still in a steady flow, though, and Burton Soul Club organised visits from **Eddie Dolman, Arthur Conley** and Lionel Ritchie's The Commodores. Sadly The Commodores didn't appear, though Arthur Conley certainly did, though whether he was actually aware of this is open to speculation. A young *Burton Mail* reporter at that time was Andy Parker who, being keenly interested and involved with the local music scene, went to interview the soul star at The Jubilee Hall. He came away somewhat less than impressed. Still able to recall the meeting, even after the passing of over 30 years, he recalls: "He was off his head".

By 1975 the old perennial Burton problem, apathy, was perhaps starting to have an effect, **Sweet Sensation** were booked for the Jubilee Club, though not by the Soul Club, but attendance at the event was described as 'pathetic'. It may just have been that the group were just too poppy for the soul crowd.

One thing is for certain, for many people Northern Soul is a permanent part of their lives. Live acts may be few and far between these days (how many of the original artists are still alive even?), but keeping the faith in Burton is still as strong now as it ever was.

Memphis Five on the Rag Parade

Gordon Band

Jade Sanctus about 1969 - the man standing on the right is Eric 'Chalky' White,
the Technical College principal.

Ken Hart

Boats and Saints.

IT'S SUNDAY
    IT'S BURTON
        IT'S BORING
UNTIL NOW !

Come and join Tom, Fudge, Phil and Gez at the Leander this and every Sunday night if you want a good time, let's all have one together. Live sounds when you want them. Bargain Booze. Bargain Sounds—See you there.

Don't forget the usual Rock Disco every Monday.   17

Bad news Tom, Fudge, Phil and Gez and everyone else, your efforts were in vain – Burton's boring again!

(Burton Mail)

Though the Burton Leander boathouse has been there since the age of Queen Victoria, putting on live music had not, to my knowledge, been a major preoccupation with club officials. However in the 60s it suddenly began to pick up on the beat/mod happenings, maybe with a bit of prompting from the younger membership. Some of the old, blazer wearing rowing stalwarts (not too dissimilar to the 'tie and a crests' that *Paul Weller* later reminded us about) may have found it most unbecoming to allow the great unwashed into the confines of the old wooden boathouse, but needs must, especially with funding needed, and they just had to bite their lips.

Its perhaps easy to overlook the fact that the atmosphere between East and West was very fragile at the time. In the same edition of the *Burton Daily Mail* you could find an advert inviting you along to a talk at the Assembly Rooms above the old Burton Baths under the ominous title 'Universal Fear of a Third World War' and one inviting you to take yourself down to the Leander Boat Club for some *'Trentside Beat'*. Some of the best of Burton's Beat Scene: *The Memphis Five and The Classix*. If we did indeed 'hope to die before we got old', then at least we would go down dancing.

Reggie Hawker recalls attending the club regularly. "A group of lads from Burton Grammar School used to play on a Saturday singing, cover versions of *Tamla Motown* songs, they were like the house band. I cannot remember their names, but for 16 and 17 year old kids I thought they were pretty good."

This would appear to be Mick Woodward's band at the time **The Wanted**. They were Grammar School, but Dovecliffe not Burton. Also in the line up were school buddies Ken Gale, Eric Cox. Phil Hughes and Jeff Bejenks. Jeff had a car so he was initially responsible for transport of the band; later still they acquired the use of a Bedford van courtesy of one of the roadies who helped out the lads, he turned up one night with the vehicle, having borrowed it off his father. To enable all the equipment to be stored in the van he had removed several items, which his father was less than pleased about, being as it was his camper van and it was actually the seats that they had removed.

Another local group who appeared at the *Leander* were The Riddle, with Stapenhill drummer Dave Hughes, and they, too, were prone to the odd transport problem. "We bought a van off Fred Gooding in Scalpcliffe Road, [but] it seized up in the middle of nowhere in the Peak District on an absolutely freezing cold night. Faced with the prospect of sleeping in the van, which we didn't fancy at all, my girlfriend and me managed to thumb a lift to Derby, (and) from there we were able to get a taxi home with my girlfriends dad paying". The rest of the band braved it in the van overnight; they are quite possibly still trying to thaw out. Dave recalls playing the Leander on New Years Eve, 1966, a good gig to get as everyone was in the party mood, even remembering the payment for the lads - £20.

Refurbishment work that same year saw the interior fitments and bar updated, while another re-fit some time later in 1973 saw the addition of the era's favourite bar upgrades – plastic keg beer dispensers.

I don't know who was responsible for submitting the club's adverts to the local press, but they certainly used the full range of contemporary soundbytes. For the 1967 visit of the 'sensational Beat group, the fantastic' **Trendsmen**, the 'fairer sex' were admitted free. Then **Section Five** 'the latest in Mod music' (in 1967?), and apparently **Mozzletoff** were 'the real rage of the with-its'.

They pushed the boat out (sorry about that one!) for the Burton Regatta in 1967. Under the heading of 'The Regatta Romp' they put on three bands: **The Traction**, who being a 10-piece band must have taken up a fair bit of the floor space, **The Gravy Train** and **Cat Ballou**, all with the accompanying 'Psychedelic Discotheque'. Like the 8 Bar Rest Club, the Leander shut down for the summer, but not before presenting **The Gass** from London's *Marquee* Club.

Jet Morgan in Munich
Alan 'Nala' Wright, Greg Silk, Dave McPherson (Roadie), Graham Ayre, 'Spike' Miller
Trina Barnes

Straight from The Stable Bar to The **76 Club**
Graham Rookyard, Mick Egan, Mick Simnett and Trina Barnes (Paine).
Trina Barnes

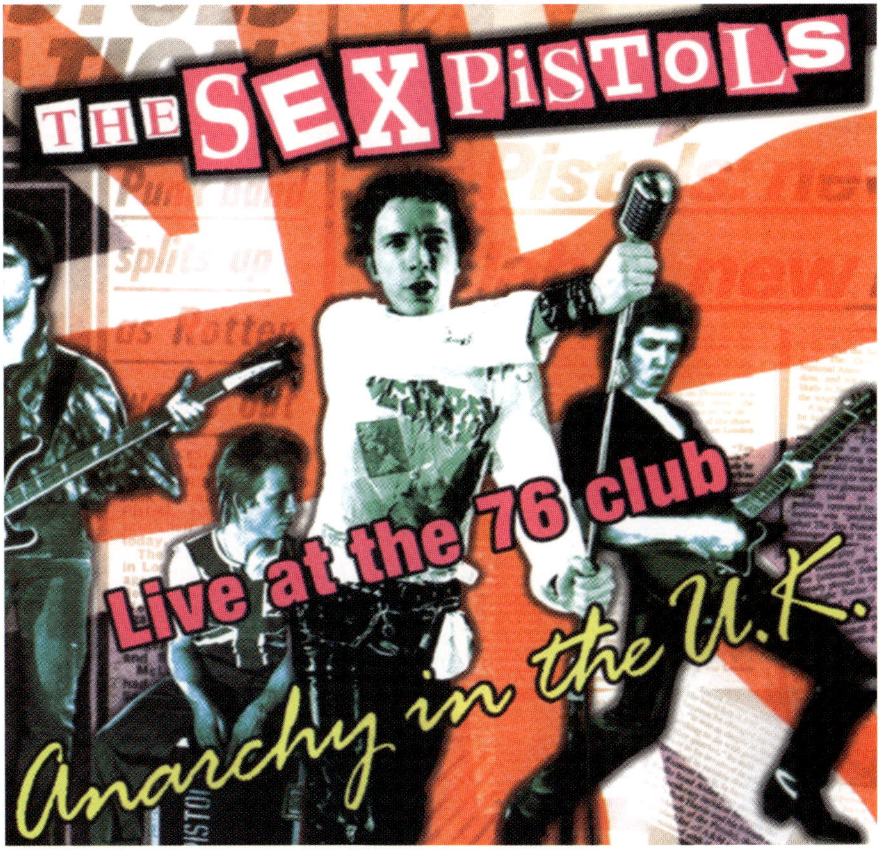

Sex Pistols at 76 Club   Copyright Prism Leisure

8 Bar Rest - The Brian Fennell Group in full swing.   Brian Fennell

The Leander Club interior, 1973

Enter the 70s, and the club was starting to draw some of the more significant names on the music scene. Veteran R & B man **Zoot Money** and his band appeared at the Boathouse, preceded by an enthusiastic advert in the *Mail*: "Did you see him on *Top of the Pops* last week?!" Well did you? In September, 1970, **Fat Mattress** and keyboard wizard **Wynder K. Frog** appeared by the riverside, though Fat Mattress were without one of its founder members, former *Jimi Hendrix* bassist and walking mass of hair **Noel Reading**. For this gig, instead of playing the club itself, the boats were moved out of the way and the band set up in the actual boathouse. Noel Redding would appear in the town with his own band a little later.

As we heard earlier, The Leander also got involved in the ever-popular soul movement. Sunday night was soul night with *Terry's Soul Explosion* Disco, though they still catered for the Rock crowd with Mondays designated as rock night. By 1973 the club was describing itself as 'The only Saturday Group Scene'. True maybe, but by this time The Paradise was already in full swing, and there were other locations to be found on the musical map of Burton-on-Trent.

By the sunny banks of the Trent, Tony Cockayne, Graham Loasby
*and Mick Mayger outside **The Leander Club**.*

(Trina Barnes)

Over on the other side of Burton, well away from the town centre bright lights, was another club trying its best to keep up with the big boys. The original Sharpes and Knights Club, was housed in the old *St Paul's Institute* by the church of the same name, an unlikely setting for some fine live performances. The classic Gothic/Victorian structure was a fine old building located in what is now, a conservation area. It would have made a great venue for modern *Goths* to hang out, and it wouldn't have looked out of place in a *Hammer* Horror film. It was such a good example of its type in fact that, you guessed it, it had to go.

Provided for the town's use in 1895 by none other than Lord Burton, it had become a youth club by 1962, something Michael Arthur Bass would have approved of, I'm sure. Burton groups were employed to entertain the youngsters, with both The Falcons and The Casuals (pre Shane Spencer) appearing there, later joined by Karl Justice and the Jury, Pete Youngman's Spidermen and The Dimensions.

After a lull of a few years, regular live music nights had returned to the venue by 1967 accompanied by the DJing talents of P T Lawrence. Pete, who has been

Johnny Byrd and the Falcons - *Burton Town Hall 1963*

Gary Barnett

Food for Thought - *1967*
Keith Poxon, Stuart Poxon and Herman Walton.

Stuart Poxon

spinning the discs since 1964, did a regular spot at the club, and recalls the particular problems that could be encountered by those using the old place.

"Everything was upstairs, so when I was setting up I used to find some of the young lads hanging about outside and employ them as roadies, taking gear up to the clubroom in return for free admission."

Pete remembers the time the club played host to **Edison Lighthouse**, who were chart toppers at the time of the visit.

"They were number one at the time (with 'Love Grows (Where My Rosemary Goes)', and took that much gear in with them that I had to set up my disco on the floor in front of the stage".

St Paul's Institute and Sharpes Brothers and Knight's Club,
St Paul's Square, Burton. *(Burton Mail)*

Kev Spiers, a name that will be familiar to everyone involved in Burton's 70s rock bands, also has fond memories of the club.

"It was run by Steve Jacks, a carpenter, and can best be described as a youth club with beer".

A number of the bands were from out of town, and Kev, from his present home Down Under, can still recall some of them.

"**Sounds** from Melton Mowbray, who played heavy rock hits of the day, **The Jaffa Band** from Mansfield, **Octopus** from London and **Medicine Hat** from Nottingham".

By 1971 the place was turning out regular, and extremely popular, band nights, **Body and Soul, Left, Right and Centre, Smoke**, Manchester's **Ma-Goo's** and Nottingham's **Roadrunner** entertaining the young crowd.

Mosaic Sunset, who had also appeared at the 76, first appeared at SBK's in 1967. Amazingly for a group, they were still going strong four years later for a return slot. it was not just out of towners down there, however: local favourites **Ginmil** were always well received, **Gremlin** played the venue in 1975 and Oakdale, under their **Backtrack** covers band guise, played there the following year.

The rumour mill at the time got word round that Black Sabbath were due to appear, the rumour was confirmed, to the obvious pleasure of the punters, when their impending appearance was announced over the microphone one week. Andy Parker recalls a huge cheer going round at the news. All to no avail though, as the Brummy metal merchants never appeared there.

Eventually the firm running the club, Sharpe's and Knights, had to move to new premises a stone's throw away from the old club. Following the move the group nights tended to be more family orientated, and so the rock fans went elsewhere for their kicks. Then the bulldozers moved in.

Paradise Found.

Starting out life as a paper store for the printers over the road, the Paradise Rooms provided, over the years, another outlet for talent, both from Burton and from further a-field.

It came into being as the Paradise in July, 1968, at the rear of what was then *The Star* Public House. The landlord, Maurice Whitbread, saw potential in the musty old room and had it converted into a club. Initially the entertainment was on a daily basis, with a mixture of singers and comedians, all catering for an older audience than in the clubs heyday a few years on.

As can be seen from the opening nights advertisement, even those who wanted a bit of lunchtime fun were aptly provided for.

PARADISE ROOM

REAR OF STAR INN, HIGH STREET,
BURTON

To-night & To-morrow

TO ENTERTAIN YOU :

MARK GERALD
Outstanding Irish comedian and
vocalist from Liverpool.

STUART STEVENS
E.M.I. Recording artiste and
instrumentalist

PLUS TED TAYLOR & HAROLD TOON
on organ respective nights
Admission 6/6

Friday & Saturday
July 26th and 27th

JONNY PEACH
Female impersonator, comedy,
vocals and impressions.

TERRY MARSHAL
Vocal entertainer

ERIC BROWN on organ
Admission 7/6

Lunch-time Dancing

MONDAY—FRIDAY   Admission 1/-
VERY STRICT ADMISSION

Snacks and Sandwiches available

NOW TAKING BOOKINGS FOR
SATURDAY WEDDING RECEPTIONS
Telephone Burton 4382   24

(Burton Mail)

The venue really was trying to provide entertainment for every type of audience: in January, 1969 punters could go along to see **Bobby Rich** – 'The Modern Songster with the Guitar' - and then, if you so desired **Mrs Shufflewick** - 'Radio and T V's Most Curious Character'. (I really can't imagine what that was all about!).

As I believe that a sufficient number of years have now passed by, and most of the audience should have suitably recovered from the experience, I can reveal to the people of this town the full horror of what was visited upon us in the same month as the previously mentioned advert:

"By overwhelming demand this excellent comedy, singing and dancing act, from Scotland…

THE KRANKIES !!

It's a burden of shame that we all have to share, but this irritating, unfunny to the point of being physically painful, duo, have been in this town.

Mystifyingly the club was trying to attract punters by declaring itself in the press to be 'Burtons only night spot'. What the 76 and, by this time, the Top Rank Club had to say about this is anyone's guess. The Paradise Room did reclaim some street cred by managing to entice *Radio Caroline* and ex-*Cavern Club* DJ Dave Terry down with his *Fantasy Disco*, and also started to provide gigs for the younger element of the town's populace with a visit from **Wild Heritage**. However, that was run a bit threadbare by an announcement that horrified many of that same younger element that were the hardcore of the audience at the venue's group nights. For the disco nights, which were now Friday and Saturday, the management placed the following announcement in the *Burton Daily Mail*:

'Tonight – Burtons own Discotron, tomorrow - P T Lawrence. Please note: strict admission for age limit 18 years and over. Collar and Tie at door. Definitely no leathers, denims, studded jackets or jeans'

Blimey!! Maybe they were trying to entice some of the clientele who went to the *Newton Park Hotel* for their disco nights, where you were not to be admitted unless you were resplendent with a collar and tie or a cravat.

It was reported in October, 1971 that platforms were being erected in the club for go–go girls. Bet they weren't wearing shirts and ties, cravats, or much else for that matter.

By 1973 the pub had a new landlady at the helm, a lady who would become part of the places folklore - Muriel Lewis. Muriel and Doug Lewis took over what had now become *The Galaxy* in 1973, Muriel having previously run the *Staffordshire Knot* just around the corner in Station Street and bringing with her a good number of that pubs punters. Muriel's sons, Ian and Chris, were both bikers (still are), so it followed that the motorbike crowd would use the place as their base.

*Taken in the Staffordshire Knot, most of the people pictured here followed Muriel to **The Galaxy**. (Note for the wary: it might not be a good idea to pour beer on the head of unsuspecting persons!).*   *(Muriel Lewis)*

Certainly when I was a lad the place was known as a grebo pub and young - would be boot boys like me usually steered well clear. As is often the case, though, reputations mean nothing: the pub regulars did all sorts to raise money for charity over the years. Yes they were mainly bikers, but as Muriel explained: "they looked after me and treated me like their mum. If anyone came in and insulted me they would treat it as an insult to themselves, and wouldn't tolerate anyone trying on that sort of behaviour". On her first day at the pub the lads all turned up to give Muriel a hand tidying up.

It had one of the most rock orientated jukeboxes in the town: "My sons used to put their own records on the jukebox, Mick Beckett, Sybil and Malc Osbourne used to tell me what records to get".

The Galaxy was also the first pub in Burton to have pool tables. Pub regulars Malc Osbourne and Mick Beckett started up the first *Burton Pool League* and organised a pool trophy with proceeds going to the Mayor's Charity Fund. Local players still compete in the *Mick Beckett Trophy* dedicated to Mick's memory.

The pub mainly concentrated on booking local groups, with Doug and Chris Lewis acting as scouts to check out potential bookings. On club nights Muriel would handle the bar while the lads organised the door and taking the money. Most nights were trouble free as the place was self-regulating, with most in attendance knowing each other well.

*Celebrating Christmas at **The Paradise** – The 'Twelve Days Of Christmas' with slightly altered lyrics.*   *(Muriel Lewis)*

P T Lawrence became involved in booking bands for the Paradise, and helped plan a 'Mini Festival' for the venue in 1975 to include: **Little Smoke**, **Hard Times**, **Hamburger Mary** and **Grand Felony.**

Despite this, support at the venue was often very hit and miss.

"The bands kept letting us down, and the audience slowly tailed off".

Another attraction was a 'Rock Rave' organised by *Galaxy Promotions*, involving the services of The Fusion Orchestra, Burton's Oakdale and **Gremlin** from Tamworth. Reporting for the *Burton Observer and Chronicle*, Roger Eversley (who in appearance was Andy Parkers identical twin), went along to see Nottingham based **Plummet Airlines**. Emphasising the *'will they won't they'* nature of the venue's punters, he said 'it was a great gig, but a meagre turnout' later venturing as far as to suggest that the band were 'the best band I've seen all year'. The next week **Chaser** played to a packed house, onlookers perhaps drawn in by the advert proclaiming that the guitarist played his instrument "through a 'talk box' *'like Peter Frampton"*.

"They weren't very good", advised the intrepid *Observer and Chronicle* scribe. One article in the newspaper berated Burton's rock fans, suggesting that *"support for Burton's newest rock venue (The Paradise) has been little short of disgusting the past few weeks."*

Still sticking to its mainly local policy, the venue booked **Arcturus**, complete with Kevin Flannery, who would later provide the *'Brick Outhouse'* cartoon strip for the *Burton Mail*, on guitar. Their style was described at the time as 'a group of science fiction songs linked by poetical passages'. Well this was the mid–70s after all.

The visit of Liverpool rockers **Nutz** was generally well attended: I distinctly recall seeing their publicity stickers consisting of a particularly shapely female pair of legs adorning various walls and windows around the Burton area for many years afterwards – there are probably one or two still knocking about.

Though it was not just groups that put on shows at the Paradise Room. *Abbey Music*, where one Kevin Spiers was employed, used to hold events there to advertise equipment available from the shop, normally on a Sunday. One super slick salesman was singing the praises of his company's latest amplifier, when he was asked would the amp pick up interference from Citizens Band radios (then unbelievably popular). 'Of course not' he confidently replied, only to be interrupted a couple of minutes later by the speakers sparking into life: 'Hello Big Buddy, you got your ears on?'

Pete Youngman took charge of the band bookings around 1976. Although still looking at giving the local bands a chance to show what they could do, he also started using the Birmingham based *Big Bear Agency*. Pete had been involved with the Paradise earlier on:

"This was before Muriel was there - it was the old landlord, Maurice Whitbread, and I was running a folk club from there. I remember one act cycling from Nottingham with his guitar on his back because he had no car!"

By 1979 Pete was moving on with his work so he left the job of booking the bands to Kev Spiers.

The Enid were a favourite with Burton audiences, and always left their mark wherever they found themselves. The band had a strange mix of styles incorporating elements of punk before it had even arrived. They played a stormer at the Paradise, as Muriel remembers well:

"The group had to hoist their electric organ up through one of the windows; they couldn't get it up the stairs. Their guitarist used to play in bare feet".

Muriel recalls serving in the pub downstairs while the group were on:

"We were licensed for 125 capacity, I don't know how many were in that night, it was absolutely packed. When the band finished their set the crowd were baying for more, stamping their feet I could actually see the ceiling moving!"

One local group, Oakdale, would generally be assured of a good reception at the Paradise Room.

They were booked up to play on Boxing Night, 1976, though the audience at the time were probably still full of the Christmas spirit, and almost drowned out the sound of the band by their constant talking at the bar. As a result the band decided to drop some of their quieter numbers.

The place was nicely packed again for **Cruiser** from Rugby and also for Burton's **Kat Magee**, the latter band later being involved in the infamous **Sassafras** 'no show' at the Drill Hall. They (Sassafras) had already played the Paradise and Chris and Doug decided to hire out the Drill Hall for them, certain they could pull in enough punters to make it viable. In the meantime the band had been to America, and when the time arrived for their Drill Hall appearance they refused to play. The official explanation was that the stage was too small (never having been a problem before) and a sign duly appeared outside the venue pointing out that 'The sheepshaggers have gone back to Wales'. Their behaviour had lost them some fans. Chris Lewis recalls that the bands attitude was one of: 'we're not playing in a shithole like this'. One of the bands excuses was that 'the stage was covered in chairs' - not very convincing. It left Chris and Doug with no choice but to pursue the matter further with legal action.

Support on the night was to be from **Sad Café** and aforementioned Paradise favourites Kat Magee. Sad Café were reportedly happy enough with the set up but couldn't play because, according to them, Sassafras had all their gear. Sassafras's manager, Tony Sherwood, said: 'The band do a full show with two truckloads of equipment, there just wasn't room to set up'. Doug Lewis pointed out that around 500 punters had turned out for the group, and most went elsewhere when they found out about the non-appearance of Sassafras. Some stopped for Kat Magee's set, but they were faced with a small audience in a venue that has the acoustic qualities of a cattle shed.

Sassafras were reported to *The Variety and Entertainments Council for Great Britain*, who warned them that if they didn't settle up with the organisers they could be facing a ban from other venues, and ruled that the stage size dispute was a no go, as Sassafras had already played successfully on much smaller stages (including the Paradise!). They were eventually re-booked to play but this time at the Town Hall.

The Drill Hall, 1971, Sassafras board outside not shown.

Back at The Paradise itself, the problem of actually getting people to come through the doors was continuing. For the visit of top guitar man **Gordon Giltrap** and **The Mackenzie Crook Band** only 30 people showed up, with a similar number to watch **Fatso** with Jim Sullivan. Many, it appears, stayed away because of increased admission charges, though as Doug Lewis quite rightly pointed out at the time, if you want quality bands you have to be prepared to pay. Talking of quality bands, the visit of perennial favourites Medicine Head seemed to resolve the problem somewhat. Their second gig at the Paradise Room in October, 1976, was described by more than a few there that night as one of the best gigs ever played in Burton. The venue was so full that many followers had to make do with listening from in the alley outside.

Soundman at the Paradise was often Roger Bird, while, on occasion when the need arose he would step up on stage with Kat Magee (Pete and Chris Webster, Keith 'Choc' Wilson, Gerald Birch and Gary 'Throb' Fisher) and join in twanging the old Jew's harp. Roger still does a lot of work with local bands, though I've yet to see him join in. Must have been okay though: 'the slickest, most original band we've seen' said the man from the *Mail*.

Roger Bird *in his element, behind a mixing desk, probably in the* ***Paradise Club***.
(Neil Spedding)

A puzzling advert appeared in the *Mail*. Announcing the arrival of the *Sophisticats* Disco at the club, it stated that this was 'The New Scene For The Over 18's – No Sex – No Dogs'. Again, if anybody knows what this was all about I'd be interested to hear.

Still the bands kept coming including Burton's very own **Lord Fishfinger and the Frozen West**, and by now Andy Parker was doing a bit of DJing down there (or should that be up there?). There is a connection with the band, I'll let you work it out.

Ken Hart, another well-known face on the Burton scene, took his band **Firefly** to the venue for their debut gig:

"We packed it out. Muriel had given us one of the bedrooms above the pub as a dressing room, and when we came off stage we all collapsed exhausted on the big bed in there. It was only then we realised that the crowd were calling for an encore, so we all had to get back up and go back in".

Jet Morgan, another Burton band, also played their first gig there. It was a very good venue for encouraging new bands up on stage, though sometimes it could be a bit unnerving as Neil Speeding, the band's lead guitarist recalls:

"Our vocalist, Greg Silk, promptly lost his voice, possibly through nerves, but carried on and we were well received".

The experience, and the way they handled it, put them in good stead with the Paradise/Galaxy crowd, they performed there many times.

The Galaxy received a facelift in 1978, with one reporter in the *Mail* gleefully emphasising that the pub 'used to be one of the roughest, toughest pubs in Burton'. There had been little live music at the club throughout the time of the alterations but once things were shipshape again a constant line up of Burton bands and performers were lined up: **The Pick Ups**, **Grand Slam**, **Pete Cliffe**, Firefly, **The Baysicks**, **Javelin** and our old friends Lord Fishfinger and chums.

The Galaxy, June 28,1978, with the hosts behind the bar.

The Pick Ups were one of the number of bands who used the Paradise as a practice room, with former Burton lad Kev Spiers on guitar in one of their first incarnations.

The Pick Ups (l-r): **Kev Spiers, Curtis Wright, Mark Clamp, Pete Dolman** *and* **Steve Barnes**.
(Kev Spiers)

One Two, One Two – **Brian Greenfield** *and* **Kev Spiers** *at* **The Paradise**.
(Kev Spiers)

Kev was by now, of course, involved with booking bands for the Paradise, and while making sure there were plenty of 'out of town' bands such as Birmingham's **Magnum** and **Leargo**, he still kept up support of local groups, including his own. Announcing the introduction of the *'Beer Town Beat'* for town music fans in 1979, a new, though very short lived, hybrid group was put together from Burton bands, **One Two, One Two** consisted of Kev, Brian Greenfield, Pete Dolman, Steve Smith and Steve Gilroy.

In her last year running the place the Paradise became *Muriels*, Muriel would be moving on to *The Punch Bowl* by the Burton end of the Ferry Bridge, where once again her loyal regulars would follow. Muriel would later run the old 76 itself, under the **Libra Club** title. Muriel was a tremendously popular host for the all her regulars, something which is not forgotten. As I write this, another get together is planned for the old boys and girls (some of them are getting on now). Muriel herself obviously has many happy memories of the Paradise, not least some of the bands who appeared there, and possibly one or two that didn't!

Screaming Lord Sutch put in probably his last appearance in the town down at the Paradise Room:

"He put on a great show, and went down a storm. After his set he stopped at the bar for a few drinks then went off to his room as he was staying at the pub overnight. The next morning he was up and about and as soon as the pub was open he was in the bar, having a drink and a chat with the lads".

Screaming Lord Sutch and band, outside the rear of The Paradise Rooms

(Muriel Lewis)

Lord Sutch became known for his *Monster Raving Looney Party*, a much-needed dig at the major po-faced political parties. His manifesto, the logic of which it was difficult to argue, included putting joggers and the unemployed on gigantic treadmills to generate cheap electricity, and during the *Mad Cow Disease* scare he urged people to eat British beef with the reassurance that 'I've been eating it for years and look at me!' Many people overlook the fact that many of the changes in British life he was campaigning for actually became law, including the lowering of the voting age to 18 years old and all day drinking. Sutch was an absolute star, and we should raise a glass to his memory daily.

Then there was the bass guitarist with **Budgie**: "He was about 26 stone and wore wellies while he played!" - and **Raymond Frogatt** turned up in a Rolls Royce" Muriel recalls that the clubs along the High Street used to have a staggered 'turning out' time to try and avoid the separate gangs of well-oiled people all gathering down the street at the same time, and the inevitable brawls that would follow. This didn't work too well as I recall, with parts of Bargates outside the chip shop resembling a Roman Gladiators arena in the early hours on some weekends. New Year's Eve was also a special time at the pub: "A Scots lad used to turn up with his bagpipes. Once he started up with the pipes he would go out on to the street and march up and down, followed by all the punters".

One visitor, who seems very elusive to track down as appearing at the club, is one *Eric Clapton*. Muriel seems sure he appeared there, though no one else, including her sons, can recall the event. Though after hearing about the possible sighting of *Cream* in *The Roebuck* maybe she has a point. Another bunch who definitely didn't play in the Paradise were The Sex Pistols: "We had booked them to appear at the Paradise Rooms, but I found out from a music paper that they used to spit at people. I didn't like the sound of that so we cancelled the booking".

Snotty little punks gobbing in Muriels' gaff? I think the lads would have had to have had a word!

Memories of a free (for some) festival.

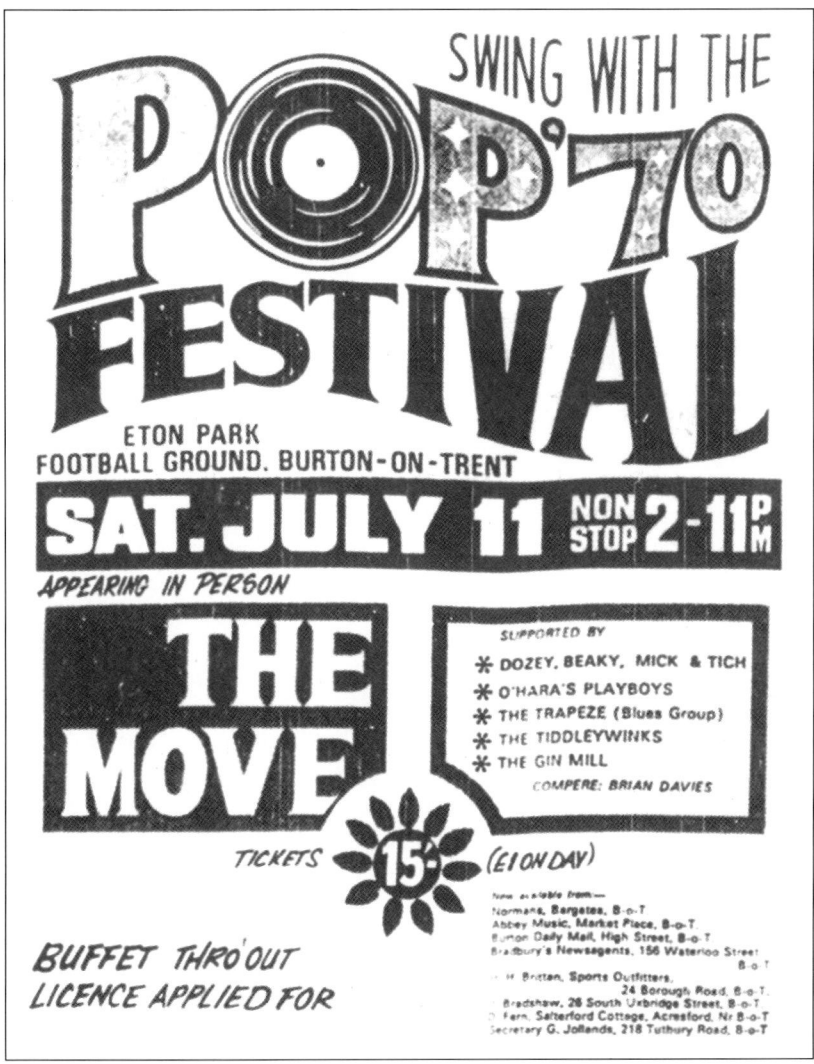

At the time of writing Burton Albion are enjoying one of their best starts to a football season for a long, long time, with one of the most impressive stadiums in the whole of non-league football (and a good many other leagues besides), they are riding high, it was not always so.

In 1970 the club, then based at its old Eton Park ground, was in desperate straights. Financially it was a spent force, and earlier the previous season it had to resign from the old Southern League because it was not financially strong enough to face another season in that league. Players were still owed wages at the end of the season for appearances earlier on, and to survive they would need a cash injection.

Those involved with the club held several meetings to try and come up with some method of raising funds. One idea - perhaps emanating from some of the younger elements involved - that was actioned, was for a music event to be held at the height of the great British summer – a *pop festival*.

Organisation of the event was soon underway. Groups' agents were contacted and a running order (as always with the music biz, down to who was the biggest draw playing as 'headliners') finalised. Topping the bill were to be The Move, who themselves were in a period of some doubt and anxiety about where they were heading. We now know, of course, that some of them were heading towards *ELO* and others, Roy Wood in particular, were heading towards *Wizard*. Ace Kefford had already parted company with the group, and a couple of months beforehand vocalist, and on stage (and off) one-man destruction unit Carl Wayne, had left for the greener grass. (I would have liked to have seen him in action at one of the Burton Tech College piano smashing events, my money would have been on him to win).

Next up we had **Dozy, Beaky, Mick and Tich**, minus the former *Bostonian*, Dave Dee. Dave had left after in fighting within the band about where they were heading, the rest of the group had decided to move away from their pop roots to try out 'a more progressive audience'.

Rumour got round the town that some of the groups advertised would not actually be appearing, and this created a certain atmosphere of apprehension, not only amongst would be festival goers, but also with some of the groups themselves. The day before the event a reassurance was given that 'contracts had been signed so there is no fear of the groups not turning up'. Whether this actually did the job, or whether the prospect of spending a nice sunny evening by the river at *The Leander* watching Zoot Money and tucking into a steak from their barbecue for 'five bob' less, swayed the great Burton publics minds is not certain.

Newhall's Tony Middleton, on his way to the festival, went for a swift one in *The Compasses* pub in Wellington Street before going on to Eton Park.

"We walked in and recognised Bev Bevan and Rick Price (The Move's drummer and bass player) sitting in there having a drink. We went over to them and they were happy to chat, but they did express a worry that they weren't actually going to get the £1500 they had asked for to play the gig".

Roy Wood, playing it down as usual and blending into the background, turned up in lurid pink car, resplendent with the number plate TOP 20H.

The attendance figures were somewhat disappointing, instead of the 5000 expected only around 600 went through the gates, although those that did turn up were well impressed.

First band up, two o'clock on the dot, were local lads Ginmil (not Ginmill as I have wrongly assumed, not just me either, the advert has the groups name miss-spelled), delivering a steady set to get the punters warmed up (musically - the day itself was sunny).

The support acts also went down well, this was to be the first gig by the Cannock based **Trapeze** as a three piece, the night before they had played live as a five piece. The band completed two sets on the day, using the opportunity to try out their audience with numbers from their first LP –'Medusa', Glynn Hardwick sums up their performance that day in one word "awesome". Dozy, Beaky, Mick and Tich may have been trying out some different stuff, but they still impressed. Tony Middleton: "good musicians – good band". **Tiddlywinks** played a series of Led Zeppelin covers, with their bass player reportedly having the type of hairstyle that looked very much like King Charles (the man not the dog).

This photo has caused much woe. Everybody recognises it as a different group, the majority think its **O' Hara's Playboy's** *though a very reliable source has it down as* **Dozy, Beaky, Mick and Tich** *(plus one!).* **Burton Albion Football Ground,** *July 11, 1970.* *(Burton Mail)*

The most eagerly awaited act though was to be The Move, and they didn't disappoint.

"Everyone moved forward when The Move came on, Roy Wood was playing a guitar that was stuffed with paper!"

Roy by this time was starting to take on elements of his visual appearance that would be part of his Wizard persona, complete with a patchwork quilt coat and a black and white cape. The band played a set of crowd pleasers, old and new, including their latest single release, the bass heavy riffing of Roy's 'Brontosaurus'. Even though this was virtually the swansong of the group the Burton crowd were witnessing a classic Move line up: Bev Bevan on drums, Rick Price on bass, Roy Wood on guitar and new boy Jeff Lynn on second guitar. Glynn: "I remember Jeff Lynne's guitar, a blonde Stratocaster. Written on the body was the message 'best wishes from Eric Clapton' ".

There was never any shortage of power when The Move played a set. Tony Middleton: "They were loud I tell yer, they could be heard that day as far away as

Geary House in Bretby Lane!" - though some reports suggest Horninglow guitar wizard Ziggy Pattress was louder still!

The *Burton Mail* was impressed, the report of the day's events summed up what those who didn't bother turning up had missed. Not sure who was doing the reporting for the event, or how much 'hospitality' they had been given, but he or she seemed very enthusiastic, and I don't think they forgot the day in a hurry:

'The place was Eton Park, the date July 11, 1970. THE DAY OF THE BIG EXPLOSION, The Move, Dozy, Beaky, Mick and Tich and Trapeze left us shell shocked, disbelieving. So that, we thought, is what live music is all about, we all know of course, that financially the day was a disaster, but what a luxurious green oasis it was in a colourless musical desert that had always been Burton.'

Steady on mate, its not *that* bad! But there could be no denying that, financially, the event had achieved exactly the opposite of what it had set out to do. 'At least 1,750 people were needed at the event to break even; the result was that Burton Albion were now in a worse financial position than at the end of last season.'

*'There was a lot more people there than the pictures suggest'. Waving at the camera in the centre of the shot is Glynn Hardwick. Also in the frame is the holder of **Paradise Club** membership card number one, in sunglasses just below the Burton Daily Mail Advertisement boarding, though she refuses to be identified!* *(Glenys Cooper)*

The event was now being christened locally as 'The Flop Festival', which was a great shame because as one of the club's directors at that time, Ken Florence, pointed out: 'I think the way the festival flopped was the most bitter blow I have ever experienced. The event was well organised and seemed certain to succeed.'

As we now happily know, the football club survived, even if some of the bands that played on the day didn't, though the reason for the poor attendance, and the subsequent financial loss of the day could perhaps have a much more simpler explanation. Nick Whittaker, modern day local author, and a youngster at the time: "We sat on the railway embankment behind the ground and watched the groups for nothing!"

Melodies Incorporated at **BTR Club**
(l-r): (Not known), **Keith Poxon, Brian Wood, Brian Draycott, Stuart Poxon**

(Stuart Poxon)

Had me a real good time…..

For many would be rock and rollers the first step up the slippery slope is taken by performing with a dance band, entertaining at company dances, or accompanying diners with pop ditties of the day. Stuart Poxon, like many other Burton youngsters, started out on his musical path by learning the accordion at the *Abbey Music* centre in Uxbridge Street. His first outing was with the accordion tinted **Aces** though as he had also learned the piano it seems only natural that he would go on to play in a group - as the drummer!

His next band, alongside his brother Keith, was **Melodies Incorporated**. Brian Draycott had been drafted in from Karl Justice and the Jury and Stuart recalls appearing at *The Midland Hotel* (now the *Grail Court*) as well as *Gresley Old Hall* and many other local venues. The band were playing regular in and around the town up until 1966 when, seeking a change in musical direction, Stuart left and enrolled new musicians to form up Food for Thought (the others stayed pretty much together evolving into **Pineapple Sun** and **The Midways**).

Food for Thought were regarded with healthy respect round the town, both for their musical abilities, which now centred mainly on a Motown/soul/pop crossover, but also for other reasons.

Mick Woodward: "Everyone in the other bands were jealous of Food for Thought, we all had vans which we loaned for the night but they had their *own* van!"

As they started out they managed to get their own gigs, making good use of their dad as a manager, in time they procured the services of an agent based in Lincolnshire. At this time that part of the country was dotted with RAF bases, so before long the band found themselves taking on regular spots there and also in the bracing air around Skegness. Beefing up their vocal sound, their line up had been augmented by two new vocalists, Herman Walton and Sonia Ellis. The much-vaunted van could have some distinct disadvantages. As they were performing around the Lincolnshire area they would often stop overnight at a campsite to avoid the long haul home.

Stuart: "We would pull up in the van on site, and before long people would come up to us and ask us what food we had for sale - the name of the band was written on the van and people mistook us for mobile caterers!"

Food for Thought about 1967. (l-r): Brian Draycott, Sonia Ellis,
Herman Walton, Brian Wood, Keith Poxon, Stuart Poxon.

(Stuart Poxon)

The group lasted for about two years, in that time they had played anywhere you could play in Burton. They also managed to pull in an appearance at Liverpool's *Cavern Club*, though they were not able to take anyone with them as they had to get the afternoon of work to get there. In a case of history repeating itself, Stuart's son, Jack, has also appeared at the famous club, as a member of Burton trio **Tilted Smile**.

Food For Thought also managed to cut a demo, a cover of 'First Cut is the Deepest', popularised by *P. P. Arnold* (though written by Cat Stevens), and *Eddie Floyds*: 'Things Get Better'. They were reduced down to a four piece again by the departure of both Herman and Sonia and later on keyboard player, Brian Wood. Ziggy Pattrass joined up as the groups second guitarist and to drum up some publicity - as all bands must - they were persuaded to pose for a photo shoot at the famous Repton School. The photographer was freelancer Archie Eduljie. On the day of the shoot he revealed to the lads that they didn't have permission to actually be within the hallowed grounds of the notorious seat of learning:

"When we asked him if we had permission to be there, Archie said 'no we haven't, but there's no point asking as they will only say no anyway."

Food for Thought – Repton School 1969/70.
(l-r): **Ziggy Pattrass, Brian Draycott, Stuart Poxon, Keith Poxon**.

(Stuart Poxon)

Ziggy also set up an audition for Geoff Noble to join the band, though by his own admission Geoff was slightly intimidated by the prospect:

"Ziggy got the audition for me though I felt the group was a bit out of my league, I was physically sick in the back of the van with stage fright, something that has been with me for many years".

However, he did pick up another trait that has also stuck him in good stead.

"They (Food for Thought) were absolutely meticulous about setting their gear up and loading and unloading the van in a certain order, that has stuck with me, I got that from them".

With the onset of the disco boom a lot of work was lost by regular gigging bands, Food for Thought being no exception, and slowly, as the work tailed off, so did the enthusiasm for performing. As a result the band slowly wound down until it ceased to exist at all.

Around about 1973 Stuart decided he would give it another try, and the brothers put an advert for fellow musicians in the paper. They soon had replies, including one from keyboard player Brian Harrigan (a journalist who penned the article *'Everyone Knows This Is Nowhere'* in the *Melody Maker*, a piece about our little home town that was less than complimentary about the calibre of musical entertainment here, we will check this one out a bit later!).

Brian worked for the *Burton Daily Mail* at this time, so he would be one of the first to spot the advert. Also trying out his luck with the band was 21-year old Kev Spiers, who brought along with him vocalist Keith Durkin (both of whom had been with Fingertricks). The trio of new signings were short lived: Brian left for his job in London with the *Melody Maker*, being replaced by Steve Benton, and Kev, Keith and the rest of the band parted company about 1975.

Brought in as new guitarist round about 1975-76 was Midway lad Pete Bowley. Pete sadly passed away a few years ago, but his widow, Linda, does recall that the band would travel far and wide:

"The band used to practice at the Poxon's house. They used to go all over the place for gigs, including army bases, where sometimes the men to danced together."

Linda also recalls that they were mainly a covers band at the time, trying out reggae stuff like 'I Shot The Sheriff', though Kev Spiers recollects that they played a song which was performed and written by the band which was called 'The Farmers Song'.

They continued in various guises for the next few years, taking on another keyboard player and changing their name to **Second Opinion**. Their regular work load now included such places as Bass's Social Club in Guild Street (remember when they had a Social Club? Remember when they had a brewery?). By the early 80s they had morphed into **Cooper**, though by now they were losing their enthusiasm for the on the road life, and finally decided to call it a day. Once they made the decision they all realised that it had been the correct one. Stuart is still involved in the local live scene though, helping out son Jack and the rest of the lads in Tilted Smile.

*The final line up, **Stroll On**.*
*(back, l-r): **Pete Bowley, Keith Poxon, Pat Kennedy***
*(front, l-r): **Stuart Poxon, Keith Durkin**.*

(Stuart Poxon)

The early 70s were a period of great experimentation. The mind bending experiences of the hippy and psychedelic movements had opened the doors for free thinking, individuality and the chance to grow your hair and let it all hang out man. Giving an outlet to numerous artists and local talent of unlimited scope, **Valve** was an idea conceived in 1971 through the combined efforts of three local 18 year olds; Nicolas Whittaker, future *Burton Mail* journalist Andy Parker, and Phil Whiteland. The lads promised the populace some 'weird, wonderful, colourful and unpredictable events', which I believe they succeeded In doing to some extent, also giving an opportunity for newly formed local groups a chance to try out their stuff in front of a real live audience.

Weekly meetings, initially under the title of The Burton Poetry Society, were held at *The Wyggeston Hotel* in Calais Road but soon switching to *The Compasses* in Wellington Street. Changing the name to Valve, saw poetry renditions, guitar work and what was termed 'electrical devices'. In July, 1972 the group staged a one-off "mammoth extravaganza" at All Saints Church Hall in All Saints Road (now the Unity Hall). This time, in addition to the usual round of poets, the audience had the chance to check out the grooves of a trio of local bands that were playing on the night: Fingertricks, **Farthingale** and Oakdale.

This was to be the debut performance of Fingertricks, consisting of Alan Sutton on drums, Dave Gibbs on bass, Keith Durkin on vocals and Kev Spiers on guitar. Kev had caught the music bug early, living in Anglesey Road he took over a paper round in the area:

"There used to be an old guy who would stand on his doorstep as I approached, he would say 'do you like pop music then? my lad plays in a group.'"

Intrigued, the young Kev asked the chap what his son's name was. 'Mick Jones' he replied 'he plays with a group called The Settlers'.

Never having heard of either Mick, or the group, Kev was somewhat unimpressed.

"That was until later, when I saw three of the group walking down Anglesey Road: Cindy Kerr, who was a leggy blonde, and two other blokes, one carrying a 12-string guitar. I was impressed!" The Settlers later produced the theme song for the 70s children's TV show *Follyfoot*, titled 'The Lightening Tree'.

At the height of the Beat Boom in 1964, on his 11th birthday, Kev was given a guitar, and promptly enrolled for lessons at - you've guessed it, - *Abbey Music* in Uxbridge Street, receiving tutoring from Phil Shuttleworth. Picking up early on ways to provide entertainment, he had a plan. The lad who he had taken over the paper round from, David Pickett, had in his possession a film projector, they managed to get hold of a film called *'Bare Beat'*, which consisted of a girl switching on a radio and taking her clothes off to the music: "very tame by modern standards, but we got a cheap LP from *Woolworths* and made a soundtrack, we charged the kids from Anglesey School 6d each, and they watched it during dinnertime".

Kev left school with a desire to be involved in music somehow. Initially he wanted to become a DJ, and there was some early *Brian Eno*-type sonic experimentation:

"The Bright brothers (Andy and Steve) had a four-track tape recorder which had three speeds. We used to tape the sound of our farts inside a 'dolly tub'". One of his cohorts at the time, Pat Kennedy, had a brother who played in local band Pineapple Sun, and Kev went along to see them at the Bass Social Club, one of the earliest gigs he can remember going to. He would make regular trips down to the club on Thursdays, and also managed to catch Food for Thought there.

Eventually he decided to ask if he could DJ down there on the Thursday nights, the answer was yes, so he set up his old *'Bobs Bargains'* modified stereogram, and away he went. It was short lived:

"One of the bands that played down there was a Leicester band, **The Power and the Glory**. They had dual vocalists who would keep things moving with comedy banter between songs. They were banned after their second appearance for being too bawdy. I mentioned the group one week and was promptly banned myself!"

Through the club he befriended local musicians like Nick Waisenfeld, Mick 'Butch' Burton and John Walker. They all used to go to the Baptist Church Youth Club in Derby Street, and Kev helped out the youth club band on bass guitar, though he was looking to form his own band. Fingertricks was the band; the debut performance was well received, so they were pencilled in for the next Valve happening, which was to take place at New Street Youth Club, where the *Comet* shop is now.

*Groovers at **New Street Youth Club** 1971*

Billed as *Valve's* first rock concert, the *Mail* sent along Mr. Harrigan to pass his opinion, which was confined to the efforts of Nick Whittaker who 'read poetry during the break between sets to the disappointingly small audience, (about 40 people)'. Geoff Noble would later also contribute to some of the poetry reading events. Fingertricks, who used to rehearse in Newhall, were picking up some good gigs, supporting Wild Turkey at Rolleston Youth Club, which Kev describes as one of the highlights of his time in bands, and Sutherland Brothers and Quiver at the SU Rag Ball, held at the Town Hall in 1973, again a particular favourite with Kev, he was a big fan of Quiver who at this time had one of *Elvis Costello's* future Attractions, Bruce Thomas, on bass.

There was a new scene in town by 1973, with the all-embracing title of **Arts Lab**. The first of these events was set up by Bonnie Ellis and John Sanders. Bonnie is very well known in music circles round the town, while John Sanders was a teacher at Dovecliffe School (nicknamed 'Scruff') who also provided poetry recitals. The venue was to be the rugby club. Music wise we had **Cod Piece** from Leeds and Fingertricks, while returning back to the town from his new base in Rhyl especially for the event, was traditional folk singer, guitarist, and ex-skiffle merchant 'Hollerin' Dave Bull, who was padding out his act with an onstage karate demonstration, breaking pieces of wood (!).

'Hollerin' Dave Bull

(Burton Mail)

This time the reviewer was taking notice of the group though, and it seems he was at odds with the audience on the night. He put forward the view that Fingertricks were 'merely trying to deafen the audience' and that 'volume is not a substitute for talent' but he did have to concede that 'they got a good reaction from the audience'. In the end he just couldn't help himself, at the end of the write up he had to slip in one last dig: 'they were noisy though'!

The Arts Lab suffered some poor attendances, and it slowly drew to a conclusion, but not before holding another session at the *Fox and Goose Pub* (now the *Bridge Brewery*) in Bridge Street, this time with another Burton favourite, Oakdale, providing the musical backdrop to proceedings.

Former Oakdale guitarist, Ken Hart is also held in respect throughout the musical fraternity in this town. He is well travelled on the club and live music circuit (when we had one here), and he is still strapping on the old *strat* and letting rip.

Ken started out in 1966 with a band called **The Colleagues**, with former *Sapphire* Derek Faulkes and a classically trained singer, Sylvia Copestake, a set up he fondly describes as "a slightly cheesy social club band". Their mainstay was working men's clubs and that sort of thing, which was ok for getting on with, but Ken was heavily influenced by *Cream*, and *Fleetwood Mac* (the Peter Green-led, blues influenced group, not the pop group they became). He started a course at Tech College and while there got in with some fellow musos Dick Wright and Joe Chapman. They were of a like mind and **Jade Sanctus** was born.

Many of their early gigs were at the Burton College itself, including performing at an SU Rag concert at the old Bond Street annexe in 1969, performing alongside Pesky Gee! and soul/ska outfit **Phoenix City Truth** from Derby. They also took part in the famous Rag Parade through the town, playing off the back of a flat bed articulated lorry:

"It was absolutely terrifying, the lorry was all over the place, we had trouble standing up!"

Kev Spiers recalls seeing Ken's band playing down at Bond Street, and also at their rehearsal rooms at *The Navigation* in Horninglow Road. He was more than a little impressed, and still is, with the quality of Ken's musicianship. Unfortunately Dick, the bass player, had to return to his native Nottingham, so the band broke up.

A brief stint with Ginmil followed. Ken was approached while at Derby's *Kedleston College* by Roy Brassington. The band at the time went under the name *United Isolation*, with Ken replacing Dave Bell on guitar. The band themselves had backed some very well known showbiz names, such as *Paul and Barry Ryan, Kiki Dee* and the godfather of soul himself, *James Brown*.

Fate always seems to play a part in these things. It turns out Ken was invited to a party held at Kev Spiers house while his parents were away. Having got talking to Kev, Ken was informed that Ginmil were breaking up, so he was actively seeking a new band. As luck would have it, Dave Kent, the original Oakdale vocalist, informed him of their plans for a new line-up for the band. Would he be interested?.

Oakdale went through many changes both during their existence and before, firstly as **Dandelion Extract**, then **Warm Jug** and finally **Lazybones**. The original Oakdale set up consisted of Michael 'Butch' Burton on bass, Nick Waisenfeld on guitar, Pete Dolman on drums, Dave Norton on vocals and Ken. Coincidently they also played their debut at the Valve extravaganza at All Saints Hall.

The band started out, as most do, as a covers band, but soon branched out into writing their own material. To get gigs they went 'on the knock', literally driving round and knocking on clubs doors and asking if they needed a band to play. Running up quite a decent local following they started to get regular slots, though soon they were minus a vocalist as Dave moved on, so the band handled the vocals themselves until the arrival of Geoff Noble (at this time still known as Geoff Bull).

Geoff was already acquainted with guitarist Nick Waisenfeld, having once been at school with him, and had already seen Ken in action with Jade Sanctus at the Robert Sutton School. He had been hooked on hearing and playing live music ever since he heard his brothers, Dave and Brian, rehearsing using AC30 amps and drums in the family living room. Also, he was a classically trained pianist, though within the Oakdale framework he would concentrate on the electric organ and vocals. Having gone down to see the band at New Street Youth Club some time before he joined, he was already on speaking terms with the band members, describing Pete Dolman as "an exceptionally good drummer" and was impressed with Nick as a guitarist: "Such a one off, he wrote some incredibly original songs".

With the departure of Dave Kent they were on the lookout for a replacement. Geoff had taken up a job window cleaning, and while busy at his work up the top of his ladder in Station Street, he suddenly felt the ladder shaking violently: "I nearly fell off."

Down below was a grinning 'Butch' Burton: "Wanna join the band mate?" he shouted.

"That was it, I was in".

Dave Gibb, Ken Hart, Geoff Noble (Bull) and **Pete Dolman**

(Burton Mail)

The Arts Lab get-togethers tended to move round a bit, and *George Street Club* was the setting for the July, 1973 event. Cod Piece were there again, as was Ziggy Pattras, but the writing was on the wall, and despite an appearance by Oakdale in October of that year the whole thing ran out of steam.

Not that this held the lads back in any way. They managed to secure a backing slot on the 1974 *Rag Rock* do at the Town Hall, alongside Chris Spedding's **Sharks** and popular Liverpool lads Nutz. It was a mixed sort of experience for Ken. It's a well known fact that support bands always get the rough end of the stick when mixing it with the bigger boys, it's expected, it's how you learn, though sometimes ego's got in the way a bit too much.

"I thought they (The Sharks) were a bit showbizzy" says Ken. "You would be on stage setting your gear up and one of their roadies would come up to you and say 'you can't put your amp there guv, he won't come on if you put your amp there".

Even so, the nights of practice down the *Great Northern* were paying off.

Geoff Noble: "We went down really well that night, really good – really tight". They may have been playing in the Conference while Sharks were in the Premiership, but they still garnered respect:

"Sharks came out towards the end of our set, and were obviously impressed. They showed us a lot of respect that night, very, very rare" recalls Geoff.

By 1975 with the band very much established in Burton and beyond, they performed one of their many stints at the Paradise, this time with The Fusion Orchestra and Burton's Gremlin, with John Brooks, who would later find a place in the final version of Oakdale, on guitar. Though there was some competition from other locals, such as **Ozone Breeze** (Howard 'Nicky' Parkin, Graham Southall, Ivan Staley and Steve Bright) and **Dude** (Steve Harrington, David McDowell, Paul Smith, Simon Stevens and Neil Inwood, who would later team up with The Pick Ups' Curtis Wright in **Glamarama**), not to mention Jet Morgan. Not too mention them now that is, their place is later in this chapter.

The Arts Lab movement just refused to lie down, re-emerging in 1976 and now bearing the title **Another Roadside Attraction**, with, apparently the same aims as previous versions. Starting out at The Paradise, the event was billed as a 'Multi–Media Concert, with an abundance of folk, mostly by local artists, experimental poetry/music, sketches and music by a local DJ'.

This being 1976, one or two of those taking part had witnessed the goings on down the 76 Club, especially when a particularly notorious and publicity seeking group had appeared down there, complete with a vocalist delighting in the name *Johnny Rotten*. So cue the appearance of Lord Fishfinger and the Frozen West, resplendent with drummer Roland de Drums, bass player *Maths Anxiety* and *Blanche Blank* on lead vocals, bionic kazoo and recorder. For their next outing they were augmented by their 'new reedsman' *Wynne de Pipes*.

Another change of personnel in Oakdale saw the departure of Geoff Bull. He had recently joined in a break-off group called Backtrack, which was Oakdale in all but name, but doing just cover versions of songs. Replacing him was Marcus Thompson.

Not for these lads the run of the mill auditions, or even advertising in the papers - how did he become the new singer Ken? "We met him in a Betting Shop!"

It would seem Marcus was just the energetic type of up front fella they needed, though in another bombshell, Nick announced he was wrapping up with the band. Again fate plays its hand. Ken: "we had moved on from practising at *The Northern*, had a stint at Scalpclffe House (by the old open air swimming pool off Stapenhill Road) and were now at the *Star and Garter* in Grange Street. Pete Bowley was in there one night, we got talking and he asked if we were looking for another guitarist". Problem solved.

They tried out their new look band at the Paradise, and it was a resounding success. They packed the place out and their new boys slotted in like they had never been anywhere else. They entered their first *Melody Maker Folk/Rock* contest with this line-up in 1975, and did reasonably well. How sad it was then, that a year later they should find themselves playing back at the Paradise, but for an entirely different reason. The band's bass player, 'Butch' Burton was fatally injured in a motorbike accident, leaving a young wife and son, Jude. The members of the band, in conjunction with other Burton musicians, organised a memorial gig for Butch at the Paradise.

Michael 'Butch' Burton, *outside Scalpcliffe House.*

(Ken Hart)

The night saw Oakdale, the **Mick Wall Band** and **Hi-Ballers** - Kev Spiers new band - take the stage and pay their due respects to the memory of Butch. At the end of the night there was a massed jam session, complete with Marcus Thompson on drums and Pete Dolman on bass. They would later perform another charity event at the same club, organised by Muriel, this time it was for the family of Steve Foster. Oakdale, **Roedene** and **The Hypists** (formerly Lord Fishfinger) would all play, and money raised was split between Steve's family and Cancer Research.

There was plenty of healthy competition between Oakdale and the Hi-Ballers. The latter group contained some seasoned local players, and had put on their first public performance at Brian Fennell's *Platform* night at the Rugby Club. Both groups had entered a rock competition that was held at the 76 Club. The competition was organised by the club's DJ, Neil Turner and stalwart Pete Youngman. Taking place at the end of March there were initially five acts on the roster, including **The Cold** and Lord Fishfinger and the Frozen West, though come competition time only Oakdale, Hi-Ballers and Roedene (formerly Kat Magee) entered. Judging was to be by both the organisers and also Dave Dennis, formerly of Oak Street but now one of **Moon**'s chief songwriters. The event was sponsored by the Musicians' Union, with the prize of a £50 voucher to spend in *Norman's* Music shop, which stood on the corner of Lichfield Street and New Street.

Normans Music Shop – *before pedestrianisation it was unsafe to walk down the High Street due to the danger from traffic! The buildings in the centre of the picture have now been replaced by a shovel.*

The winners on the night were to be the Hi-Ballers, who played three of their own songs, one written by Kev and two by Nick Waisenfeld. Both Roedene and Oakdale suffered serious sound problems during their numbers, with the PA system going on a bender during Oakdale's set, Andy Parker reported in the *Mail* that "the PA reduced their set to a wall of sound which was difficult to listen to." This resulted in only two songs being attempted. The winners were also given a Friday night spot at the club (it was very unusual during the 70s for local bands to appear down there), so on Friday July 8, the band took their place on the cramped stage and took the faithful through a fine set, which included 'Never been to Memphis', 'Hard to Handle' and 'Higher Higher'. The crowd enjoyed it, the band enjoyed it. Hardly anyone left the front of the stage for the bar during the set, a sure sign that you had done a good job down the 76.

Confidence was high in the Hi-Ballers' camp so in September they entered the *Sounds Spectacular 77 Rock Contest* held at Nottingham Tiffany's, taking with them a full supporting cast of fans. But all to no avail, surprise, surprise a band from Nottingham won.

Oakdale continued with yet more changes, Pat Kennedy taking over on bass as a temporary measure, eventually letting Dave Gibbs do the honours. Also Pete Dolman wanted to move on so fully-fledged Keith Moon fan, Andy Pegg, took over behind the kit. They entered the *Melody Maker* contest again, but by May 1978, the band made the mutual decision to split up, the loss of Butch Burton had left a void.

Oakdale – just before the final split 1978. **Andy Pegg, John Brooks, Dave Gibbs, Marcus Thompson** *and* **Ken Hart**.

Ken Hart: "After Butch died the heart seemed to have gone out of the band – he was such a big part of the band's spirit, it was like trying to mend a broken egg". Eventually the band members all branched off into different projects.

Ken kept the momentum going. Along with bass player Dave Gibbs he formed up Firefly, re-recruiting the services of Andy Pegg on drums.

"We decided to start again after Oakdale, we played a combination of rock, power pop and our own stuff".

They appeared at The Paradise, and also at the Drill Hall, on one occasion as support for Burton band **Ginty**, although The Drill Hall was not exactly the favourite venue for any of the groups that tried to put on a show down there.

"The Drill Hall was a dreadful place to play, the louder you played the worse the sound got".

Again the usual shuffle round of faces took place within the band, Ron Harvey took over from Andy Pegg with Joe Horwich drafted in on keyboards to fill out sound-wise, though even the use of keyboards would have been wasted in the cavernous atmosphere of the Drill Hall.

Firefly at the Drill Hall 1978
Ken Hart, Ron Harvey, Dave Gibbs and **Joe Horwich**

(Ken Hart)

Neil stayed with his next band Ginty for six years, constantly gigging in, and around, the town.

"We were pretty loud and raucous, playing lots of Thin Lizzy and AC/DC type stuff".

Initially they retained the services of Spike on bass, with Measham-based vocalist Paul 'Ginty' Johnson (you can see where the band got their name from). Johnson had an extremely powerful voice, which he would put to good use.

The next version of the band had a dual guitarist approach, with Tim Smedley's contributions giving the overall sound a definite *Lizzy* feel. With the steady rhythm section of Stuart Truman on drums, and Gary Fisher on bass, the band produced a powerful heavy rock sound.

*Ginty – **Gary Fisher, Stuart Truman, Paul Johnson, Paul 'Ginty' Johnson, Neil Spedding** and **Tim Smedley**. I don't know where this is, but judging by the weaponry on the wall behind, you wouldn't be wise to turn your back on the audience.* *(Neil Spedding)*

As a thank you to their supporters after their first successful year in existence they arranged a birthday party at the Paradise Room, described in the Mail as *"lively and thoroughly entertaining, Ginty romp through their set with an infectious sense of fun"*. Joining in was sound man Roger Bird, jettisoning the Jews harp for something a bit more substantial, he treated the audience to a harmonica solo called 'Traintime', which the *Mail* reporter found 'breathlessly impressive'. A good summing up of what the band were all about was again provided by the reporter: *'...the band enjoy themselves, and make sure their fans do the same'*.

Plans were under way for the band to get their sound down on record, though its was relatively low key, the whole thing being designed to be available to their local fan base, with no real thoughts of setting the charts alight.

"We made a record at the *Ginger Recording Studios* in Aldridge, and they managed to get the track listing wrong on one side. A lot of local pubs put the record on the juke box". The disc has Lennon and McCartney's 'I Am The Walrus' on the A side, with two self-penned numbers on the B, Spedding/Johnson's 'Say You Don't Mind' with 'A Little Understanding', written by Tim Smedley and 'Ginty' Johnson.

Their appearances at the 76 (and later the Libra Club), as well as places like the *British Oak* (the one that was in Byrkley Street, now *The Cottage*) often had the places packed to the gunnels, but by 1985 Neil had seen enough. He left the band and has sadly never - to my knowledge - performed live since.

Ginty get on Disc – 1980

Keep them Freaks a rollin'........

The interior of the **76 Club**, *October 1, 1971.*

(Burton Mail)

'Come and join the Swinging Guys and Groovy Girls' said the advert. This being 1970, that was the way (some of us) talked, and 'swinging' meant a different thing entirely to its modern connotation. Not everybody was willing to throw off their Kaftans and join in the fun. A letter found its way to the Mail, signed by 'Newtimer'. It said:

'A common complaint is how dull Burton is for young people, they have to go to Derby, Leicester etc...'

Hasn't it always been so? If the letter writer is still in town how exciting does he/she think it is now? If they had but known it at the time, the town, and particularly the 76 Club, was about to enter a purple patch, with a regular supply of good live music, culminating in the mid to late 70s bonanza of top flight groups appearing at the club.

A survey conducted by the *Mail* at the time threw up some - it has to be said - fairly predictable conclusions. The girls of this town 'didn't mind long hair as long as it was clean'. Clean or not, they weren't too fussed about skinhead's; - there 'weren't very many nice ones about'.

One young lady, who had recently arrived from Canada, found Burton men 'very friendly, having recently got to know 104 of them'(!). Another girl had obviously been upset by the local lads 'I find the Burton male leaves much to be desired, the majority are ignorant, self indulgent and lacking in sensible conversation', maybe she had a good point. In reply, one young Burton lad pointed out that as long as the young girls had 'plenty of loud music and several rum and cokes, they seem to be contented'. Well they could get all that, and more, at the 76.

*Re-opening night at the **76**, September 18, 1971. Regulars check out the new look club.*
(Burton Mail)

The club had recently undergone another of its many facelifts, reopening on September 18, 1971, with a promised 'New sounds, New Décor, New Scene'. Moving away from the purely disco format that had been slowly taking over, the club promised regulars a return to Friday night live music. Sue Smith reported in the *Mail* that: 'The special effects in the club are aluminium wall sheeting – lighting is linked to the sound system, and therefore gives the fantastic effect of flashing to the beat of the records'. It all sounds very quaint now, but at the time it was cutting edge stuff.

The soundscape to the Friday night live events were provided by the *Aquarius Disco*, alias Neil Turner. Neil had started going down the club in about 1967, and was mates with Tom Broster's son, Terry. At first he was just another regular, but having started doing disco's at a youth club in Newborough he found himself being asked to start DJing at the club (Terry himself had sometimes donned the DJ hat if a particular act never showed).

Neil Turner: "I used to ring record companies up, and they would send me free records. They would turn up from Virgin, A & M, CBS, Warner Brothers, all of them with armfuls of LPs. I would ring up visiting bands' agents as well, and they would send me all sorts of stuff down".

The doorman was Dave Roberts, fondly remembered by many as 'The Penguin' or 'Dickie Bow' because of his sartorial preference for a bowtie, white shirt and black evening suit, Dave had formerly run the door at the Jubilee Hall and had been involved with the Mocambo Club. Dave's son, Ian, would later become part of the team at the club. Ian recalls that some of the punters wouldn't always wait to get home before they started getting to know each other.

"I started work there part-time when I was about 15 years old, working in the cloakroom for 30 bob a night. I once walked in there and caught two people 'at it' - in the cloakroom!"

Later on Joyce Veal would be employed in the cloakroom, with Gordon Band's daughter Karen, taking the entrance money on the door. Karen remembers that the club would often get a visit from the local constabulary, all in the interests of public safety of course.

"The police used to nip in occasionally and have a drink at the bar. (How times change). One copper in particular used to drop by on his beat, take a seat in the cloakroom and hide his pint under his conveniently shaped helmet, whether it was on his head or not!"

Ian recalls a visit on another occasion from some out of the ordinary gentlemen.

"We had booked a disco from abroad one particular night. Apparently they had been involved in all sorts of stuff while abroad, including a lot of fraud. Some gentlemen from Interpol were waiting expectantly at the club for them to appear". They must have got wind of it somehow, because needless to say they never showed up!"

Many different people have served behind the bar at the club, including the two Teds – Pullen and Tedder, and as we heard earlier on, should any type of trouble break out, Tom Broster would soon be on the scene.

Club regular Reggie Hawker: "Tom was a great bloke, he knew most people by name, sorted out any trouble and also acted as DJ if there was no one else around. I think the guy on the door was Ted (sic) Roberts, who was in charge of security, although I can never remember him actually getting involved in any fisticuffs, preferring to leave any fighting to big Tom!"

Occasionally the security services in the club were sometimes put to strange use. Another club member at the time, Weg Smith recalls one particular incident that still causes him no small amount of mirth.

"The funniest night must have been when **Brown's Home Brew** played. They were rubbish and no one was listening to them, but Joe Brown told us that if we didn't listen and give him the respect he deserved he'd take the band off. We all shouted for them to go, but because it was the famous Joe Brown the doorman, known as Penguin, stood in front of the stage to ensure everyone listened! They didn't do an encore."

Andy Parker refers to the same night: "Joe Brown actually threatened one of the audience". It's safe to say that this was the exception rather than the rule, though. In Andy's opinion most of the visiting bands enjoyed playing down there.

The first band booked to appear at the new look club were **Kilroy**, followed later by the ever popular **Peppers Machine**, who played twice at the club in 1971. Into 1972 and **Black Widow** (formerly Pesky Gee!) were treading the boards. The group had courted a certain amount of infamy by their stage show, which included elements of *black magic*, and the presence, on occasion, of a naked female on stage.

There's no talk of such goings on at the 76. There were plenty of people in there that night, some 200, and Gordon Band did note that 'there were a lot older people in the audience than usual that night' - attracted by the band or the naked lady? Black Widow were due to play again in March but were replaced by **Raving Rupert**, apparently Scunthorpe's 'Top Elvis Impersonator'. Those who attended surely only did so out of pure curiosity, they were not disappointed - by all accounts he was a passable substitute in the absence of the great man himself.

Definitely not just for the curious was **Vinegar Joe**, a very highly rated band, containing eye candy for both sexes in the form of vocalists Robert Palmer and Elkie Brooks. The late, great, Robert went on to find massive fame as a solo artist, managing to leave us with one of the most sexist, non PC videos ever produced in 'Addicted to Love'. I know ladies who go visibly weak at the knee's at the mere mention of the man's name. Elkie Brookes was a very upfront vocalist in a *Tina Turner* sort of way, very popular with the lads in the audience.

In that audience on the night, and still full of the memories after all these years, was ex-Burton lad Weg Smith: "Saw Vinegar Joe and joined in with the shouts of 'Show us your legs Elkie. She wouldn't have got on Radio 2 back then!"

Neil Spedding: "Mick Dyche had got word back to Burton that we should get down there for *Vinegar Joe*, he said 'you've got to go down and see them'. If someone with the musical knowledge, and contacts, like Mick had was impressed, you could be assured they were good live act. "They were really good, a brilliant night".

Supertramp were also given a good reception down the club, as indeed were Trapeze, still extremely popular, though it was touch and go whether the group could actually appear. With the country being affected by power cuts, a rota would appear in the *Mail* letting people know when the power was likely to be going off. The Town Hall had already had to cancel functions.

The 76, following the last re-working of the interior, had the stage situated to the left hand side as you walked in, at a right angle to where it would eventually end up after the final re-fit in 1975. This reduced the size of the stage somewhat, resulting

Steady lads – **Elkie Brooks**

(Pete Youngman)

in one or two performers being less than happy with the set up. According to legend, **Chris Farlow**, the top 60s vocalist, walked into the club, attired in a large leather coat and matching leather hat.

"He walked out on to the stage, took a look around, muttered 'no f*ckin' chance' and walked straight off again".

Stan Webb, of Chicken Shack fame, would always lead off with the same question on entering the club: 'where's the bar?' On one occasion he never even got that far though. Like many others he claimed to be having trouble getting his equipment down the club's entry, he made a decision to abandon the gig, much to the annoyance of those present.

"He pissed off, and the crowd wasn't too pleased, it wasn't his amp that he couldn't get down the entry, it was his ego!"

Others were more than pleased with the little club. A visit from the **Mick Abrahams Band**, fronted by the former Jethro Tull guitarist, would virtually guarantee a full house. Other favourites were the Raymond Froggatt Band, with many eager to catch them to see what sort of guitars the band would be showcasing. They had a reputation for making their own instruments, with some bizarre and eccentric models on display, one was rumoured to have 'at least 18 strings on it!'

A visit from Roy Young was always keenly anticipated, Pete Youngman: "Roy Young is a terrific showman, and he can sing like Little Richard".

Praise also came from the club's owner himself, Gordon Band, enthusing that the 1973 appearance of the Roy Young Band at the 76 was 'the most successful booking to date'. No wonder the bloke likes coming here.

Jude were a combination of some well seasoned performers on the rock circuit: former *Procul Harum* guitarist Robin Trower, Clive Bunker, ex-Jethro Tull, former Stone the Crows bass player Jim Dewarn, and top gravel voiced Scottish vocalist Frankie Miller. The group's roadies couldn't get their sound unit down the famous entry. Undaunted they were offered - and hats off to them, used - the clubs own PA system. Inevitably they had sound problems as a result, but at least they had a go.

Also high in the 'value for money' entertainment stakes were **Patto**, the band formed by Mick 'Patto' McGrath (soon to be part of the Neil Innes-led Beatles piss take, *The Rutles*). They would often perform their own version of *Johnny Kidd and the Pirates* 'Shakin' All Over', with the whole song played at a just about audible whisper level and the final 'power chord' provided by drummer 'Admiral' Halsey, launching his drumstick at a cymbal from somewhere in the audience.

Phil Seamen's lifestyle finally overtook him in 1972, and he died of drug related problems, 'Beat Poet' Pete Brown, sometime lyricist for *Cream*, had teamed up with multi-instrumentalist Graham Bond, forming **Bond and Brown**, and they dedicated their appearance at the 76 in November, 1972 to the memory of Phil, a Burton-born true genius.

Doing nothing to dispel the rumour that some bands just took themselves too seriously, **Renaissance** managed to get everyone in the audience to sit cross-legged on the floor, the epitome of everything *prog rock* was about. As Geoff Noble points out "there were a lot of 'Great Coats' in the audience that night".

Never, ever, being accused of taking themselves too seriously were **Kilburn and the Highroads**, who made their 76 debut in 1973 and provided a link between good old fashioned rock and roll, and the soon come punk attitude. Ian Dury's band were putting smiles back on to the faces of fans after some of the more po-faced elements of early/mid seventies music while also providing sartorial guidelines for the punk main players - it was Ian who first wore safety pins in his ear.

Kilburn and the Highroads, *with 'the rather strange looking' Ian Dury,*
extreme left, and Keith 'Steel Hat and Socks' Lucas, second from right.

(Burton Mail)

The *Mail* described them - quite rightly - as 'one of the most unique set-ups on the rock scene'. Once witnessed, they were never to be forgotten.

Pete Youngman: "The band would all come on stage wearing a combination of tin hats, macs and boots. On completion of their set Ian would shout 'Spider!' - that was the cue for his minder to clear a way through the crowd for him".

The Kilburn's would liven any crowd up, with the punters as vital a part of the *Kilburn's* live experience as the band members themselves. The conclusion of the bands set would often consist of the whole audience being led round the club doing the Conga. This was not lead by Ian himself, though: polio had seen to it that he had a very limited mobility, but what he lacked in movement he more than made up for with on stage wit and banter, and of course some terrific lyrics. Kilburn and the Highroads went through many personnel changes throughout their existence, and it often seemed that a new additions appearance were as important as their musical ability. Ian delighted in confronting people with things that they may have found uncomfortable, a drummer arriving on stage with crutches, a bass player who appeared to be a midget. Many local musicians would make sure they were down the club for a visit from the band, though they were often bemused by elements of the groups look on stage.

Geoff Noble: "I couldn't figure out whether he (Ian Dury) had got a wooden leg or what. I do recall on one occasion the bass player was paying a visit to the gents before going onstage " - pre gig nerves maybe? A nervous *pish* before he went on? - "He was having a dump. He came out and commented to those around 'Phew! I wouldn't go in there!' and with that on he went!"

What appealed to many of those watching was the fact that the band were not trying to be 'psuedo American', with no mid-Atlantic twang to their vocals. They were definitely English, and delighted in making sure everyone was aware of it.

To save on expenses a good number of performers at the club would be put up for the night round someone's house, and after watching what P T Lawrence describes as "a brilliant gig" he was more than happy to provide Ian Dury with overnight accommodation. He would later do the same for AC/DC. The Kilburn's did once manage to upset Gordon Band, who threatened to take legal action against them after they had been booked to appear at the club but failed to materialise, their excuse being that 'they were taking a holiday in Jamaica'. We now know that this was the last throw of the band before they re-emerged as *Ian Dury and the Blockheads*.

The quality of the bands was a constant factor throughout the mid to late 70s. One of the main reasons was the use of London based agents. With Pete Youngman now living in London he was in an ideal position, checking out bands' live performances and give a good reference on the suitability.

"I went to a committee meeting with Ivan Fearn and Tom Broster, and they gave me a list of bands from the *Sherry Copeland Agency*. Because I lived in London they asked me which one's they should book. I told them they should sign them all. I later phoned the agency and arranged it so that they would send down good bands on a regular basis".

Most people who were keeping track of events - music wise - across the country would have already been well aware of the quality of a band like **Thin Lizzy**, who had set out to be 'the best guitar band in the world'. Many would argue that this goal was achieved.

It was the original three-piece version of *Lizzy*, complete with lone guitarist Eric Bell (who would appear at the club with his own band later), and they were starting to garner some of the success that had been predicted for them. They were described in the advert heralding their appearance at the 76 as being 'Number 24 in the *Radio Luxembourg* charts' and did, in fact, reach number six in the UK charts with 'Whiskey in the Jar' the same month (January).

Expectations were high amongst the 76 crowd, and no one went home disappointed.

Neil Spedding: "'Whiskey in the Jar' was high in the charts and we were shoulder to shoulder in the club. The band were absolutely shit hot. They played 'Whiskey' twice, with Phil Lynott also playing guitar instead of bass on the song, a Fender".

Phil Lynott's old group, **Skid Row**, had already appeared at the club, and the **Gary Moore Band** were to play there later, Gary would be one of the number of guitarists figuring in the dual guitar approach favoured by the group once Eric Bell had left.

Beckett were one of the many bands who, though plenty good enough, just didn't have the lucky break needed to make it big. They had recently supported 'boot boy glam rockers' *Slade* on tour, and they impressed at the club.

Weg Smith: "They were really good, doing an excellent version of Neil Young's 'Southern Man' "(the one that upset *Lynrd Skynyrd* so much), though that particular group were BIG favourites down the 76, their masterpiece guitar epic 'Freebird' being almost the clubs unofficial anthem due to regular turntable airings from DJ

Beckett *in action down the 76*

(Trina Barnes)

Neil Turner.

Some of those regulars may have viewed another of the bookings with a certain amount of trepidation. **Suzi Quattro** was part of the 'Glam Rock' stable after all, but they needn't have worried. Suzi's image, that of the tough leather clad rocker, was not an image at all, she was just that; a tough Detroit rocker. The publicity machine had introduced her as 'for the glitter fans, she wears a silver suit on stage, topped off with purple hair!' but once on that stage she was nobody's fool.

"The whole bands performance on stage was very polished, she would let the blokes in the band have it with both barrels, with some very fruity language, if they messed up. She was obviously going places".

Though one of the places she nearly didn't go was the 76 itself.

Doorman Ian Roberts: "I was on the door that night, I could see what I thought was a young girl walking up the High Street from The Queens." (The diminutive Suzi was either stopping there, or had been for a quick livener before the show). "She walked up to the entrance and I told her 'you can't come in here you're too young'. She tried to explain to me that she was 'the turn' for the night, I wasn't having any of that so I told her 'I don't care, you aint coming in'. With that she pulled a flick knife out. It was at this point that a rather large gent appeared, who turned out to be Len Tucky, her lead guitarist and (then) husband, he managed to calm her down a bit and persuade me that she was genuine!"

Suzi held no grudges, she did a belting show for the club, and afterwards shared some time with Gordon Band.

"She had been booked for some time, but come the time of the gig had hit Number One with 'Can the Can'. I was beginning to wonder whether she would actually show up. True to her word, she said she had signed up to play, and that's exactly what she would do, for the original fee as well".

Gordon repaid her loyalty in the time honoured 76 fashion.

"We got her some fish and chips after the gig, and she sat and ate them with us!"

Looking at the quality of the bands down the club that year, 1973 must be regarded as one of, - if not *the* - defining vintage year for the 76. This was the year **UFO** first appeared there, and while some in the audience found them a bit 'cold', others still remember them as "very, very loud". Each time they put in an

A quiet night at the **76** *(l-r): Mick Egan, Graham Rookyard (with pint), Ron Palfreyman, Brian Clarke, Nigel Broomfield, Mick Simnett and DJ Neil Turner* *(Trina Barnes)*

appearance at the club they would have a new guitarist. One of these being *axe meister*, Michael Schenker. For their first visit, vocalist Phil Mogg was joined by guitarist Bernie Marsden, soon to form Wild Turkey, who themselves would ensure a packed night in the club, something that Mick Woodward would remember, but for a different reason.

"It was absolutely solid the night Wild Turkey played the 76. However, I had to leave half way through as it got a bit uncomfortable for my wife, she was heavily pregnant".

Michael Shenker would be a vital part of the 'Cosmic Rock' image UFO were trying to project, complete with 'stack heel boots, armbands, glitter and leather trousers!'.

Alex Harvey had started out on his musical career as a singer in showbands, in his native Scotland. Teaming up with former *Teargas* guitarist, Zal Cleminson, he formed **The Incredible Alex Harvey Band**, who formulated heavy visual theatricals to augment their set, to get the full effect witnessing a live show was essential. This had the desired effect on their Burton audience.

Bob Whetton: "Absolutely amazing, one of the best live sets I ever saw".

How could anyone fail to like a band who included in their set a song called 'There's No Lights on the Christmas Tree Mama, They're Burning Big Louie Tonight'. Asking those in his audience 'Do you believe in ecology?…well stop pissing in the water supply!'.

76 Club *Interior.*

(Burton Mail)

Because of the compact size of the club Alex Harvey was in his element.

Mick Woodward: "What made this particular gig so good was the fact that Alex was able to get in amongst the audience, because of the size of the club".

Although some could have found that intimidating, once the throbbing pulse intro to 'Faith Healer' was sparked up, the bands intro music, everyone would be more than ready for what was to follow.

A visit from **Sarah Gordon and Little Free Rock** could also bring in a few punters, though not necessarily for the music. The delightful Sarah had a habit of removing several items of clothing, an old trick, but one that seems to work still.

Quite definitely not having to rely on clothing removal antics were the white funk soul brothers, the **Average White Band**. Their polished sound, which sounded nothing less than terrific in the club, made them a firm favourite. Pete Youngman would also offer bands a place to lay their heads for the night after the show.

"They (AWB) performed a brilliant gig, and were supposed to be stopping at my house afterwards. I told them the number of the house, but by the time they arrived they got the wrong number, getting no reply they proceeded to kick the door in of the house next door". Which obviously slightly annoyed his neighbour.

"The next day my neighbour collared me: 'I want a word with you, some Scotsmen were here last night trying to kick my door in'. At this point the neighbours daughter appeared, she knew that it was the band who had been attempting to gain entry. 'But dad, it was the Average White Band, they're famous! 'That's alright then' said the neighbour.

The man would now be able to tell all and sundry for years to come that the Average White Band kicked *his* door in!

Not everyone was as happy as Pete's neighbour though. Word got round, mainly through the press, that plans were afoot to open up a new disco at the old bowling alley in Bargates. The *Mail's* Brian Harrigan had received a letter regarding the prospect of this, the author of the letter felt 'disgust and amazement that Rank: '...were to waste the premises ..on another disco, that by no stretch of the imagination qualifies as entertainment'.

He also has a quick dig at the lack of room for manoeuvring equipment down the legendary 76 entry, and sums up by pointing out (in his view) that: 'the town certainly does not need another monster disco'.

Though he does confess that: 'it would be nice to see *King Crimson* in Burton, eh?'

All to no avail, we now know that *Adams* threw open its doors, and invited in their smartly dressed, nay, 'smart but casual please' clientele to revel in its delights. (Because it's a well known fact that people wearing shirts and ties never get involved in fights when they're pissed do they?).

Before long they were working their magic on the town's younger elements, who could resist the invite to a 'Best Dressed Chick in Town' Competition? *King Crimson* never showed up either.

I just steam in but......

76 CLUB
HIGH STREET BURTON

FRIDAY 17th

MOON

PLUS DISCS FROM AQUARIUS
9.0 p.m.-2.0 a.m.

FRIDAY 24th

SEX PISTOLS

PLUS

DISCS FROM AQUARIUS

You can't sit on the fence, you couldn't then, you can't now: you either love 'em or you hate 'em. That's the way of things with the Sex Pistols. They set out to cause a reaction, any reaction would do, positive or negative, as long as you didn't just stand there and do nothing. The 76 crowd didn't disappoint, they almost unanimously hated them.

Before the group's appearance at the club there had been some advance publicity. Whether this was down to their manager, themselves, or just a music press that was starved of sensational stories is open to question, but at this time you had to have been studiously keeping your eye on that press for information about a new movement that was ready to break in pretty spectacular style across the media, and therefore, the country.

The *Pistols* had already played over a good deal of the country, albeit keeping very low key, with only their growing contingent of hangers on, including the infamous *Bromley Contingent*, in on the act. They were deliberately flying in the face of the whole rock music set up, which at that time, had become stale, predictable and - to many people - just plain boring.

Gordon Band was given the opportunity to put the group on at the club. As ever, he was more than aware of the *kafuffle* that would precede the group's appearance at any venue. They were not a safe bet, anything but, but that was the whole point, - their style of audience confrontation was a totally alien concept at the time, and though it was often misinterpreted as goading, the idea was to bring about a halt to complacency amongst the audience. Gordon must have had to weigh up how his 76 regulars may react.

The Pistols had performed at the *100 Club Punk Festival* just four days earlier. There was a certain amount of violence at that event, but no more than your average Saturday night over at *Eve's* disco.

Gordon Band: "I'd heard about the group, and knew exactly what I was doing booking them. They were on their way up here to play, Nottingham I think. I was offered them for the Friday, so took them on".

Sex Pistols *at Manchester Free Trade Hall - a couple of months before their 76 appearance.*
(Paul Walsh/Penetration Fanzine/I Swear I Was There-David Nolan)

The group were pencilled in for the September 24, 1976. Many of the 76 regulars would go down on a Friday night irrespective of which group were booked to appear. Bands were accepted on merit, if they were good and went down well, they were asked back. If they stank, that was it, you were very unlikely to have to suffer them again.

Nick Whittaker had started to get wind of the *Pistols*.

'I remember a rumour going round that the band – who no one had ever heard of then! – were accompanied by two strippers! Was it just us getting the wrong end of the stick – or had some clever publicity wallah deliberately spread the rumour in order to attract more punters?'

It was probably a combination of things. One of the groups London gigs had been at the *El Paradiso Strip Club* (bass guitarist, and supposed would be Beatles fan, Glen Matlock, has given a rather vivid account of the, shall we say, 'clean up' that had to take place amongst the stage front area before the gig). Another likely reason for the rumour may have been the appearance of soon to be *Banshee* leader, Siouxsie Sue, parading at gigs in topless leather and lace outfits, which some found questionable when the only really questionable item included was the swastika armbands. Yet another factor may have been the on-stage disrobing of *Pistol* person Jordan at a gig in Watford, all carefully arranged by their publicity conscious manager.

The group had with them a number of the Bromley lot, faces who subsequently became minor celebrities in their own right. Encountering the strangely garbed southerners caused a bit of comment among the locals.

Kev Spiers: 'The Sex Pistols had some followers up from London, walking around in PVC jackets and chains hanging from their nose to their earlobes. We were all walking round with beards, lumberjack jackets and flared jeans. That culture shock hadn't hit Burton at that particular time.'

Don Jones: "Siouxsie and Adam Ant were there, Adam had on a PVC Levi jacket with fake Pound notes hanging off it".

As to the actual numbers of home town boys and girls in there that night, the number seems to have gradually risen with the passing years (not unusual for an early *Pistols* outing), though Paul Dennis puts the turnout as "no more than 100 people in there that night, a high proportion of those were Pistols hangers-on".

Come show time, and all preconceived ideas of what you were about to witness were out the window. The band was introduced by resident DJ, Neil Turner, who can be clearly heard on the subsequent recordings of the gig urging on the Burton faithful: 'Lets hear if for the Sex Pistols, come on!'

Nick Whittaker: '(We were) not overly impressed by what seemed to us a bunch of talent-less, loud-mouthed idiots. Spitting at the audience didn't help (we didn't realise it was meant to be a privilege!), and so scuffles broke out. We didn't pay entrance money to be insulted like that".

Singer John Lydon's reason for gobbing while on stage, according to him, was that he suffered from sinus problems, and he would gob at the side of the stage to clear the phlegm. This was later taken as a sign of appreciation by some of those in the audience, so they would let groups have it back, by the bucketful.

Other witness's couldn't get their head around the attitude of the band. Being used to a steady supply of professional bands, who would get upset or annoyed by technical hitches, or a less than smooth transfer from one number to another, they found it hard to grasp where this lot were coming from.

"They came on, did two songs, then Johnny said 'that's it, I'm f*ckin' off', and off he and Steve Jones went, leaving the drummer and the bass player on stage. They eventually came back on, only to see the other two walk off – they were crap!"

Others, though few in number, were initially taken aback by the band's unconventional behaviour, but were gradually starting to feel a certain amount of affinity with what the band, particularly the singer, were doing.

"We had all taken a step back from the stage front, I couldn't believe the singer, he was crawling round on his hands and knees throwing beer at the audience. I thought it was great!"

By now the atmosphere was a bit fraught. The stage set up at the club enabled the audience to directly face up to any band, there was no boundary between performer and spectator. Luckily almost the whole event has been recorded for posterity (more of which later), and on the recorded versions (there's plenty to chose from), you can clearly hear someone in the crowd - I know who it is but I'm not at liberty to divulge – shouting at the group 'f*ck off, **Eddie and the Hot Rods**', a reference to the individual's preference for the group that had appeared at the 76 in July.

Eddie and the Hot Rods – *remnants of the pub rock/blues scene, one of the forerunners of punk.*

Johnny Rotten, sensing maybe that he was working the audience well, not in the conventional sense, but in the way *he* enjoyed doing it, made a sneering comment during the gig in his own imitable style: 'What a great set!'

Again, at some stage in the proceedings a very Burtonian sounding voice can be heard shouting out 'Piss Off you morons!'

Graham 'Weg' Smith recalls: 'Johnny getting a shock off the mike stand which made him jump up, only to hit his nose, cutting it on the boarding above the stage'.

As many of those in the audience were musicians themselves, they would often be checking out their counterparts in the visiting bands, sussing out the qualities, or otherwise, of those they were watching. Pete Youngman was assessing the situation. His verdict? "I thought they were crap! Steve Jones had a Fender amp, he (or maybe somebody else?) had spray painted 'Guitar Hero' across it".

Pete himself confesses to buying 'Never Mind the Bollocks' when it came out - maybe the guitar hero had impressed him after all. Pete also remembers another moment, which is heard with perfect clarity on the recordings: "Johnny got his hanky out and, blowing his nose, said, 'they don't like us'. This you can hear just before the PA starts to splutter and feedback out the start to - coincidentally enough - 'Problems'.

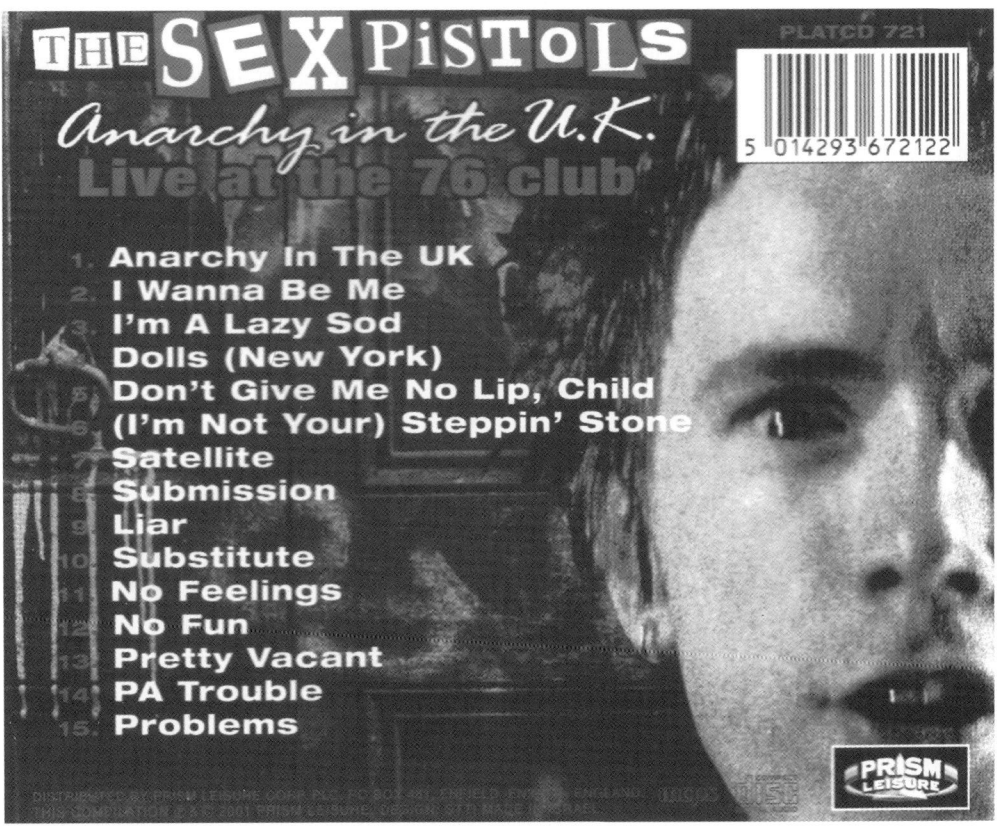

One of the many CD/LP's available of the gig at the 76

(Prism Leisure)

Almost all were impressed with the drumming of Paul Cook, though nobody has really mentioned the qualities of Glen Matlock, who is widely regarded as the only 'musician' in the group. We will leave a summing up of the nights events to 'Weg' Smith. At the end of the set, the bands vocalist informs the punters: 'If you want an encore you'll have to ask', which a good number of the audience that night most certainly did not. Undaunted, in Wegs words: "I seem to remember that they got booed off and came back on to do an encore. Class!"

In the lead up to the gig, the *Burton Observer and Chronicle's* music correspondent, Roger Eversley, had obviously been tracking the group's rise to infamy. His article in the newspaper the night before the event, hinted at what might be on the cards in an ever so slightly 'taking the piss' sort of way, under the banner headline *'How can anyone write about the unprintable?'*

Right on the mark though, he summed up the sort of trepidation that often preceded a Pistols outing: *'There's a band on tomorrow night at my regular Friday nightspot the 76 Club. I've a feeling it's going to be …well, lets say bizarre'*. Roger then gives the reader a brief run down of the band and it's members, including the news the name of the bands singer: *'..is Rotten. Yes, Rotten'.*

He doesn't seem to have been looking forward to experiencing the band at close quarters though: 'All this gives me headache. I think this band are going to be at least outrageous and probably bad'.

However, having been in the audience that night, he was putting forward an altogether different point of view by his next piece for the papers readership:

'It was the end. The ultimate in Rock. The culmination of five years or more of tastelessness, thoughtlessness and decadence in popular music'.

Far from regarding the *Pistols* as tasteless, here was someone seeing the group live and having his eyes opened, in the parlance of the Pistols camp he was 'getting it'. Reading the reaction of the majority of the audience, and probably sensing that future events would put this group out of bounds to their fans, he observed that it would be the groups first – and last – gig in Burton. Highlighting *'the mixture of dumb surprise, unsuppressible scorn and vociferous derision'* he seemed to delight in revealing that *'it was also very funny. A great joke to see an audience brimming with indignation; nay fury'*, the Filth and the Fury indeed!

He really was climbing on board, and thought the band were *'fulfilling a role demanded by the current trends in rock 'n' roll…they played exceedingly loud…and attempted to play in a fashion not far removed from the early Who (in fact including one of that groups early hits, can't remember which one it was though)'*. It was 'Substitute'.

The Sex Pistols were, of course, due to play at the *Kings Hall* in Derby as part of the *Anarchy Tour* package. We all know what happened after the *Bill Grundy* TV bun-fight, and the Derby gig with *Johnny Thunders Heartbreakers, The Damned* and *The Clash* was cancelled after the group refused to appear before a panel of indignant, and self-righteous, Derby councillors (no doubt of a similar age group to Mr Grundy, who had goaded the group in the first place). All those who had forked out the £1.60 ticket price returned to the *R E Cords Record* shop in the High Street to get their refund.

Also available in the shop, a couple of years later, was the first of many copies of the live recording of the 76 Club gig. 'Indecent Exposure (Its' A Dirty Business)' on Rotten Records, released as a Bootleg LP in 1978, with *R E Cords* 'swamped with requests for the record'. At the time mystery surrounded how someone had managed to record the band's set with such, apparently good sound quality. We now know it was recorded straight through the mixing desk by the bands sound engineer, Dave Goodman. At the time of release though things were less obvious. Gordon Band had his own theories, and he was quick to notice a difference between the nights actual events, and what turned up on record. 'The crowds noises have been taken out, and its of unusually good quality for a Bootleg'.

The crowd noise, or lack of it, is an argument that still surfaces every now and again. Those who were there on the night remember clearly the stunned silence from the 76 regulars that greeted most of the songs.

Andy Parker: "It was shocking, awful – nobody clapped between the songs, the crowd noises have been added." On the recorded version there is much whooping and clapping between numbers, which may well have been 'imported' from the Chelmsford tapes, another live recording of the band done at a similar time.

Paul Dennis backs that up: "It (the recording) was pretty much as it happened, apart from the fact that extra crowd noise has been added later on".

Due to the presence of the *Pistols* followers it was not all stunned silence. Roger Eversley noted it was the type of music that was likely to get you *'bashing yourself against the wall, or, as a few people did, to leap and cavort foolishly about the club'*, confessing *'I suppose I was one of them'*. Eversley was, in fact, an early witness to pogoing, allegedly a Sid Vicious invention.

Indecent Exposure – the first 76 Club outing on vinyl.

(Sam Parker)

Sid, later the *Pistols* bass player, was at the time a follower of the group (whether he was there on the night is open to guesswork). It has been well documented that he was given the nickname 'Vicious' because, by all accounts before it all went to his head, he was anything but. There was an intriguing item in the *Mail* advertising the visit to Derby of the band *Jupp* from Southend, it was reported that the band was led by Mickey Jupp, hence the name, along with guitarist *Sid Vicious*! This was February, 1976.

Some years later Sid's mother, Anne Shirley, ended up living in Swadlincote, succumbing eventually in 1996 to the same fate as her photogenic son.

With the punk movement gaining momentum more bands became available for booking, though a number of these bands had made the transition from pub rock, derided by some at the punk barricades but nonetheless a vital schooling ground for many. Pioneer punks *The Damned* were advertised to appear at the 76 in November, but were replaced by London's **The Vibrators**, who had come through the pub circuit themselves, a reputation they have had to constantly defend. They were billed as Chris Spedding's backing band, Chris having been involved in the *100 Club* showcase, and having played on the Vibrators 'Pogo Dancing' single. He was regarded as an honorary punk by the New Wave elite.

The Damned advertised, but didn't play.
Going down the 76 for **Charlie**?

(Burton Mail)

It was often very hard to distinguish between punk, and what was just good old-fashioned pop. Promising Londoners **Bethnal** played the club in January, 1977. They were a hybrid of styles and nationalities, and although included a very non-punk violin in their line-up, they were definitely classed in the rock category. Others like *power* poppers **The Motors**, were remnants of the former **Ducks De-Luxe** and no strangers to the 76 in that previous guise, were promising to 'bridge the gap between *New Wave* and *Barry White*!'

Leading up the doo-wop revival were **The Darts**, who were very much enjoyed on the night they appeared at the 76. Members of the group achieved a certain amount of notoriety in the town a couple of years later when staying at the *Riverside Hotel*. They were over-nighting there after completing a gig in Wolverhampton and, using up some of the nervous energy that was still coursing through his veins afterwards, one of the ensemble managed to cause a certain amount of damage to property in the hotel (room wrecking being part of the rock and roll lifestyle). Damage was caused to a chandelier in one of the rooms, though this was no mindless act of vandalism, this was an *educational* accident. When up before the courts he was asked to explain how the damage came about. He told the bench: "I was attempting to explain how Bobby Charlton scored in the European Cup Final by heading the chandelier".

Opening up to the prospect of a whole new generation taking themselves down the 76, the club introduced a New Wave night on Wednesdays, with Andy Parker on hand to spin the discs. He was confidently predicting a Top Ten hit for *The Clash* with their debut 45 'White Riot', and was suitably impressed with *The Damned's* first LP.

First up on the New Wave nights, from the USA, was one time *Bowie* squeeze, **Cherry Vanilla**. Curiosity seemed to be the order of the day, and the place was packed. The lady, along with her backing group, caused a bit of a surprised reaction amongst the critics in the audience. By all accounts the act went down well, being 'more proficient than imagined'. That's hardly surprising though, considering the rhythm section on the night, bass and drums, consisted of one Gordon Sumner, better known as Sting, and Stewart Copeland, two members of the - soon to be bleached blonde popsters - *The Police*.

Many of the groups booked by Gordon Band were on the roster of the London-based *Sherry Copeland Agency*, one of the partners, Ian Copeland, being Police drummer Stewart's brother. Ian passed away in May 2006.

The half expected anarchy that some feared would accompany these new wave acts never materialised, partly because it was midweek and some of us had to get up for work the next day.

As Andy Parker pointed out: "There was very little trouble amongst club regulars, most of it came from the groups themselves, either fighting with each other or the audience".

Some members of visiting band **U Boat**, found themselves in the Monday morning 'Bad lads' line up in front of the Burton Magistrates, for taking part in a 'free for all' with, what had a few minutes before, been their audience outside the club.

Sadly, the new wave nights suffered from poor attendances, and by the time of the visit of *999* it was decided to call a halt. This was a shame, as the quality of bands like 999 exceeded the usual expectations. They were accomplished musicians - guitarist Nick Cash had been a member of Kilburn and the Highroads, perennial 76 favourites (albeit under his previous stage name of Keith Lucas). They played some high-energy stuff, I know I was there (sorry Gordon I was underage!), though one or two seemed to miss the whole point of the music genre. Colin Carr, writing in the *Mail* found the group too loud. I found them loud as well; the difference being that's why I was there. I wore my 999 badge proudly for many months afterwards.

999

Many people were less than enamoured with the new hard-hitting style of music. A reviewer of *Sham 69's* debut 12 incher found his aural pleasure being battered by 'a painfully monotonous bunch of jerks'. However he found some comfort in the impressive fact that 'the singer can count to four'.

With the demise of the short-lived new wave nights we had to go elsewhere for our kicks, mainly Derby Kings Hall in my case. I have since found out that both *Squeeze* and *The Buzzocks* were intended for the 76, only to be cancelled along with the Wednesday night sessions - our loss not theirs.

The influence of the punk movement showed up in some of the new bands that started up in Burton at the time, though most of them had a more new wave leaning than out and out punk. The likes of **The Crazy Quilts**, **Darrell and the Chaperones**, **Whizz for Atoms**, **Fatal Dose** and **Diorama**, all appeared in the town at venues such as *The British Oak* in Byrkley Street and above *The Locomotive* in Station Street.

Ian Hewitt was involved with a number of Burton bands. In the tradition of many involved in music he went to art school, and meeting many like minded individuals decided to form up a group and become part of 1978s thriving punk/new wave scene.

Ian Hewitt: "I remember the first gig I played. It was at the British Oak with the Crazy Quilts, who we were support for. The punk scene in Burton was really good, everyone was like minded and we would normally get a good reception".

This is view supported from a member of the old guard, Geoff Noble, who reveals that the hippy ideal was sometimes anything but love and peace.

"When the punk think came in there was an honesty about it, which I liked. The early 70s could be really nasty, a very spiteful sort of period".

Another favourite of the punk groups was **The Continental Club**, or Conti to those who frequented it. The club would often put on punk/reggae nights in keeping with the new-found kinship between followers of both movements. The club also put on reggae acts. In 1976 they had Derby band **Big Six**, and **Count Blackbeard**, while the following year saw a visit from **Sir Nata**. Even with punk's 'we'll play in your garden shed' attitude there was still one place they unanimously disliked though, "The Drill Hall – it was crap!"

Fatal Dose's Paul Latham (Lavvy), recalls the set up at *The British Oak*: "We had to pay for the room hire and used to get a share of the door receipts, so we had to rely on getting a good few down. We used to ask Steve (the landlord at the time) how much we were going to get. He'd say 'Lets go and have a look round' as we went through the room he would reel off the deductions: 'doors off its hinges £3; toilets broken £5; 20 glasses broken £2.... We never got much!"

Maybe most of the people in these groups hadn't been at the 76 the night of the *Pistols* visit (quite a few people in the town who claimed to be there that night weren't), but the Pistols shock tactics had been effective in giving impetus to those who 'got off their arses' and formed groups. What Rotten and Co thought of their gig at the 76 is not recorded, its highly unlikely they gave it any more thought once they were on their way, but at a later date John Lydon (formerly Rotten) did comment that 'some of the best gigs we ever did was in front of stone cold silence'. I think the night at the 76 probably comes within that category.

The Small Bar, **76 Club**, *1975*

(Burton Mail)

At the end of the alley…

As can be seen from the picture, and to quote from the *Mail* at the time of the last re-fit in 1975: 'The general theme of the design is somehow Oriental'. It was envisaged that the club would return to its halcyon days, providing entertainment for at least five nights each week. Sundays would feature pop and soul with veteran local DJ *Barmy Barry*, on Wednesday nights it was proposed to re-visit groups 'from yesteryear' - those who were perhaps past their prime, but still able to belt it out live - while live music was to continue on Friday and Saturday nights (though later this would be Friday nights only) with a new resident DJ 'Sartori'. The Burton Jazz Club would be making a welcome return to its Thursday night slot, with Monday and Tuesday reserved for 'private functions'. That was the plan anyway. To quote directly from Andy Parker's piece in the *Mail* again: 'Live music is to be the foundation on which the club builds its future – and surely in the world of entertainment there can be none stronger'. Well it certainly lived up to that over the coming years.

Not everyone was happy to pay for the privilege though, the two fire doors that you can see either side of the bar in the previous picture, would often be utilised as an alternative entrance. It was a bit of a ball ache getting to the doors from outside, but if you had an accomplice situated in the club, free entry would be ensured by the door being quickly opened, at a pre-set moment. Another popular trick for those who couldn't afford the entrance fee (or those who just wanted more money for booze and, er, other things) was to arrange for someone already in the club to lean over and dial a number on the phone (was it 191?) in the cloakroom at the ideal moment, usually when the bouncers were otherwise engaged, causing the phone to ring. This would mean the person on the door, usually Karen, had to get up and go and answer it, with no-one on the door to stop you, in you went!

The New 76 CLUB SCENE

IT'S ALL HAPPENING!
Live Groups — Disco's

Future Attractions !
BURTON'S SWINGING
NEW JAZZ CLUB
OPENS THURSDAY, APRIL 3rd
★
FROM FRIDAY, MARCH 21st
DRINKS & MEALS
WILL BE SERVED UNTIL 2 a.m.

Friday, March 14th—
Now on tour!
UPP
plus Aquarius

Saturday, March 15th—
Live groups!
BABY Plus Satori

Sunday, March 16th—
Top Midlands D.J.
BARMY BARRY

Thursday, March 20th—
Burton Technical College
Rag Dance
NUMEROUS D.J's

Friday, March 21st—
Your favourite group
HUSTLER Plus Aquarius

Saturday, March 22nd—
One of the top groups
around!
KILBURN & THE HIGH
ROADS
plus Satori

Sunday, March 23rd—
Top Midlands D.J.
BARMY BARRY

Friday, March 24th—
Tim Rose's backing group
THE MOVIES
plus Aquarius

Saturday, March 29th—
Big Sounds from a Big
Group
FUMBLE plus Satori

Sunday, March 30th—
All your sounds around
from
CARL DENE

HIGH STREET, BURTON-ON-TRENT

For some reason the guitarist with **Baby** was minus a vital piece of equipment: "Kev Spiers lent Mick Pirri - the bands guitarist - his Les Paul. After he had done he put the guitar down at the side of the stage and someone kept flicking fag ash on it, much to the annoyance of Kev!".

Gary Holton found great popularity as part of the extremely successful 'Auf Wiedersehen Pet' TV programme playing a chirpy East End Cockney 'wide boy' -

not difficult as that is what he was. Before that he was guitarist in the **Heavy Metal Kids**. His antics - onstage and off - would eventually lead to him being ousted from the band, but many recall his style at the 76.

Geoff Noble: "Gary Holton would be out amongst the audience, taking the piss, not in a nasty way, but baiting them a bit".

Unfortunately, his offstage problems got the better of him and in 1983 he died, the result of a drugs and alcohol mix. Other group members recall the little club with no small amount of affection. Drummer Keith Boyce:

"I recall playing there with the *Kids*. The main thing that sticks in my mind is the changing room/chip shop bit. We thought it hilarious at the time; we used to say that we were off for a bit of *chip shop rock*. I also remember the alley and the small club, with the roadies always complaining as it was a joke trying to get our huge PA and lighting rig down there. Why we didn't take a scaled down rig I don't know - trying to be clever I suppose!"

This was the same for many bands. The obvious answer, as Gordon Band had already pointed out, was to take less equipment. Keith Boyce again: "It was always a good crowd down there though, what few they could squeeze in".

Keith later joined **Bram Tchaikovskys Battle Axe**, but he still hadn't learned his lesson.

"I played there with Bram, this time my huge drum flightcases wouldn't go down the alley!"

With *Adams* now going full tilt, competition for the loyalty of the young adults in Burton was hotting up. *Adams* publicity machine was working well, firing off a press release reporting that the club was 'just what the people of Burton want'. Not all of them it wasn't, although they did start putting on live bands occasionally - in 1974 they had chart act and one hit wonders Yellow Bird and 'doo woppers' **Yaketty Yak**. More competition came from **The Allied Breweries Social Club** in Belvedere Road (now *The Belvedere Park Club*).

The *Allied Club* had a strong membership base - the brewery was a big employer in the town at that time - resulting in some pretty heavy-duty names playing there. These included acts as diverse as Acker Bilk and **Eric Delaney** and fading glam rocker Alvin Stardust, though to be fair to Alvin (no stranger to Burton), his star continues to burn, even including a stint on the legendary, and *uber cool, Stiff* Record Label. Allied also gave an outlet for some Burton performers who could rely on a good, and abundant, following. Kat Magee were to appear there, as were **Rock Revival**, Mick Morris's 50s-style rockers. Mick claims to have appeared in just about every club and pub in Burton. Growing up listening to continuous airings of *Elvis* and *The Shadows* tracks, some of it was bound to influence him.

Rock Revival used to practice in the back yard of Mick's parents' house in Wellington Street, his parents also managing the group. They would get many gigs through *The Castle Entertainment Agency*, this would often take them out of town, on occasions finding themselves in some close scrapes.

Mick Morris: "We once played at US Air Force base. Once inside the base, thinking it was a road, we managed to drive the van straight on to the runway. Trundling along we didn't realise we were heading for a close encounter with a B17 Bomber! Very soon some pretty serious looking US Military Policemen appeared, and we were then promptly arrested".

Freed up shortly afterwards - they had received a serious bollocking - they were allowed to carry on with the gig.

"Not long into our set two GIs started fighting. Nothing unusual about that, but what we couldn't get over was the bouncer - he must have been at least 7 ft tall. He ran up, decked both of them, then dragged them both out of the hall by their trouser belts!".

Mick Morris – *wearing his influences on his sleeve*
(Mick Morris)

Events at *Allied Club* were generally a bit quieter; members were treated to a visit from Jamaica's 'Number One Soul Brother' **Desmond Dekker**, and, in 1977 **Magazine**. Surely not Howard Devoto's Manchester New Wavers? No, this lot were a pop group from Birmingham.

The prospect of some top groups appearing at the 76 club, brought a certain level of expectancy to the rock fans in Burton. Highlighting this a piece appeared in the *Burton Mail*, an obvious retort to some of the mutterings of boredom, that state that seems to accompany growing up.

'For a long time the cries and moans of boredom….have seemingly been largely unanswered. But now with the prospects of things getting better the cynics have been silenced.'

You couldn't silence them better than with a healthy dose of the **Steve Gibbons Band**, who were late replacements, on this occasion, for **Strider**. Pete Youngman: "Strider didn't show up, so Steve Gibbons took their place, and they were amazing. I spent the whole evening thinking I had been watching Strider, and was very impressed, and it turned out to be Steve Gibbons!"

Everyone who saw bands at the club has an opinion on whether they were any good or not, though it was all a matter of taste. One punter who witnessed **The Kursaal Flyers** was unimpressed: "They got booed off the stage, people thought they were crap.

However another has this to say about the same band: "As I recall, and this could be time playing tricks on the memory but I don't think it is, they went down pretty well. They were a great bunch of lads!"

A few weeks later they were in the charts with a hit record. The fickle world of pop!

Good Habit, the band that would eventually become **Racing Cars**, were not easily forgotten.

Glynn Hardwick: "they all came on stage wearing Monk's habits, apart from their guitarist, who was wearing pyjama's and a chicken mask. We found out later on he was having a breakdown".

Such shenanigans weren't always confined to the groups, sometimes those in the audience made their own fun.

Glynn again: "One of the bands I played in had a bass player who always wore cowboy boots. He was really pissing us off one night so we got hold of him in the club and hung him upside down. We removed his boots and he spent a good time walking round with no boots on".

Anyone who has frequented the club will know this wouldn't have been a pleasant experience underfoot; there would always be a lot of beer over the floor.

"Eventually we let him have one boot back, so he limped round the club. Unbeknown to him, his other boot had spent all this time revolving round on one of the DJ's record decks. At long last he spotted it, and, visibly relieved, he retrieved the boot and slipped it back on. It was at this point that he discovered that we had filled it up with beer and chicken wings from the Jolly Fryer".

One group who would have whole-heartedly endorsed that sort of behaviour was **Neil Innes and Fatso**. Neil had been involved with both the *Monty Python* team and surrealist humorist's *The Bonzo Dog Band*. Not forgetting the later *fab four* piss-take *The Rutles* (known as 'The Pre-fab Four' for the film). Entertainment was at a premium when Neil and band, described as 'one of the funniest set ups on the rock circuit', was in town. Neil would often make his stage entrance with a blow-up doll strapped to his back.

How is it possible to make someone laugh just by playing a guitar? I don't know, but this man can do it. Try and sit through *The Bonzo Dog Band's* 'Canyons Of Your

Mind' guitar solo without breaking into a smile. Mixed in with the humour, though, is often a more serious message. Check out his lyrics for 'Dear Father Christmas' - he's got a good point there.

Neil Innes - *Possibly one of the funniest musicians alive.*

(Pete Youngman)

Very much in the same vein as Neil Innes Manchester's **Alberto Y los Trios Paranoias** (who later shortened their name to *The Alberto's*), first brought their own take on the absurd to the 76 in 1975. They would manage to take some of the pomposity out of the music business by taking the piss, out of others and themselves, as Geoff Noble recalls.

"They would pull the plug out of a guitar and it had a fag lighter on it. They had two drummers, one of which would perform with a contraceptive on the end of his nose".

The *Alberto's* main man, C P Lee elaborates. "In 1975 we did have two drummers, Bruce Mitchell, who now plays with the *Durutti Column* (and has done for decades), and the Mighty Mongo aka Raymond Hughes. Mongo's stage antics were summat to behold – his stage gear consisted of a woolly hat and pyjama bottoms (with a cushion stuffed down the front for effect), and he would be led on stage with a rope around his neck. (Guitarist) Les Prior had a cigarette lighter gaffer taped to a guitar lead jack-plug for his demonstration of how to be a 'perfect' rock guitarist".

Admittedly, events that took place over 30 years ago at the 76 are now a little dim, though he hasn't forgot one thing: the beer. "Burton-on-Trent would have figured in our mentality because of the ale, but if my memory serves me at all the club didn't sell 'proper' beer – much to our disappointment".

The group were able to parody any type of music - have a listen to their 'cheesy 70s disco style' funk of 'Put The Funkin' Kettle On'. Secretly, of course, they are quite accomplished musicians.

Bringing their own brand of weirdness down the club were **The Doctors of Madness**, fronted by the aptly named Kid Strange. The Kid would perform with his eyes closed, having taken the trouble to have eyes painted on his eyelids!

All this wasn't nearly entertaining enough for one - now ex-resident - of the town, Brian Harrigan was writing for what I would describe as 'the thinking persons music paper', *Melody Maker*. For reasons known only to himself, Brian launched a bit of a rant against his former home, and in particular the 76 Club, telling anyone who cared to listen what a drab awful place it was. He then goes on to let the reader know some of the top groups that had played here recently, totally defeating his own argument, Kid Strange indeed.

The article appeared on the May 1, 1976:

Page 34—MELODY MAKER, May 1, 1976

Everybody knows this is nowhere

So you thought your town was a rock desert? Let BRIAN HARRIGAN guide you through Burton-on-Trent — Desolation Row

● " Everybody do the disco stomp " — Hamilton Bohannon

● " Down at the club, you're gonna say that it's all right " — Drifters

● " Cruisin' and playing my radio/ With no particular place to go " — Chuck Berry

CHRIS SPEDDING: "One night, when the late-lamented Sharks played the 76 Club, I filtered into the dressing room to get a closer look at the enigmatic guitarist. The dressing room turned out to be half of the chip shop."

Describing Burton as *'the sort of place where you ask the taxi driver's where the action is'* - wouldn't you do that in any strange town - on he went *'to anyone from a big city, Burton is Toytown...Musically its Desolation Row'*.

Then, in one sentence, he manages to capture the essence of what made the 76 so good.

'Its cramped, loud and the beer's not so great, but God has it got an atmosphere'.

So, all agreed, the 76 was a good club for live music. He even mentioned Burton's most famous son.

'Burton's one and only famous musician, drummer Phil Seamen, had the right idea when it came to making it big. He got the hell out'.

Which is what Brian had done himself, having a go from the safety of the big city, being the big city boy now. Though, again, in the final part of the piece he defeats his own summing up of the place, questioning a *'Socialist Worker'* vendor (the 70s equivalent of *Big Issue*), he enquires of the lad: *'Guess you must get fed up with encountering the small town mentality here?'* to which the would be revolutionary replied *'You mean Burton? Listen, I come from Loughborough. Compared to that place Burton **is** the big city!'*.

Old favourites Sassafras were paying a visit to 'Desolation Row', one of many such visits, and it was a hot steamy night in the 76, another reason that the club was well suited as rock venue.

Terry ' Beefy' Bennett, Sassafras vocalist – *'Burton is very strong for us'*.

(Burton Mail)

The reviewer, at the 76 Sassafras gig, made a comment on the type of conditions to be found in the club on a good night:

'During the Sassafras gig the waves of heat from the masses at the front of the stage began to affect both the masses and the band'.

Leather clad rockers Judas Priest were 'stormingly received' at the 76, playing most of their 'Sad Wings of Destiny' LP, as were **The Hellraisers**, with the crowd enjoying 'the sight of five slightly ageing, unspectacular greasers'.

More activity from music fans in the local press. In a response to an idea for an open air blues/rock/soul festival on the Ox-Hay, and with perhaps thoughts of the 1970 Eton Park affair still in mind, a letter to the *Mail revealed* that 'The majority of Burtonians prefer to sit in public houses drinking and 'talking shop', rather than go to any live event'.

Earlier in the year the *Mail* had run a competition, with the prize being copies of Mike Oldfield's orchestral opus 'Tubular Bells'. All the entrants had to do was provide the answer to one simple, open ended question: 'I think the best way to improve the entertainments scene in Burton would be…'. Number of replies? Two!

Come 1976, and things were certainly livening up on the music scene. Former *Bay City Roller* heartthrob and tartan terror, Les McKeown was cleared of shooting a fan with an air rifle (now someone attempting it the other way round I could understand), though as a headline 'Pop Star cleared of shooting fan' does have a bit more gusto than one of our local efforts, 'Pop star buys suit in Burton' (it was Dave Berry in 1972, the 'no news day' to beat all 'no news days').

The **Scorpions** got soundly booed off the 76 stage by the faithful, but not before all raised a laugh at the site of the bass player, who was so tall "you couldn't see his head!". The departing comment of the band's singer still remains with many of those who supplied the catcalls: 'We don't need to play your little club, next time we play Wembley.' And they did.

Another group that has played Wembley and the 76, and just about every venue in between, are Scottish/Aussie hybrid AC/DC. Their night at the club was a never to be forgot experience.

Andy Parker recalls interviewing the group in the *Jolly Fryer*, before the gig. They pointed out that they don't normally play the smaller type of club nowadays. Though those who were there are sure glad that they made the exception for us.

Paul Dennis: "The AC/DC gig was packed to the gunnels – and they nearly lifted the roof off!"

In what we now know as classic, AC/DC stage showmanship, guitarist Angus Young *'threw off his cap and raced around the audience on Bon Scott's shoulders. The group rolled, leaped and shook around the stage'.* Not all of it was intentional though, Pete Lawrence recalls that Angus (who later stopped round Peter's house) fell off the stage during the gig. Being in close a proximity to the stage, and therefore Angus's gymnastics, the audience in the 76 were getting more than just feeling the vibes off the band.

Geoff Noble: "I was stood at the front and got covered in everything that was flying off Angus,. They are everything a rock band should be, they were absolute dynamite."

'The gig was an absolute stormer – 'the outrageousness of a 17 year old guitarist who came on stage in a school uniform, and spent the rest of the night trying to blow everybody's brains out with some surprisingly good playing'. By unanimous decision the 76 regulars agreed, 'they ripped the joint'.

THE AUSTRALIAN/SCOTTISH group AC/DC who make a special appearance tomorrow at the 76 Club.

AC/DC – 'tore the roof off the place'
(Burton Mail)

Perhaps at the other end of the scale from the Aussie rockers, The Enid were a bit more 'off the wall'. Ken Hart says of the bands set up: "They had wall to wall equipment, all around the club, including synthesisers".

Mick Woodward agrees: "They had loads of equipment, three keyboards, guitars and a drummer, they were weird".

Having so much tackle in a club the size of the 76 meant that they had to make sacrifices, one keyboard operative had to play with his back to the rest of the band, and therefore the audience. To ensure that everyone got the full benefit of the performance the group had an unusual method of getting your attention.

Andy Parker: "They used to make everyone in the audience sit down!".

Others that appeared had other methods of grabbing your attention, even if it was not planned that way. **Max Merritt and the Meteors** were another Aussie import, with the *Mail* elegantly describing their leader as *'an Aussie Bricklayer'*.

Pete Youngman: "The band had been involved in some sort of train crash, and some came on stage complete with crutches".

You have to admire their determination. Their efforts were somewhat in vain though, they failed to get an encore, with audience apathy being the suspected reason, though nearer the truth would have been the fact that, on this particular night, there were a large number of non-regulars in the club, the result of a temporary closure of *Adams*, over the road.

Proving that - no matter how immune we think we are - sex sells, some decidedly non-PC advertising alerted the 'testosteroned' young men of the town to the fact that one **Dana Gillespie** (the *'Dishy Dana Gillespie'*), would be in town, along with her band. She had already displayed her female charms in films such as 'The Lost Continent' and Ken Russell's 'Mahler'. There were plenty of pre-publicity photos of Dana, attired in a rather becoming basque, the bait had been set, and everyone was biting.

"We were all looking forward to the night. We had all seen the photo's of her and were ready for a treat. Come the time for her appearance she strolled on stage in a sweater and jeans!" Ha Ha! Ever get the feeling you've been cheated?

The reason for *Adams* being shut was simple, it was being turned into *Eve's*, with the PR men releasing the blurb 'and from Adam came forth Eve, and it was good' (no it wasn't). It was now being promoted as the ideal place for 'the young executive type of person' - strange that they should pick a band as *teenyboppy* as **The Dead End Kids** to put on a show then. They quite rightly got a pummelling from the local press for even attempting to do a lacklustre cover of *Dr. Feelgood's* 'Roxette'.

Rank had splashed out £60,000 on the re-fit, with management promising to weed out the trouble causers, warning: 'the bottom 20 per cent of hardened regulars who caused a lot of the disturbances will not be allowed in'. There was always more trouble in that place than the 76.

One particular group of revellers caused a stir without being admitted to either venue. Whether these gentlemen were young executives is not known, but on the night they would have been refused entry to most places. Having been to a wedding party earlier, they walked down the entry to the 76, but were turned away. What was the problem, was it that they had no membership cards? Had Big Tom ejected them from the club the week before? No. 'You can't come in!' Why? Because you're all naked!'

Many of the acts appearing at the 76 now came complete with a more new wave sort of vibe, many were just adapting to the trends, though some were quite definitely new wave sons. Ultravox were born out of a mutual interest in the *Kraftwerk* mode of *synth pop*. Playing the club in 77, their line up at this stage was pre Midge Ure.

Bass and synthesiser player, Chris Cross: "Actually I do remember the 76 Club, it was a gig that bands would often remark on, ie, 'did you ever do the 76 club?' It was very difficult for the crew, but as far as I remember we had a good time"

His recollection of conditions for the bands inside the club is quite vivid.

"I remember the fish shop part and a very small space where we couldn't use any lights or maybe one or two. I think the stage was in an alcove at the side. Very small is the memory. It's a gig that could be described as 'character building' but is now in the file marked 'do you remember when' and 'coated in nostalgic fairy dust'.

"It definitely provided lots of laughs with other bands in dressing room anecdotes. 'The crowd were small but well formed,' 'not many there but the chips were good' and 'more gherkins than punters'. Those small gigs were very important as they really helped bands to get experience that pays off in the long run".

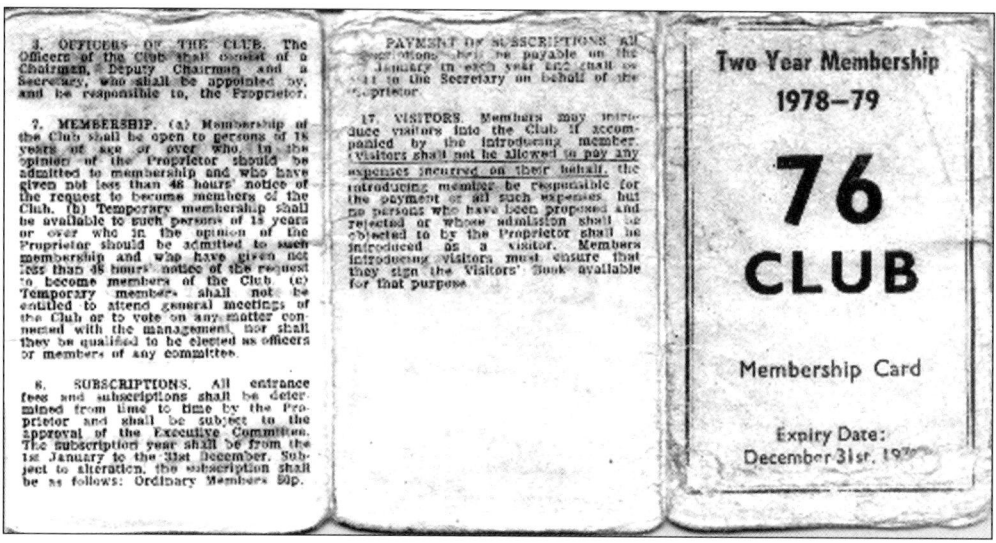

A membership card in this condition suggest plenty of use – and plenty of good nights at the club!

(Pete Brown)

I'm still not sure of this band's correct title, they are either simply called 'O' or A Band Called O, but no matter what the name, they used to turn up and do their set with their dog in tow, and the guitarist played a Gibson Flying V, allegedly the property of one Mr Keith Richards, who (allegedly) had the item stolen from him some time before.

Clayson and the Argonauts, who I am reliably informed have a Burton connection, though I've yet to discover what it is, had invented their own dance which they encouraged punters to try out at gigs, the group provided *'a mixture of pathos, comedy and reality. The dance was the Masso, in which you tried to hurt yourself in as many ways as possible'*. According to the *Mail* there were not many takers for the dance, quite the opposite *'they were treated with apathetic disinterest by the crowd'*. The group's leader, Alan Clayson is now a very successful author, producing books on many rock legends, including Keith Moon.

If you need some serious noise pollution then Motorhead would probably be your weapon of choice, and it took a brave fellow to stand in front of that group's speaker cabinets in a place like the 76, though surprisingly they did not win the vote for loudest group at the club. That particular honour went to **Def Leppard**, who by all accounts set their sound system for the Sydney Opera House. It didn't wash with the 76 crowd.

"They were terrible, definitely a studio band where all the rough bits could be taken out. We used to call them 'Stone Def Leppard' as a result of their 76 showing".

Speaker cabinets at the club could also have other uses. I know of one young lad who, feeling that wave of nausea that heralds the onset of a drink fuelled vomiting session, released he wasn't going to make it to the gents in time. As he was stood next to a speaker cabinet, he did no more than stick his head through the open front of the unit, and hurled copious amounts of bile and diced carrott's inside. Giving the roadies a few more problems getting the speakers out of the place. You've got to admire the lads improvisational skills though.

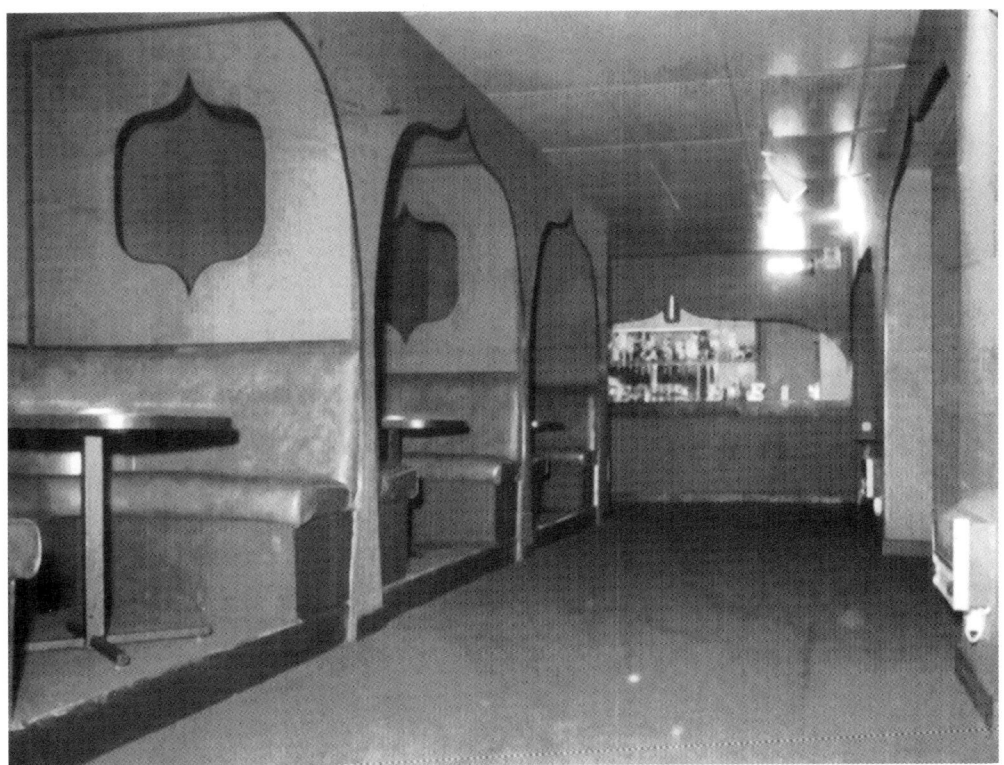

The only E you got down the 76 was Worthington's

(Burton Mail)

For some reason **Dire Straits** were thought by many, myself included, to be an American band, although why this should be I don't know. They played the club in 1978 and those that were already familiar with them, mainly through their 'Sultans of Swing' chart hit, were not disappointed, a thoroughly polished performance was witnessed with the lads running through most of their first LP, though the band were not sure.

Pete Lawrence: "I was there for Dire Straits - they felt that they hadn't been received too well, so they left early."

Reggie Hawker was also in the audience: "I can only presume that Dire Straits had been contracted to play before 'Sultans of Swing' went to number one in the charts. They put on a good show and ended with their chart topper. What they thought about their changing rooms in the Jolly Fryer I dread to think!"

It didn't matter how much equipment you tried to wheel down that narrow alleyway, sometimes the gremlins got to work. **Buster James**, who were (and still are) a tremendously popular live act, had been recalled to the 76 'by popular demand'.

Pete Youngman: "Buster James were fantastic. We had seen them down the club before and wanted them back. The next time they came the soundman discovered that all the microphones were missing. Not only that, the PA system refused to work. After much time messing about with all the stuff the soundman gave a shrug of his shoulders and gave the whole lot a good kick, at which point the whole thing promptly sprung into life!"

At least they were prepared to give it a go. **Cado Belle** were due to play at the club, but, in the time honoured fashion, their roadies kicked up about having to try to manhandle all the gear down the entry. They refused to even unload the van, so Gordon Band, used to all this sort of nonsense, phoned up one of the band members. The band duly appeared and did the unloading themselves.

By the end of the 70s the musical climate settled again. Punk/New Wave was on the decline, being replaced by more user-friendly (and music biz controlled) genres, although the sense of rebellion was carried on by what we now know as *The New Wave of British Heavy Metal (NWOBHM)*, which had no small amount of influence on matters Stateside in the late 80s and early 90s. **Samson** were one of the leaders in this movement. At the time of their 76 visit they were fronted by Bruce Dickinson, later the tattooed millionaire of **Iron Maiden** fame, who would later put in an appearance themselves. Barnsley's heaviest, **Saxon**, also gave the place the full on heavy metal noise treatment.

Not so impressive though were **The Roy Hill Band**. "They must have played 'George's Bar' at least six times", with the punters seeing through the scam they treated them in the time honoured 76 fashion: "we booed them off".

Earning everyone's respect were **Girlschool** - maybe most of us there that night went out of a sense of curiosity, the prospect of an all girl rock band not being particularly new (remember *The Runaways?*). But this was no manufactured girly act, this lot were out and out rockers, and most of us went home more than impressed. *Lemmy's* a big fan, what more needs to be said?

Now we must turn to one of the 76's legendary stories, re-told many times, which has passed into Burton folklore, and though it did not actually take place inside the club, it no doubt involved some of the clientele. Here is a witness's first hand account.

"I never saw any trouble inside the club itself in the 70s, but one night I had just come out of the club's entry and there was a police car parked outside. The police had been called to the club for some reason, some youths came out, noticed the police car, walked up to it, and each taking a grip on the car, rolled it on its side and then calmly strolled over to the chip shop to get some chips. A police woman came out of the club, saw what had been done, turned to us all stood outside and asked 'what's happened?' Of course nobody had seen anything! Within seconds there must have been 13 police cars on the scene, but still nobody had seen anything". Inside the club itself many were there to witness the re-entry of the lady, but her pleas for assistance went unheeded. 'Someone's tipped the police car over!' she announced to all and sundry, to be met firstly with bemused silence, then the sound of raucous laughter.

Simple Minds became one of the biggest bands on the planet, their type of sound being particularly suited to the type of *Stadium Rock* that would later epitomise them, along with *U2*, as the band of the 80's. Their appearance at the club heralded the start of the 80s, with CD's instead of vinyl, and a move away from live music in pubs and clubs. The likes of Simple Minds would be hard put getting their equipment, never mind themselves, into a place the size of the 76 nowadays.

Formerly Johnny and the Self-Abusers, **Simple Minds'** *turn at the 76 saw us out of the 70s, and eased us into the 80s, and the finale to this story.*

An intriguing entry for 1979 has a visit from *The Invaders* booked up for the club - was this *Madness* in their earlier formation? Once the furore of events in the late 70s had died down (and the multi national record companies were firmly back in control of things), there seemed to be a great demand for regurgitating some older musical styles. Apart from the burgeoning heavy metal movement, (if you were going down the club to see **Witchfynde**, **Sledghammer** or **Anglewitch**, I think you pretty much knew what sort of band to expect) and established rockers like **Eric Bell** and Girlschool, the impetus seemed to be behind re-hashing *Mod/Ska* and *Rockabilly* genres.

With a whole new audience to cater for, some of these bands delivered the goods more than adequately. Pete Townsend's protégé's **Straight Eight** were steady enough but failed to take off, while Birmingham's **The Quads**, were extremely competent, but were somewhat restricted within the *Mod* parameters. **The Lambrettas** are fondly remembered down the 76, both by those punters in the sweaty, heaving – skanking – mass in front of the stage, and by the staff.

Ian Roberts: "When they played Poison Ivy the whole place was going mad, there was that many dancing that we had to stand behind the bar with 'the two Teds', holding on to all the bottles and glasses, they were all leaping off the shelves!".

Welsh group **Seventeen** were in the process of advancing from their punk roots and embracing the new - so called - *power pop* phenomenon, on the way to becoming *The Alarm*, though it was the presence in the little club of 'Rockabilly Rebels' **Whirlwind** and 50s style Welshmen **Crazy Cavan and the Rhythm Rockers** that brings our story full circle. Their use of the moves and grooves, in 1980, that were first put into action by their skiffle cousins in the late 50s proved the old adage - there is nothing new in rock and roll.

This is where our tale must end. Music was being steered towards the synthesiser-based sound of the *New Romantics*, and from that, an evolutionary progression to *plastic pop*, and manufactured boy and girl bands, none of which made for a particularly invigorating live experience. At the time of writing, I think it is fair to say with fingers crossed, that we have come through the other side, and young, innovative – live – bands are with us again, along with those that never went away, who just sat back and waited their time until the latest fad was spent. The 76 club itself continued for some time, initially as *The Libra Club* then as *Javs*, though this is not just about one club in Burton, it has – hopefully - covered all the places in Burton where young hopefuls strapped on a guitar, plugged in and turned to face an expectant audience. Where we could all stand and see, and hear, some of the best bands of the day.

All the clubs and most of the bands mentioned in this book are now but a memory. I hope that I have rekindled those memories for those that were there, and in the case of those that were too young, and those that now have to travel to all corners of the country to see a good group live, this is how it used to be in this town, in your town. This town rocked!

The following pages contain lists of groups and artistes who appeared in the clubs of Burton-on-Trent, and surrounding areas, during the period covered by this book. This list has been compiled using information from various sources, and is mainly concerned with the clubs mentioned throughout.

It is not an exhaustive list, and again there will be errors and omissions, but – broadly speaking – it is as good a representation of all those who have appeared in the town as you will get.

I have attempted to list all the names that various groups were known by. Where a group were known to have changed their name this symbol appears:

→ followed by the new name.

Subsequently, their former names will be indicated by this symbol:

← followed by their previous name.

For example **Mike Everest and the Alpines** became **The Memphis Five:**

Mike Everest and the Alpines → Memphis Five.

Memphis Five were formerly **Mike Everest and the Alpines:**

Memphis Five ← Mike Everest and the Alpines.

The main clubs are all listed, if a band appeared there, the year that they appeared at that club will be found in the relevant column.

Appendix 1... 1950s Groups in Burton

Group	Origin	Kevin Ballroom	Town Hall	Cambo Club	Swad Rink	Notes
Alpines, The	Burton			Dec. 59	Apr. 59*	* Rock Party
Arctic Skiffle Group	Derby		May 58*			* Skiffle Group Contest
Bill Roulstone & his Band	Burton					various venues
Black Cats Skiffle Group		Nov. 57*				* UK Skiffle Champions
Blackjacks Skiffle Group	Burton			Dec. 59		Star & Garter Jan. 58
Blue Stars Dance Band						various venues
Cy Laurie & his Band						Jubilee Hall - Oct. 57
Davengers	Burton		May 58*			* Skiffle Group Contest
Hard Hitters, The	Stapenhill					Grove Hotel 58
Joe Fearn & the Esquires	Burton					Numerous venues
Joe Loss & his Orchestra		1959				
'Kids Skiffle Group'	Burton	Mar. 57				
Moonshines	Derby		May 58*			* Skiffle Group Contest
Musical Sputnics	Derby		May 58*			* Skiffle Group Contest
Norman Willey Group	Burton					8 Bar Rest 1959
Outbacks	Burton		May 58*			* Skiffle Group Contest
Red Rockers, The	Newhall				Mar. 58	Donisthorpe Mar. 58
			May 58*			* Skiffle Group Contest
					Apr. 59*	* Rock Party
Ripchords, The						Stapenhill Inst. Feb. 58
Rockets	Nottingham		May 58*			* Skiffle Group Contest
Ronnie McRae & his Red Rockers					58	
Roy Norton	Burton					Various venues
Roy Tilley & his Party Band		Apr. 57				Rock & Roll Party Dance
'Roy, Ronnie & All the Boys'		Feb. 57				
Sid Phillips & his Band		Apr. 57				+ 7 other bands
'Skiffle Nights'					Jan. 58	
Sydney Roy & the Ripchords					Apr. 57*	* teen & twenty night
Tony Reynolds & his Metro Orc.	Burton					Various venues
Trent River Ramblers	Burton		Feb. 58			Star & Garter Feb. 58
						Tatenhill Village Hall 59
			May 58*			* Skiffle Group Contest
			Apr. 58*			* SU Dance
Victor Silvester & his Orchestra			1959			
Wee Willie Harris	Scotland				June 58	
Wintones, The	Burton					
Worried Men Skiffle Group	London					Jubilee Hall – Oct. 57

group/artist	origin	76 Club	Cambo	8 Bar	Jubilee	Town Hall	Co-op	Rink	Tut Pall	Notes
1,2,3,4,Fives	Geordie Land	64								
3 Spirits	Tamworth	64								
3. 0 am Blues		67								
4 Aces	Derby	64*							64	* with Gene Vincent
4 Beats										NCYC 65
6 Times Table		69								
8 Bar Orchestra	Burton					62*				* Dance Band Jamboree
87th Precinct		67,68								
Acker Bilk & the Paramounts						67*				*Burton Abbey Round Table
Adges Convention		68								
Advel										1965?
Agency, The		67								
Allisons, The	Liverpool?							63		
Alpines	Burton	62	60 +	60,62	61*(x3)	60(x2)		62		*with Joe Brown S/Hill Inst., Stretton Village Hall 60
Alpines, Mike Everest & the	Burton	62(x3)	61+		62*(x3) 63(x3)	63		63(x2)		*with Emile Ford Stanton Village Hall 62 → **Memphis 5**
Ambassador Trio*	Burton	61								*Joe Fearn
Amboy Dukes	Nottingham	68								
Andy Wade	Pittsburgh US	62								
Andys Clappers	Birmingham	65								
Angel Pavement		68								
Anglias, The	Lichfield							64		
Ann & the Countdowns										Shobnall Fields 65
Answers, The		67								
Apaches, The										Winshill CH 63
Applejacks, The	Solihull	65								
Appollo's	Burton?									1965?
Arnhem Blue										Leander 68
Art Gallery, The	Sheffield	68,69								
Ashes, The	Nottingham	65,66								
Astonaires, The	Birmingham									Tech. College 63
Atlantas, the	Derby	63(x6)								
Atlantix, The	Burton/Derby	62(x3)				60,62	61			St.Chad's CH 62

Appendix 2... 1960s Groups in Burton

group/artist	origin	76 Club	Cambo	8 Bar	Jubilee	Town Hall	Co-op	Rink	Tut Pall	Notes
Atlantix, The with Chris Goodhead	Burton/Derby	63(x5)				62,63				BoT Carnival,Stretton 60 St.Johns CH, Broadholme 63
Atlantix, The - with Kik	Burton/Derby									St. Chad's CH 63
Atlantix, The with Mick Previtt	Burton/Derby					62*				* Top Tune Time
Avengers, The (1)		63(x2)			63		63			
Avengers, The (2)	Birmingham	68								
B.B. Jones & the Trojans		69								
Bachelors, The	Eire				63*					*with Mike Perry & The Outlaws
Baker Steet Ltd		68								
Bakerloo (Line)	Tamworth	68								← Bakerloo Blues Line
Baltimore Switch		68								
Band, The		68								
Baracuders, The		63								
Barbara Ray		62								
Barron Nights	Leighton				64*					*Big Beat Night
Barry De-Arm & the Sonics	Birmingham	64								
Barry James Show		63								
Bartenders, The		63								
Basin Street Soul Band	Birmingham?	68								
Bead a Row Walk		69								
Beat Ltd	Birmingham				63					
Beat Merchants	Brighton	64,65								
Beat Peddlers	Nottingham	66								
Beat Squad, The	Manchester				64					
Beatmen	Nottingham	64,65,66								
Beatnicks	Rotherham							64		
Beatroots	Nottingham	65								
Bedrocks, The	Leeds	69								
Bernie & the Raiders	Burton	63							64	St.Chad's & Wins.CH 63
Beryl Marsden & the Challengers	Liverpool						63			
Bettie Smith Group							63			
Beverley Brown		66								Cabaret Artist
Big Idea, The		67,68								

Appendix 2... 1960s Groups in Burton

group/artist	origin	76 Club	Cambo	8 Bar	Jubilee	Town Hall	Co-op	Rink	Tut Pall	Notes
Big Three, The	Liverpool	63,65								
Big Ugly & the Diamonds	Mansfield	64,65								[Big Ugly Dane & the]
Billie Davis					63					
Billy Campbell & the Mighty Sparrows		69								
Billy MacMichael		62								
Black Diamonds, The	Derby					63(x2)				
Black Eagles										Cresta Club 64
Black Jacks, The	Burton		60+							
Black Orchids					63*					*with Vince Everett
Blackwells, The	Liverpool	64								
Blades, The		68								
Blondell		69								← **Gospel Garden**
Blue & Roots	Nottingham			65						
Blue Jays		66								
Blue Kats Klan		68,69								
Blue Spots		67								
Blue Tones, The		65								
Blues by Five		65								
Bo Street Runners		66								
Bobby Ash Sound		68								
Bobby Christians Crusaders								63*		see Christians Crusaders
Bobby Dean & the Diamonds					63*					*Rock Jamboree
Bobby Shafto & the Cyclones		66								
Boll Weevils										Top Rank Club 66,67
Boogaloo Band, The		69								
Boots, The		69								
Boulevards	Nottingham	64,65								
Brambles Army		69								
Brand, The										Leander 67
Bread & Butter Band										[SU] Drill Hall 67
Breakthrough, The		68,69								
Breakthru		68								
Brian Fennell Quartet	Burton			60-65		62*				*Dance Band Jamboree
Brian Gullivar & the Travellers	Birmingham	64								
Brian Howard & the Silhouettes		64								
Brian King & the Four Aces	Derby	64			64			63		
Brian Neale					61*					*Rock Jamboree

Appendix 2... 1960s Groups in Burton

group/artist	origin	76 Club	Cambo	8 Bar	Jubilee	Town Hall	Co-op	Rink	Tut Pall	Notes
Brian Poole & the Tremeloes	Dagenham	63,66								
British Standard		67								
Brooklyn Pigeon Flyers		68								
Brooks Brothers		62,63			63	63				
Bruce Turner (Jump) Band		63						63		
Brum Beats	Birmingham	64							65	
Bryan Martin & the Marauders					63*					*with Vince Everett
Buddy Britten & the Regents					62*			60#		*Teenbeat, # Solo
Bumble Hum	Scotland?	69								poss. Humble Bum (Billy Connolly)
Bumps in the Night		66								
Bystanders, The		66								
Calmen Waters, The	Grimsby	69								← The Aztecs
Candy Bus, The		69								
Capital Systems	Birmingham	67								
Caravan	Canterbury									SU Union Street 69
Carl & the Cheetahs	Birmingham	64								
Carl & the Teddybears	Burton									St. Paul's Inst. YC 64
Carl Pagan & the Heathens		66								
Carls Fables		69								
Carol Laine								60		
Carpet Baggers		66,67								
Casuals, The	Burton				64	63		63		St.Paul's Inst, Gresley Old Hall 62 St.Chad's & Wins.CH 63
Casuals, Shane Spencer & the	Burton	62(x10) 63(11) 64(x2) 65,66			63* 63# 65	62(x2) 63(x2) 65,66				*with Billie Davis # with Gene Vincent Cresta Club, NCYC 64
Cat Ballou										Regatta Romp 67
Cavemen, The		64								
Centors, The	Derby	64								Tech. College (Rag) 66
Chads, The	Birmingham	64,65								← The Sundowners
Chances Are		68								
Changing Scene, The										Leander 67
Chapter 6										Top Rank Club 69
Chasers, The	Nottingham	66								

Appendix 2... 1960s Groups in Burton

group/artist	origin	76 Club	Cambo	8 Bar	Jubilee	Town Hall	Co-op	Rink	Tut Pall	Notes
Checkmates, The								63,66		
Cherry Blossom Clinic		68								
Chevrons, The									64	
Chicago Line, The		68,69								
Children, The	Nottingham	65,66								
Choice, The		68								
Chris Barber & his Band										Bargates (opening of) 66
Chris Farlow & the Thunderbirds		68,69								
Christians Crusaders		64								
Chuckles, The	Manchester	66,67								
Cindy & the Sapphires		63								
Circle Line, The		67								
Classics, The	Stoke									Winshill CH 64,66
Classix, The	Stoke?				65					NCYC 64
Cleveland Fox	Manchester	69								
Cliff & the Rebel Rousers	Slough				64					
Clifton All Stars	Rugby	64								
Cliftones					63*					*with The Fortunes
Clockwork Notion, The	USA	69								
Clockwork Orange		67								
Clockwork Toys		68								
Coalitions, The	Coalville	64								
Cobwebs, The	Derby	65								
Coffee Pot Percolators, The		66								
Coins, The		67								
Colin Storm		63								
Colin Storm & his Whirlwinds			60							
Colleagues, The	Burton									Late 60's
Combine Action	Birmingham	66								
Commanches, The		66,67								
Complex, The		68								
Connoisseurs, The	Liverpool	67								
Conspiritors, The	Stoke	67			64					
Cortinas, The		68								
Corvettes, The		62,63								
Country Gentlemen, The	Manchester							63		
Crescendos, The	Canada	66								

Appendix 2... 1960s Groups in Burton

group/artist	origin	76 Club	Cambo	8 Bar	Jubilee	Town Hall	Co-op	Rink	Tut Pall	Notes
Crescents, The (1)	Crewe	63,64								
Crescents, The	Canada	66								
Crestas, The	Manchester	66								
Crew, The		67								
Critics, The		66								
Cosbys, The	Liverpool	65								
Crusaders, The	Burton	66(x2)			62	62*				* Top Tune Time
Crusades, The					61					
Cuby & the Blizzards	Netherlands	68								
Cupids Inspiration	Stamford	69								← The Ends
Currants, The		69								
Cy Laurie & his Band					63					
Cyclones, The (1)	Derby	63(x6)			63					Tech. College (Rag) 66
		64							64	Leander 66
		66								Top Rank Club 69
Cyclones, The (2)	Bristol	63			64					Silver Kettle Café 63
Dairy, The		68								
Dalesmen, The	Mansfield	65								
Dandelion, The	Birmingham	69								
Daniel L. Jackson	USA									Peel Croft 68
Dankworth, Johnny & Cleo Laine		??								
Danny & the Renegades	Nottingham	64,65								
Danny Collins					63*					*with Jimmy Crawford
Danny Davies & the Tennesseeans								64		
Danny King & the Mayfair Set	Birmingham									Tech.College Lawns 66
Danny Rivers & the Echos					63					
Danny Satan & the Sabres		64								
Danny Storm	Leicester	63			60,62			60		Roger Chapman
Danny Storm & the Strollers	Leicester	64								
Darleks, The		64								← The Rainchecks
Dave Berry & the Cruisers	Birmingham							66		
Dave Dee & the Bostons	Wiltshire	63								
Dave K & the Dykons	Nottingham	64,65,66								
Dawn & the Dee Jays	Lincoln	65								
Dean Rivers & the Beat Makers										Winshill CH 64
Dean Rivers & the Crusaders	Overseal	62(x4)								
		63(x4)			64	64				→ The Beatmakers

240

Appendix 2... 1960s Groups in Burton

group/artist	origin	76 Club	Cambo	8 Bar	Jubilee	Town Hall	Co-op	Rink	Tut Pall	Notes
Dean Wayne & the Wadermen		64								
Decoys, The		69								
Defenders, The		64								
Defiants, The	Mansfield	65,66								
Delmont 4, The		63								
Delroy Good Band		67								
Delroy Williams		68								
Demons, The		64			63					
Denims, The	Birmingham	66								
Dennisons, The	Liverpool	65								'Jack Sugden'
Denny Bruce 5, The		66								
Denny Laine & the Diplomats	Birmingham	63,64								Bev Bevan
Devarks, The									64	
Diamonds, The		62(x2) 63			62					Hartshorne WMC 63
Dickens Set, The		66								
Dictionary of Soul		69								
Dimensions, The					65					St. Paul's Inst. YC 64
Dimples, The		67								
Dolphins, The	Burton	61 62(x10) 63(x3)	61		61	60,63(x2)	61			St. Margaret's CH 60 + Wins.CH & Shobnall 63
Dolphins, Bernie & the	Burton				63					
Dominators, The										Baths Assy. Rooms 64 Grammar Sch.BBQ 66
Doug Sheldon								63		
Downland Brothers, The		63						63		
Downlands, The		65								
Druids, The		65								
Dual Purpose		68								
Duke Demont & his Detonators	Burton?				63				64	NCYC 64,65
Duke Demont & his Dominators	Burton?				64					Cresta Club 64
Dwellers, The	Birmingham	64								
Earl Prestons Realms	Merseyside	66								
Earl Royce & the Olympics	Liverpool	64,65								
Easter Man		68								
Easybeats, The	Sydney, Aus.	65								George Young

Appendix 2... 1960s Groups in Burton

group/artist	origin	76 Club	Cambo	8 Bar	Jubilee	Town Hall	Co-op	Rink	Tut Pall	Notes
Ebonies, The	Denmark	69								
Ebonites, The	Birmingham	68								
Eddie Krome & the Phantoms	Nuneaton	63								
Eddie Sex								60		
Edisons Phonograph	Leeds	68								
Emile Ford & the Checkmates		62								
Emporers, The	Birmingham	64								Linton Red Lion 63
Enth Degree, The										Tech. College (Rag) 67
Epics, The	London									Leander 66
Escorts, The	Liverpool									Top Rank Club 67,68
Exchequers, The		64								
Expressions, The					66					← **Ricki Topaz & the Diamonds**
Fab Sounds		65								
Factotums, The	Liverpool	64								
Falcons, The	Burton	63(x3)			63	62(x2),63				St.Paul's Inst. 62
Falcons, Johnny Byrd & the	Burton	63(x9)			63	63				
Family, The	Leicester	67,68								← **The Farinas**
Farinas, The	Leicester	66								→ **Family**
Farren Kirsty Big 6, The		64								
Farons Flamingos	Liverpool	63			63			63		
Fashion, The		66								
Favourites, The		69								
Faze & Reality										Peel Croft 69
Fearns Brass Foundry	Leicester									Rugby Club 68
Felix Taylor Show		68								
Fentones, The*	Mansfield	65								*see Shane Fenton
Few, The	Liverpool	64								
Fitz & Startz	Merseyside	65								
Five, The		66								
Five by Five										NCYC 64
Fix, The	Liverpool	66								
Flamingos, The		66								
Flee-Reckers, The (Nelson Keene)	Holland	62,63,64								
Fleur de Lys	London	69								
Flowers, The		66,67								
Force Five, The		64								

Appendix 2... 1960s Groups in Burton

group/artist	origin	76 Club	Cambo	8 Bar	Jubilee	Town Hall	Co-op	Rink	Tut Pall	Notes
Fortunes, The		64#,67			63*					*with The Clifton All Stars # with The Cliftones
Four + One	Nottingham	65								→ **In Crowd, Steve Howe**
Four Reasons		66								
Four Seasons, The	USA							63		
Four Strangers, The	Birmingham	65								
Fourmost, The								66*		*replaced The Fortunes
Fox, The		68								
Frank Kelly & the Hunters								63		
Frankenstein & the Monsters	Manchester	66						63	64	
Fred Karnos Army		66,67								
Freddie & the Dreamers		?			?					no date
Freemen, The	Nottingham	63								
From the Sun		67,68								
Futurists, The										Cresta Club 64
G Clefs	Roxberry,USA	69								
Gamblers, The	Newcastle	63,64								Billy Fury's backing band
Garnett Mimms	Virginia, USA	69								
Gary Levene & the Avengers	Birmingham	62,63 x5 64			65					'Roy Wood'
Gass, The	Manchester									Leander 68
Gay Gordons, The	Scotland	62								
Gene Vincent	Virginia, USA				63			63		
Gene Vincent, with The Shouts	Virginia, USA	64								
Gentry, The	Sheffield	66								
George.E.Washington & his Congressmen		65								
Georgettes, Georgina & the	Ashbourne	64			64				64	
Gerry & the Pacemakers	Merseyside				nk					
Gerry & Lee		63*								*with Barry James
Godfreys Grit 'n Soul Band		66								Barley Mow 66
Gospel Garden		68,69								← **The Dimples** → **Blondell**
Graham Bond Organisation	Romford	66,68								
Gravy Train, The	Lancashire	67								
Great Odell, The		62*								*Cabaret
Groove, The										Leander 67 → **Souls a Go Go**

Appendix 2... 1960s Groups in Burton

group/artist	origin	76 Club	Cambo	8 Bar	Jubilee	Town Hall	Co-op	Rink	Tut Pall	Notes
Group, The		66,67								
Group Three, The	Leicester					64				
Guess Who?	Canadian?								64	
Guy Hamilton & the Sensations		65								
Hal. C. Clarke Band										Peel Croft 68
Halfway There	Nottingham	66								
Halliard, The		69								
Hammer, The	Hull?	68,69								
Harris Moran Band	Burton			60						
Harvey Brookes Shuttle	Hull	68								
Harvey Stuart Blues Combo		67								
Haveys Team		67								
Hawker Beat Unit, The									64	
Hawkers, The	Derby	64								
Hearts Art		69								
Heathers, The		66								
Heatwave, The		67								
Hedgehoppers Annonymous		68						66		← The Trendsetters
Heinz & the Wildboys	Germany	65,66								Ritchie Blackmore
Hells Bells	Nottingham	65,66								
Heralds, The		66								
Herbies People	Wolverhampton	67								
Herd, The		69								Peter Frampton
Hermans Hermits	Manchester	64								
Hickory Sticks		65,66								
Hi-Fi's, The		64								
High Numbers, The		65								[possibly didn't appear]
Highwaymen, The	Stoke	63(x2)								
Hilta Max		69								
Hipster Image	Stoke	65								→ Climax Blues Band
Hollies, The	Manchester							65		
Honeycombes, The		64			64					
Hoo Doo's, The		67								
Hooties, The	Birmingham	65								
Hound Dogs, The	Nottingham	65,66								
House of Lords	London									Leander 68
Huckleberries, The		67								

Appendix 2... 1960s Groups in Burton

group/artist	origin	76 Club	Cambo	8 Bar	Jubilee	Town Hall	Co-op	Rink	Tut Pall	Notes
Humphrey Littleton		66				66				
I. S. Bronzo		68								
Idle Race	Birmingham									Newton Park Hotel 60's Jeff Lynne
Illiad[s], The		66								Top Rank Club 66
Illusions, The		69								
Immediate Pleasure		68								
Impacts, The	Stoke	64								
Imps, The	Derby	65								
In Betweens, The	Wolverhampton	66								[N'Betweens] → Slade
In Crowd, The	Nottingham	65,66,67								← Four + One
Inmates, The	London	65								
Inner Mind, The		68								
Innocents, The								63		
Inside Out		67								
Interns, The									64	
Invaders, The		63								
Ivy League								66		
J. J. Jackson (with Rico?)	New York, USA	68								
J. T. & the Libertines	Wallsall	65								
Jacci Lewis & the Dominators						64				
Jacki & the Leytons	Nottingham	66								
Jackie Lynton		63								
Jackie Simms	Shrewsbury	64								
Jacks Union		69								
Jade, Chris & Dean					63*					*Big Beat Show
Jakes Blues		65								
Jalopy Ride		68								
Jam Sandwich		68								
Jamie & the Silhouttes										Winshill CH
Janie & the Angels		63								
Jaybirds, The	Nottingham	65								Alvin Lee
Jeannie & the Big Guys	Merseyside	65								
Jeff Hunter & the Apaches	Lichfield	64								
Jeff Silvas & the Strangers	Birmingham	64								
Jeff 'Wild Bill' Cody		63								
Jenny & the Delmonts	Merseyside	64								

group/artist	origin	76 Club	Cambo	8 Bar	Jubilee	Town Hall	Co-op	Rink	Tut Pall	Notes
Jenny Wren & the Jackdaws	Birmingham	65								
Jesters, The									64	
Jet Blacks, The		63								
Jet Wayne & the Cavaliers	Nottingham	64								
Jets, The	Derby				63					
Jethro Tull	Blackpool									Rugby Club 68
Jimmy Crawford (Package Show)					63					
Jimmy Crawford & the Shantells		64								
Jimmy Parker & the Soul Supply		68								
Jimmy Powell					63*					* Big Beat Show
Joan Lee		62								
Joe Brown & the Bruvvers	Swarby, Lincs	62			61*					* Working Mens Club
Joe Fearn Band	Burton	62 (x2)				62(x2)#				* #*SU & # FNF Dance
Johnny Washington & Congressmen	Birmingham							64		
Johnny Fox & the Hunters		63(x2)								
John Smith Affair		67,68								→ The Which What
Johnathon Kane & the Freemen	Nottingham	65								
Johnny & the Redcaps	Walsall	63								
Johnny Bev		63			63					Tech. College 63
Johnny Byrd & the Avengers						64				
Johnny Carr & the Cadillacs	Bristol							63		
Johnny Congress & Whitehousemen	Sutton Coldfield	60								
Johnny Dean & the Crestas		63(x2)			63					Tech. College 63
Johnny Gentle	Liverpool	63								Tech. College 63
Johnny Johnson & the Bandwagon	USA									Peel Croft 69
Johnny Knight & the Sonettes	Birmingham	64								
Johnny Neal Sound		67								
Johnny Paradise & the Vikings		64								
Johnny Peel & the Avengers		63(x5)				63				
Johnny Tremane & the Liberties		63								
Johnny Washington					62*					*Big Beat Show
Johnny Washington & Congressmen					63(x2)					
Jokers, The		63								
Judds Mates									64	
Jude Brown Trust	Burnley	68								
Jules & the Ghost Squad		63								
Julie Grant		63*								*with Mark Allen Group

Appendix 2... 1960s Groups in Burton

group/artist	origin	76 Club	Cambo	8 Bar	Jubilee	Town Hall	Co-op	Rink	Tut Pall	Notes
Jumping Jacks	Birmingham	64								
Just Five, The	Lichfield	64								
Kane & Co.	Nottingham	65								
Karl Justice & the Jury	Burton	63(x4)			63	63				Wins.CH, St.Paul's Inst. Stretton Village Hall 63
Kavemen, The	Burton									NCYC 64
Keith Powell & the Valets	Birmingham	63,64,65								Measham Miners Gala 64
Ken Mar-Gerisson Band	Burton						62(x2)*			*with The Falcons
Kensington Mews		67,68								
Kim Martine		62								
Kings Things		66								
Kinks, The	London				64*					*with The Vibrons
Kleek, The										Leander 67
Knights of Sin	Ashfield	65								
Kontikis, The									64	
Koobas, The Fabulous	Liverpool				66					
Lady Jayne & the Royalty		67,68								
Lance Fortune	Barnsley	63*								*with Jimmy Crawford
Lance Harvey & the Kingpins	Stoke	64								
Land of Love										Top Rank Club 69
Larry Avon & the Presidents	Stoke	63				64				
Laurie Jay Combo					63					
Lawmen, The	Birmingham	62								
Leander Beat Group					66*					*Leander Club Dance
Lee Christian & the Consorts	Birmingham	62								
Lee Christian & the Sinners	Birmingham	64								
Lee Rogers & the Strangers	Birmingham	65								
Lee Stirling & the Bruisers	Birmingham									Tech. College (Rag) 64
Legacy										Leander 67
Lemon Honey Introduction, The		69								
Lemon Tree, The		68								
Leroy & the Avengers										Cresta Club 64
Leslie & the Majestic Six	Manchester	67								
Letter, The	Stoke			65*						*Market Hotel
Light, The (featuring Dipper Kent)		68								
Limits, The									64	
Lincoln Casuals, The		65								

Appendix 2... 1960s Groups in Burton

group/artist	origin	76 Club	Cambo	8 Bar	Jubilee	Town Hall	Co-op	Rink	Tut Pall	Notes
Litter, The	Stoke	64				64				
Little Lambs of the World		67								
Liverbirds, The	Liverpool	63								
Locomotive, The	Birmingham	67,68								
Lonnies Few	Stoke	67								
Lovin, The		68								
Loving Kind, The		66,67 x2								
Lubi Soul, The	Manchester	68								
Macbeth, David		63								
Mack Sounds	USA							66		
Magazine, The		67,68								
Manchesters Playboys	Manchester	66								
Mandy & the Girlfriends	Hull	68								
Mandy & the Millbeats	Derby	64								
Mansfields, The	Mansfield	65,66								
Marcus & the Aliens										Winshill CH 64
Mark Allen Group (with Lee Terri)	Birmingham	62(x2) 63(x6)			63*			63		*Screaming Lord Sutch
Mark Dean Combo		63						63		
Mark Fayne & the Fountains	Mansfield	65								
Mark Peters & the Vetones	Nottingham	65								
Mark Raymond & the Rayvons		62(x2)			63					[Mark Rayvon?]
Markus		66								Cabaret/Comedy
Martin Rayner & the Secrets	Birmingham	65								Clifford T. Ward/Vocals
Matadors, The		67								
Matchbox 5	Manchester	65								
Maurice Harper Quartet	Burton			60		62*				*Dance Band Jamboree
Max Bear & the Chicago Setback										Leander 67
Max Hollyman & the Demons					63					
Medicine Hat		69								
Meece, The		67								
Memphis Five, The	Burton	64(x5) 65(x3)			64 65*	64(x3)			64(x3)	Overseal Village Hall 64 *with The Dimensions NCYC, Leander 65 Odeon Cinema ← Mike Everest & the Alpines

Appendix 2... 1960s Groups in Burton

group/artist	origin	76 Club	Cambo	8 Bar	Jubilee	Town Hall	Co-op	Rink	Tut Pall	Notes
Mersey 4, The	Merseyside	65								
Messengers, The					63*					*with Jimmy Crawford
Merseybeats, The	Liverpool	64				64				← **The Mavericks**
Miar Davies		64								
Michigan Express		67								
Middle Earth		68								
Midnight Shift		66								
Mighty Avengers		65								
Mike Berry	Northampton				63*					*Big Beat Show
Mike Berry & the Innocents	Northampton							63		
Mike Berry & the Luvvers	Northampton	66								
Mike Everest & the Rapids		64				64				
Mike Sagar & the Quiet Three		64								
Mike Sheriden & the Night Riders	Birmingham	63,64								Roy Wood
Mint, The	Leicester	68								
Miss Tracey & her Diamonds	Sutton Ashfield	65								
Mojo's, The	Liverpool	63(x2)						66		← **The Nomads** Lewis Collins (bass)
Monday Morning Glory Band	Leeds	68								
Money Jungle, The		69								
Montanas, The	Wolverhampton	67								
Mood Indigo, The										Leander 67
Moods, The		64								
Moody Blues, The	Birmingham	68								Tech. College (Rag) 67
Moonrakers, The		66								
Mosaic Sunset		68								Sharps & Knights
Mozzletoff										Leander 67
Mysteries, The			61					64		
Nashville Teens	Weybridge	64						65		
Naturals, The	Harlow				64					
Nemkais, The										Rugby Club 68
Nero & the Gladiators		62						63		
New St. Station										Drill Hall 67
Nightriders, The	Birmingham	63(x2)			63					Roy Wood
Nite-Riders, The	Birmingham	63								[Mike Sheriden & the?]
Nocturns, The	Birmingham	65								
Notations, The	Liverpool	66								
Notions, The	Merseyside	66								

Appendix 2... 1960s Groups in Burton

group/artist	origin	76 Club	Cambo	8 Bar	Jubilee	Town Hall	Co-op	Rink	Tut Pall	Notes
O, The		63								
O Hara's Playboys	Sheffield	67,68								
Olympics, The	Birmingham	64,65	61							
One Inch Rock		69								
One Step Beyond		67								
Orange Pips, The		67								
Orbeats, The	Stoke								64	
Organised Chaos	Birmingham	66								
Orluvus Incorporated	Mansfield	65								
Oscar Toney Jnr.	Alabama, USA	68								
Our Young		66,67								
Outlaws, The (1)	Coalville	63(x14)		62	63(x3)*					*with The Bachelors Broadholme 63 Winshill CH (x3) 63
Outlaws, The (2)	London							63		
Outrage, The	Manchester	66								
Outward Bounds, The		66								
P.J. Proby		?								
Pacifics, The		66								
Page Four		67								
Pandoras Box										Leander 68
Paper Bag		69								
Paperback Edition		67,68								
Paramounts, The	Southend	64								→ **Procul Harum** Robin Trower
Parchment People		67								
Passion Forest	Birmingham	69								
Pat Kellys Solution		68								
Pat Wayne & the Beachcombers		64								
Patti Labelle & the Belles	USA	68								
Peeps, The	Coventry									Leander 67
Peighton Checks	Scunthorpe	68								
Penny Farthing		68								
Penny Peep Show		67								
Peppermint Creams		68								
Peppers Machine	Derby	66 (x3) 67,68,69								Corporation Arms 68 Peel Croft 69

Appendix 2... 1960s Groups in Burton

group/artist	origin	76 Club	Cambo	8 Bar	Jubilee	Town Hall	Co-op	Rink	Tut Pall	Notes
Pesky Gee!	Leicester									Leander 67
										Rugby Club 68* 69
										* with Jethro Tull
Pete Lloyd & the Strangers		64								
Pete Trent & the Travellers	Rugeléy	63,64								
Peter & the Persuaders						64				
Peter Jay & the Jaywalkers		66*						66		*with Memphis 5
Peter Lee Stirling & the Bruisers								64		
Petrus Booncamp		69								
Phantoms, The (1)	Birmingham?	63								
Phantoms, The	Leicester							63		
Pheonix City Truth		69								Peel Croft 69
Phil Ryan & the Crescents	Crewe	63,64,65								
Phil Seamen	Burton			63 #		64*				* Dance Band Jamboree
										# with Brian Fennell
Pieces, The	Liverpool							64		
Pinkertons Colours		66								
Pitiful Souls	Manchester	68								Peel Croft 67
Pitifuls, The	USA	67								
Planets, The								66		
Planets Mini Band, The		66								
Plastic Penny, The										Peel Croft 69
Power & Glory		67								
Presidents, The					64					
Prim and Proper		66								
Primitives, The	London	65								
Puppets, The	London	64,65								
Purify, James and Bobby	Florida, USA	68								
Q, The	Nottingham									Leander 66
Questions, The		66								
Quotations, The		68								
R & B 5									64	
Raging Storms	Manchester	66								
Raiders, The	Burton				64				64	Overseal Village Hall 64
Rainbows, The										Peel Croft 69
Rainchecks, The	Liverpool	63								**→ The Darleks**
Ramrods, The		60								

Appendix 2... 1960s Groups in Burton

group/artist	origin	76 Club	Cambo	8 Bar	Jubilee	Town Hall	Co-op	Rink	Tut Pall	Notes
Rapids Big Roll Band		66								
Rapids, The	Derby/Burton?	63x2,64								
Rave, The										Leander 67
Raven Hutch & the Legends						64				
Raver		69								
Raw Meat Blues Band		68								
Ray Dane & the Diamonds	Nottingham	63								Cresta Club 64
Reaction, The		66(x2)								Top Rank Club 66,67
Red Rockers, The	Newhall							60		Red Lion Linton 63, Hartshorne WMC 64
Red Star		68								
Reds, The	Merseyside	64								
Reg James Explosion	Manchester									Leander 68
Remo 4	Merseyside	66								
Renegades, The	Birmingham	63(x3) 64(x4)								Cresta Club 64
Rhythm & Blues Inc.	Burton				63,64x2	64				→ **The Atlantix** Winshill. CH, Red Lion Linton 63 Hartshorne 63
Rhythm & Blues Quartet	Birmingham	63(x2)			63	63				→ **Spencer Davis Group**
Ricci Norman & the Electrons	Stoke	62(x3)*								* with Vince Eager
Ricki Fever								60		
Ricki Fever & the Avengers	Rugby							63		
Ricki Fever & the Electron[ics]s	Burton/Stoke?	63			63(x3)*					* Big Beat Show
Ricky Ford								64		
Ricky Valance	South Wales	62								
Riddle, The										Leander 66
Rikki Topaz & his Diamonds	Burton	63,64x4			64					Wins.CH 63>Expressions
Rikki Topaz & the Diamonds with Glen Gold	Burton					64*				* Top Pop Time
Rinky Dinks		64								
Rip Van Winkle Rip It Ups	Liverpool	65								
Rivals, The		64								
Rivers, The								66		
Roaring Jaguars, The									64	
Robert Parker	New Orleans	68								

Appendix 2... 1960s Groups in Burton

group/artist	origin	76 Club	Cambo	8 Bar	Jubilee	Town Hall	Co-op	Rink	Tut Pall	Notes
Rockin' Berries, The	Birmingham	64						63		
Rocking Blue Venoms, The	Birmingham	64								
Rockin Henri & the Hayseeds		63			63					Cresta Club 64
Rocking Renowns, The	Birmingham	63,64,65								
Rocking Saltaires, The		62,63x2								
Roger & the Dodgers					63					
Roger James					62*		63			* Big Beat Show
Rogers, The	Nottingham									Corporation Arms 61
Rondos, The	Nottingham	65,66,67								
Ronnie & the Redcaps	Walsall				63*			63		* Big Beat Show
Root & Jenny Jackson	Leeds	68								
Rory Storm & the Hurracaines	Liverpool	63								
Roy Dave & the Debonaires										Woodville WMC 64
Roy Norton & his Band (appeared at many venues)	Burton					60* 62	#			*Carnival Dance # Dance Band Jamboree
Roy Stewart & the Tremors									64	
Rufus Rebels	Derby	64								
Rufus Stax Outrage										Peel Croft 69
Rustics, The		64								
Sabres, The		62(x2)								
Saints, The (Combo)	Birmingham	64,65								→ **Spencer Davis**
Samara the Wonder Girl		61								Cabaret
Sammy King & the Voltaires	Yorkshire								64	
Sandalwoods, The	Solihull									Leander Folk Club 66
Sandy & the Beachboys	Cornwall	64								
Sapphires, The	Burton	63			63	63	63	63	64(x3)	NCYC, Tech.College 63 Shobnall, Broadholme 63 St.John's CH 66
Sapphires, Ian Little & the		63(x2)			63,64x2	63(x2),64			64	George St Club Room 63
Sapphires, Roy Chantell & the		63(x3)								Cresta Club 64
Satin Finish										Drill Hall [SU] 67
Scarlet Religion		68								
School, The		66								
Scott Gibson Five, The		66								
Scott Williams Combo	Manchester								64	
Scotty Wood Combo		63			63(x3)					
Screaming Lord Sutch & the Savages	Middlesex				62,63	67			64*	*with The Raiders

Appendix 2... 1960s Groups in Burton

group/artist	origin	76 Club	Cambo	8 Bar	Jubilee	Town Hall	Co-op	Rink	Tut Pall	Notes
Sea, The										Peel Croft 69
Sean Campbell & the Mysteries	Stoke	64								
Searchers, The	Liverpool							63		
Second Time Around		68								
Section Five										Leander
Seed, The	Birmingham	67								
Seftons, The	Liverpool	66								
Selmer Sound										Top Rank Club 67
Semitones, The		62*								*with Brooks Brothers
Senators, The	Nottingham							64		
Seven Eight Set, The	Birmingham	67								Top Rank Club 66
Shakeouts, The	Nottingham	65,66								
Shakes, The						64				
Shane Fenton & the Fentones	Mansfield	64								→ **Alvin Stardust**
Shane Spencer	Burton									Corporation Arms 68
Sharon Tandy	South Africa	69								→ **Fleur de Lys**
Sheila Deni & the Diamonds	Wolverhampton	65								
Shetlands, The					64					Hartshorne WMC 63
Shondells, The	Stoke?USA?	64								
Sight & Sound	Birmingham	67,68								
Silk Cut		67								
Silkie, The	Hull	65								
Sirius & the Planets		65								
Six Across	Stoke	66,67,68								
Skatalites, The	Kingston, Jam.	69								
Skeleton Clock										Top Rank Bowls 69
Skillets, The	Burton									Barley Mow Folk Club 66
Skin Deep		68								
Sky Blue Pink										Corporation Arms 68
Sleepy Talk	Norwich	69								
Small Change		67,68								
Solitaires, The		64								
Solo's, The										Stretton Village Hall
										Barton Village Hall 62
Solo's, Rick Savage & the						62*				*with Joe Fearn
Sombreros, the	Birmingham	67								
Sons and Lovers	Nottingham	67								

Appendix 2... 1960s Groups in Burton

group/artist	origin	76 Club	Cambo	8 Bar	Jubilee	Town Hall	Co-op	Rink	Tut Pall	Notes
Sons of Adam	Nottingham	65,66								
Sorcerors, The	Sutton Coldfield									1964 ?
Soul Express		68								
Soul Movers		67								
Soul Package	London	68								
Soul Seekers	Liverpool	65,66								
Sound Advice								66		
Sounds of the Echo's		67								
Sounds Incorporated	Kent	63								
Soundtracks, The		65						63		
Source of the Power		69								
Span, The		68								
Spartans, The								66		
Spectres, The	London	66								→ The Traffic [Jam] → Status Quo
Spidermen, The	Burton				61,62					Stretton 61 St.Paul's Inst 62
Sporting Life		67								
Starlights, The	Stoke	64								
Starliners, The		62(x2)								
Steeplejacks		66							64	Linton 64
Steve & the Veldens	Birmingham	63(x3) 64,65								
Steve Allen	Burton				61					
Steve Brett & the Mavericks	Wolverhampton	64								
Steve Raven & the Thunderbirds										Linton Red Lion 64
Steves Fix	Coventry	69								
Stonewall Jackson		69								
Stop Look Listen		68								
Stormbreakers	Nuneaton				63					
Story Book	Stoke									Top Rank Club 69
Story Tellers		67								
Strange Days										Top Rank Club 69
Strangers, The	Birmingham	63,65								
Strangers Incorporated		63						63		
Strollers, The (1)	Birmingham	62			62,63					
Stroller, The (2)	South Derbys				64			64		Linton 63, Cresta 64 (x2)

Appendix 2... 1960s Groups in Burton

group/artist	origin	76 Club	Cambo	8 Bar	Jubilee	Town Hall	Co-op	Rink	Tut Pall	Notes
Style, The		66								Hartshorne WMC 64, Winshill CH 65
Sue Carr & the Telstars	Birmingham	64								
Sugar Machine		68								
Sun Trolley		68								
Sundowners, The	Folkestone	64								
Sweet Charity		67								
Swinging Chimes, The		62(x2)			63					
Symbols, The	Essex	67								
Take Five					63					
Tanya Day	Walsall	62,63*								*with Barry James Show
Taylor Upton Big Band	London	67								
Techniques, The		66,67								
Ted Taylor & his Orchestra	Burton					62*				*Dance Band Jamboree
Tee Set, The		66								
Teen Set		67								
Templers, The		64								
Tempo Victors, The		65								
Tennessee Teens	Nottingham	65								
Terry & the 'D' Men					64					
Terry & the Scott Gibson 4					64					
Terry King & the Saints	Stoke	62(x2)				64			64	
Terry Macleod & the Chets	Derby	65								
Terry Macleod & the Delfonts		66,67								
Terry Macleod & the Spartans		64								
Them	Belfast	65								Van Morrison
This End	Tamworth	66								
Three Spirits, The	Tamworth	63								
Tick-Its	Nottingham	65,66								
Tierneys Fugitives	Black Country	68								
Tiffany Show, The	Liverpool	66								
Tiffany with the Thoughts	Liverpool	65,66								
Tiffany's Dimensions	Liverpool	65								
Time, The		68								
Tiny Davies Souls a Go Go		67								Leander 67
										← The Groove
Tommy Bruce & the Bruisers	Birmingham?	63								

Appendix 2... 1960s Groups in Burton

group/artist	origin	76 Club	Cambo	8 Bar	Jubilee	Town Hall	Co-op	Rink	Tut Pall	Notes
Tommy Burton (Combo)		62(x2)								
Tommy Quickly & the Remo 4	Liverpool	65								
Tony & the Countdowns	Nottingham	65								
Tony & the Extras									64	
Tony 'D' & the Shakeouts	Nottingham					65			64	
Tony Jackson & the Vibrations		?								
Tony Kaye & the Huckleberries	Stoke	63,64								
Tony Reynolds Band	Burton					60,62*				*with The Dolphins
Tony Rivers & the Castaways		?								
Tornados, The		66								
Toyshop, The	Yorkshire	68								
Tracey Lind	Burton					65				
Tracey Martin & the Beatmen					62					
Traction, The										Leander 67,68
Tradesmen, The										Leander 67
Traffic, The		66(x4)								Drill Hall [SU Dance] 67
Trakk, The	Chesterfield	67								
Trane, The										Drill Hall[SU Dance] 67
Travellers Express	Sheffield	68								
Treacle, The	Hull	68								Mick Ronson ← **The Rats** → **David Bowie**
Trekkas, The		65								
Trentside Four	Nottingham	63,64								
Trevor Burton & the Everglades	Birmingham									Cresta Club 64 → **The Move**
Triads, The										Leander 67
Tribe, The	London	66								
Tri-remes, The (with Susan & Sue)	Nottingham	65								
Tuxedos's, The	Birmingham	63,64,65								
Twopenny Dream		68								
Under Milk Wood		69								
Undertakers, The	Liverpool	67								
Underwater Sunsets										Drill Hall [SU Dance] 67
Uneeks, The	Birmingham?	65								
Union Blues		67								
Urchins, The	Leek	64								

Appendix 2... 1960s Groups in Burton

group/artist	origin	76 Club	Cambo	8 Bar	Jubilee	Town Hall	Co-op	Rink	Tut Pall	Notes
Val Terry		66								Cabaret
Valiants, The		63(x2)						63		
Vampires, The					63*					* with Jimmy Crawford
Variations, The	USA?	68,69								
Varsity Rag	Birmingham	67,68								
Vendo Soul Band		69								
Vibrons, The	Derby	63(x3) 64(x2) 65x2,66			63* 64*(x2)			65	64(x2)	* with Brooks Brothers * with The Kinks NCYC 65
Vibrons, Dave & the	Derby	66								
Vicky & the Kordettes	Stoke	65								
Victor Brox Blues Train	Manchester	67								
Victor Sylvester						64				
Victors, The		64								
Vigilantes, The	Mansfield	61,65,66								
Vince Eager	Grantham	62(x2)								
Vince Eager & the Shouts	Grantham				63*					* Big Beat Show
Vince Everett					63*					* Big Beat Show
Virginia Wolf		68								
Vogues, The		67								
Vostock Five, The	Walsall	65								NCYC 64
Vulcans, The	Derby	64								
Wanted, The	Burton									Winshill CH 65
Warriors, The	Manchester	66								
Watch Us Grow	London	68								
Water Melon Men		67								
Wayfarers, The	Liverpool	65								
Wayne Gibson & the Dynamic Sounds	London	64								
Web, The		76								
Wellington Kitch Jump Band	Birmingham	67								
West Point Supernaturals		67								
What the Dickens	London	65								
Wheelers, The	Sheffield	64								
Wheels, The		64,68								
Which What, The		69								← John Smith Affair
Whisky Max		67								Leander 68

Appendix 2... 1960s Groups in Burton

group/artist	origin	76 Club	Cambo	8 Bar	Jubilee	Town Hall	Co-op	Rink	Tut Pall	Notes
Wild Flowers	Canterbury	67								Robert Wyatt
Wolves, The	Wolverhampton	64								
Woodpeckers, The			60							
Woody Kern	Mansfield	68								
Wot Dat Dare		67								
Wynder K. Frog (Mick Weaver)	Colchester									Rugby Club 68
Yakks, The	Derby	65,66								
Yanks, The		65								
Zero's, The										Measham NCYC 64,65
Zodiacs, The										NCYC 62

Appendix 3... 1970s Groups in Burton

Group	origin	76 Club	Paradise	Town Hall	Drill Hall	Vaults	Rolleston YC	Notes
999	London	77						
AC/DC	Aus./Scotland	76						
Academy	Birmingham					1972		
Ace	Scotland?	73,74,75						
Acker Bilk								Allied Club 77
Advertising		78						
Afro			1974					Burton Soul Club
AFT	Burton?	76						Automatic Fine Tuning
After the Fire		79						
Alan Bown		72(x2)						
Albatross	Burton							British Oak 72
Alberto Y los Trios Paranoias	Manchester	75						→ **The Albertos**
Alex Harvey Band	Scotland	73						
Alkatraz		75,76,77						← **Man & Neutrons**
Alvin Stardust	Mansfield							Allied Club 77 ← **Shane Fenton**
American Gypsy	USA	75						
Amphioxus	Burton							Rugby Club [Platform] 76
Andy Wall Band	Burton		77*					BTR Folk Concert 77
Apricot Nought		70						
Aquarius, The	Birmingham							Eton Park Club 71
Arbre		76						
Arcturus	Burton	75						
Armada		72						
Armageddon	Tamworth	75						
Arthur Conley	Atlanta,USA							Jubilee Hall 75
Asylum		79						
Average White Band	Scotland	73		73				
Baby	Leicester	74,75						
Back Door	Yorkshire	76						
Backtrack	Burton							Eton Park Club 76<->Oakdale
Backtrack								Sharpes & Knights
Barabas	Burton							Rag Processsion 70
Barbara Dickson								Barley Mow Folk Club 72
Barley							71	
Barracuda								Leander Club 73
Barry Andrews Band	Swindon	79						← **XTC**

Appendix 3... 1970s Groups in Burton

Group	origin	76 Club	Paradise	Town Hall	Drill Hall	Vaults	Rolleston YC	Notes
Batti Mamzelle	Trinidad?	73,74						
Be Bop de Luxe	Wakefield	74						
Beano	Liverpool						77	
Beckett		74						
Bed	Burton?						73	(with Chicken Shack)
Bedrocks, The	Leeds	70						
Bees Make Honey	London/Irish	73,75						
Beggars Opera	Scotland	73						
Bethnal	London	77						
Big Six	Derby				76			Continental Club 76
Bishop	Burton							?
Bitter Suite								SU Rag Week 72
Black Sabbath	Birmingham							??
Black Widow	Leicester	72(x3)						← **Pesky Gee**
Blakes Bang Bang		72						
Blast Furnace & the Heatwaves		78						
Blazer Blazer		78						
Blitz		76						
Blodwyn Pig		74						
Blue	Glasgow			74 [SU]				
Bodacea	Newhall							1973?
Body & Soul								Sharpes & Knights 71
Bombadis								Leander 74
Bond & Brown	London	72						
Brakes, The		78						
Bram Tchaikosky's Battle Axe		78						← **The Motors**
Bramstoker						71		
Brendon							78	
Brett Marvin & the Thunderbolts	Crawley	75						← **Terry Dactyl & the Dinosaurs**
Bronco		72,74						Hatton YC 71
Browns Home Brew	Lincoln	73						Joe Brown
Bruce Ruffin	Jamaica				73			
Brush		73						
Budgie	Cardiff	72,73		71				
Bulletts, The			79					
Burlesque			76					Adams Disco 75

Appendix 3… 1970s Groups in Burton

Group	origin	76 Club	Paradise	Town Hall	Drill Hall	Vaults	Rolleston YC	Notes
Buster	London						74	
Buster James		78						
Byzantium		74,75(x2)						
Cado Bell		76						
Californians, The								Adams Disco 74
Camel	London	72						
Capability Brown		73						
Cargo	Burton						72	(with East of Eden)
Casino	Yeovil	76(x2)						
Chairmen of the Board	Detroit, USA							Jubilee Club 74 [BSC]
Champion		78						← Wings
Chants, The		76						
Chaos	Burton							British Oak 79
Chapter Six								Eton Park Club 70
Charge				70				
Charlie		76						
Chaser			76					
Cherry Vanilla	USA	77						Sting & Stewart Copeland
Chicken Shack	Birmingham	72					73	
Chill Willi & the Red Hot Peppers	London	74						
Choice							71	
Chrome Molly							78	
Cisco			75					
City Boy	Birmingham	75						
Clancey	London	75(x2)						
Clayson & the Argonauts		78			77			
Clear Blue Sky	Acton, London	72						
Cleveland Fox	Manchester	70						
Clockwork Toys		70						
Codpiece	Leeds							Rugby Club 72 [Arts Lab]
Colours of Love		70						
Communication							nd	
Conkers		75						
Copper Mine		71						
Count Bishops, The	London	77(x2)						
Count Blackbeard								Continental Club 76
Cowboys International	London	79						Terry Chimes

Appendix 3... 1970s Groups in Burton

Group	origin	76 Club	Paradise	Town Hall	Drill Hall	Vaults	Rolleston YC	Notes
Crackers	London						76	
Crazy Caven & the Rhythm Rockers	Wales	79						
Cruiser	Rugby		76					
Cycle								British Oak 79
Daddy Long Legs	New York, USA	74						
Dakotas, The	Manchester							Adams Disco 75
Dana Gillespie Band	USA	76						
Darts, The	London	77						
Dave Lewis Band	Northern Ireland	78						
Dead End Kids	Scotland							Eves Disco 77
Def Leppard	Sheffield	79						
Deke Leonards Iceberg		77						
Del Bromham Band	West London	79						
Delegation								Eves Disco 77
Desmond Dekker	Jamaica							Continental & Allied Club 76
Desperate Dan			76*					*Galaxy Inn
Destiny		71						
Dire Straits		78						
Dirty Tricks		76	76					
Doctor Strangely Strange				?				SU?
Doctors of Madness		75						
Dodgers, The		78						Jubilee Hall 76 [with 'O'Band]
Dogs Body	Nottingham	71(x2)						
Doll by Doll		79						
Don Hendersons Election		72						
Dozy, Beaky, Mick & Tich	Wiltshire							Eton Park Pop Festival 70
Druid		76						
Ducks de Luxe		74						→ **The Motors**
Dude	Burton		75					
Duke Wally	Birmingham				76			
Earl Shilton's One Way System	Leicester	70						
East of Eden		75					72	
Eastwood							71	
Eddie & the Hotrods	Southend	76						
Eddie Holman	USA							Eton Park Club 74
Edgar Broughton Band	Warwickshire	77						
Edison Lighthouse								Sharpes & Knights 71

Appendix 3... 1970s Groups in Burton

Group	origin	76 Club	Paradise	Town Hall	Drill Hall	Vaults	Rolleston YC	Notes
Egg	Canterbury	72						
Ellis		73						
Emery Chase		71						
Energy							79	
Enid, The		76	76		77			
Equity								Sharpes & Knights 71
Eric Bell Band	Dublin	78,79						**← Thin Lizzy & Noel Redding**
Eric Delaney Band								Allied Club 76
Ewan MaColl								Barley Mow Folk Club 70
Fable	Wolverhampton					72	74	supporting Fusion Orc.
Fabulous Poodles		77						
Fairfield Wells							76	
Farthingale	Burton							All Saints CH 72
Fast Buck		72,76						
Fat Mattress (with WynderKFrog)								
FBI		75,76			76			
Federation							76	
FF & Z		72						
Findo Gask	Scotland	75						
Fingertricks	Burton							All Saints CH, Rugby Club 72
Fingertricks	Burton				72*			*support. Sutherland Brothers
Fingertricks	Burton							New Street YC 71
Firefly	Burton		78*		78			*Galaxy
Fisher Z	Manchester	79						
Flash Cats		79						
Flesh		73						
Flying Aces		76,77						
Flying Saucers		79						
Fogg								Adams Disco 74
Food for Thought	Burton							**← Melodies Incorporated** Rolleston YC, BTR Club
Foundations, The	West Indies							Adams/Eve's Disco 76,77
Foxglove							79	
Frankie Millars Full House	Scotland	76						
Freddie Mack	USA	74						
Freedom		72						

Group	origin	76 Club	Paradise	Town Hall	Drill Hall	Vaults	Rolleston YC	Notes
Freedom Suite								Top Rank Club 70
Freight								Hatton YC 71 / support. Van Der Graaf Generator
Frost		70						
Fruup	Eire/Belfast	73(x2),74						
Fumble		74,5,6,7						
Funky Bunk		71						
Fusion Orchestra [Jill Sawards]		72(x2),73	75			72,75		Jubilee Hall 75
Fusion Orchestra [Jill Sawards]		74						
G. T. Moore & the Reggae Guitars	London	75						
Galliard				70				support Medicine Head
Gary Glitter	London							79 Allied Breweries Club
Gary Moore Band	Belfast	73						
Genesis	Charterhouse							70,71Hatton Youth Club
George Hatcher Band		77	76					
Geranium Cake								71 Rugby Club
Gerry Marsden	Liverpool							76 Allied Breweries Club
Giggles		74						replaced Hustler
Ginger Bread		70						
Ginmil	Burton							Eton Park Pop Festival 70
Ginmil								Sharpes & Knights 71
Ginty	Burton	79	76,79	79				79 British Oak
Girlschool		78						
Glencoe	London	73 (x2)						
Good Habit	Wales?	75						71 Hatton Youth Club
Gordon Giltrap	Tonbridge		75					with McKenzie Cooke Band
Grand Felony	Birmingham		74					
Grand Hotel		79						
Grand Slam	Burton		78					
Gravy Train, The	Lancashire	74						
Greenslade				74*				*SU, ← **Colloseum, Alan Bown**
Gremlin	Burton		75					Sharpes & Knights 75
Grizelda						70		
Gryphon		76,77						
Gullivar Quake							71	
Gypsy	Leicester	72(2),74(2)						

Appendix 3... 1970s Groups in Burton

Group	origin	76 Club	Paradise	Town Hall	Drill Hall	Vaults	Rolleston YC	Notes
Ha Ha Ha	Sweden						73	
Hackensack		72,73,74						
Halcyon	Worcester	73,74						
Half Breed	Newcastle	75						
Hamburger Mary	Birmingham		74					
Hard Times	Birmingham		74					
Head Over Heels		78						
Head Waiter		78						
Heads Together	Yorkshire	75						
Headstone		74,75						
Heartbreakers, The								Jubilee Hall 74
Heavy Metal Kids	London	73						
Heinz	Hagen, Germany		79					
Hello	London	74						Adams Disco 74
Hellraisers		75						
Helter Skelter	Burton							70's
Heroes	Burton	78						
Hi-Ballers	Burton	77(x3), 78	76,77					Eton Park Club 75
								Rugby Club 77
'Hollerin' Dave Bull	Burton							Rugby Club 72 [Arts Lab]
Hollywood	USA	74						
Hooker		77						
Hot Wire	Burton/Sth.Derbys.	77?	77?					
House Shakers, The	London	72						
Hunter		78			78			
Hurdy Gurdy		71						
Hustler	London	74(x2),75						← Flesh
Huxley Mushroom							71	
Ian Campbell				72				
Ice Cream	London						74	
Imagine							78	
In the Beginning		70						
Incas, The		70						
Inmates, The	London	79						
Invaders, The		79						
Iron Maiden	London	79						
Isaac Guillory & Pure Chance		75						

Appendix 3... 1970s Groups in Burton

Group	origin	76 Club	Paradise	Town Hall	Drill Hall	Vaults	Rolleston YC	Notes
Isotope Band, The	Burton?							Jubilee Hall 75
Ivy League								Allied Breweries Club 76
J. J. Barnes	USA	74						
J. J. Jackson	New York, USA	74						with Rico?
Jack the Lad	Geordies	74,75						← Lindisfarne
Jaffa Band		70						Sharpes & Knights 71
JALN Band							77	Eves Disco 77
Jamerson Raid	Birmingham	79						
Jasper Carrott	Birmingham							Barley Mow FC 71,72,74
Javelin	Burton		78*					*Galaxy
Jelly Bread		72(x2),73						
Jenny Darron		78						
Jenny Haans Lion		77(x3)						
Jeruselum			72*					*Rag Concert
Jet Morgan	Burton/Derby	75	74,75(x3)					
Jigsaw							76	
Jo'Burg Hawks	South Africa	73,74						
John Cougar	USA	78						later Mellancamp
John Grimaldi's Cheap Flight		78,79						← Argent
Johnny Johnson's Bandwagon	USA						73	
Johnny Nash	Houston, USA				72			
Joint Sensation		70						
Jonesy		76(x3)						
Judas Priest	Birmingham	74,75						
Jude		72						Robin Trower & Frankie Millar
Juicy Lucy		72						← Wild Flowers
Junior High & the Rockets							75	
Kat Magee	Burton			76	76*			Allied Club 76,*Sassafras
Kellys Eye		75						
Ken Nicol & Easy Street	Lancashire	75						
Kenny Ball & his Jazzmen		71						Burton Grammar School 72
Kevin Birch Band, The		79						
Kevin Coyne	Derby	79						
Kilburn & the Highroads	London	73,74,76						→ Ian Dury & the Blockheads
Kilroy		71						
Kipper							78	

Appendix 3... 1970s Groups in Burton

Group	origin	76 Club	Paradise	Town Hall	Drill Hall	Vaults	Rolleston YC	Notes
Krakatoa	Brighton	77,78						
Krazy Kat		76,78						
Kursaal Flyers	Southend	75						
Lamplight		74						
Late Show		78						
Lazy Bones	Burton							70? ← Warm Jug - → Oakdale
Leapy Lea								Central Club 76
Leargo	Birmingham		79					
Lee Fardoh Band		78						
Left, Right & Centre		70,71(x2)						Sharpes & Knights 71
Lemon Cream, The		70						
Lew Lewis & his Band		77						
Lew Lewis & Reformer		79						
Libertines, The								79?
Light Fantastic							77	72,77
Limit			79					
Limmie & Family Cooking	Alabama, USA	74						
Lindisfarne	Geordies							Hatton Youth Club 71
Lion			76					
Listen to the Warm		70						
Little Acre	Black Country	76(x2),77(x2)						
Little Acre	Black Country	78,79						
Little Bo Bitch		79						
Little Bob Story	France	77						
Little Smoke			74,75					
Lord Fishfinger & the Frozen West	Burton		76,78					
Love Affair						76		
Loving Awareness		75,76						← Glencoe
Madata	Burton?					75		
Magazine	Birmingham							Allied Breweries Club 77
Magnum	Birmingham		79*					*Murials
Ma-Goos, The	Manchester							Sharpes & Knights 71
Major Lance	USA	74						
Marseille	London	78						
Marsh's Easy Street	Lancashire	75						
Marty Wilde								Newhall Labour Club 77

Appendix 3... 1970s Groups in Burton

Group	origin	76 Club	Paradise	Town Hall	Drill Hall	Vaults	Rolleston YC	Notes
Matumbi	London				76			
Max Merritt & the Meteors	Australia	75,76						
Maxim								Adams Disco 75 <-Spasm
Meal Ticket		77	76					
Mean Street Dealers		79		79				← School Sports
Medicine Hat		70						
Medicine Head	Burton/Stafford	70,73,75						
Medicine Head	Burton/Stafford	76(x2),77	71,76	70	72			
Medusa								Hatton Youth Club 71
Mick Abrahams Band		72(x2),73,75						← Jethro Tull & Pig
Midways, The	Midway?							Eton Park Club 70
Mike Storry Band		75						
Minx	Rolleston YC						72	
Mojo Hannah	Atlanta USA?	73						
Montanas, The	Midlands						77	
Moon		76,77						
Morgan		72						← Love Affair
Mosaic Sunset		68,70						Sharpes & Knights 71
Mother Superior			76					
Motorhead		78						
Motors, The		77						← Ducks De Luxe
Move, The	Birmingham							Eton Park Pop Festival 70
Mr. Big		76						
Mungo Jerry								Allied Breweries Club 76
Mutations Creations								Eton Park Club 71
Nasty Pop		76						
Neil Innes & Fatso		75,76						← Bonzo Dog Do Dah Band → Rutles
New Pennies, The							73	
No Dice		77						
Noel Redding Band		76						← Jimi Hendrix Band
Notations, The								Eton Park Club 70
Notations, The								Sharpes & Knights 71(x2)
Nucleus						78		
Nutz	Liverpool	73,74,75(x3)	75	78*				*SU
Nutz		76,77(x2)						
'O'	Jersey		74,77(x2)					Jubilee Hall 76

Appendix 3... 1970s Groups in Burton

Group	origin	76 Club	Paradise	Town Hall	Drill Hall	Vaults	Rolleston YC	Notes
'O' Hara's Playboys	Manchester							Eton Park Pop Festival 70
'O' Hara's Playboys	Manchester						72	
Oakdale	Burton	77	76,77					All Saints CH 72
Oakdale	Burton							Fox & Goose 72 [Arts Lab]
Oakdale	Burton							Rugby Club 73 [Arts Lab]
Oakdale	Burton							Jubilee Hall 75 [Supt.Fusion]
Oakdale	Burton			74*				*support Sharks [SU]
Octopus								Sharpes & Knights 71
Odinstorm								Leander Club 73
One Hundred Highways						76	76	
One Two, One Two	Burton							1979?
Oscar Toney Jnr.	Alabama, USA	70						
Ozone Breeze	Burton							Eton Park Club 76
Paladin	London	72			72			
Pancake		70						
Panties		78						
Paper Lace	Nottingham						73	
Paradox	Birmingham		79*					*Muriels,Rolleston YC 78
Pat Travers	Canada	76						
Patto		72						← Timebox
Peggy Seegar	USA							Barley Mow Folk Club 70
Pepper Village								Adams Disco 75
Peppers Machine	Derby	71(x2),72,73						
Pete Browns Back to Front		77						
Pete Websters Band	Burton		77					← Kat Magee
Phaetons Funeral	Burton							Rugby Club 76 [Platform]
Phil Whiteland	Burton?							All Saints Church Hall 72
Pick Ups	Burton		78,79					
Pieces Fit	London						73	
Plummet Airlines	Derby	76,77	76					
Pockets								Adams Disco 76
Polytechnic Show		71						
Pondersend		78,79						
Principle Edwards Magic Theatre	Exeter University	73,76					74	
Probe							71	
Punishment of Luxury	North East	79						
Quartz	Birmingham	79						

Appendix 3... 1970s Groups in Burton

Group	origin	76 Club	Paradise	Town Hall	Drill Hall	Vaults	Rolleston YC	Notes
Quicksand	Wales	74					74	
Racing Cars	Manchester	76,79	75					
Radio Stars		77						
Rain	Derbyshire						75	
Rainbow Valley								Adams Disco 75
Rare Bird		74						
Raving Rupert	Scunthorpe	72						'Elvis' Impersonator
Raw Material		73(x2)						
Raymond Froggatt Band	Birmingham	72,74(x2),77	76					
R-D-B		77						
Real Thing, The	Liverpool						74	
Records, The		78						
Red Brass				76				
Remus Down Boulevard		78						
Renaissance		72						
Richard Digance								Barley Mow Folk Club 74
Ricki Cool & his Icebergs		79						
Ricky Valance	South Wales			79				
Road Runner	Nottingham	71						Sharpes & Knights 71
Rock Island Line			75					
Rock Revival	Burton							Allied Breweries Club 76
Rockin Goose		74						
Roedene	Burton	77	77					
Roogalator		76,77(x2)						
Roy Hill & his Band		78						
Roy Young Band		72,73		72*				*support - Average White Band
Roz			74					
Rubber Rhino				75*				*support Trapeze
Salt		77						
Sam Apple Pie	Walthamstow	73,75						
Samson		79						
Sarah Gordon & Little Free Rock		73						
Sassafras	Wales	74(x3),75,77	76	75,76				
Saturi		75						
Savoy Brown		75						
Saxon	Barnsley	79						
Scorpions, The		76						

Appendix 3... 1970s Groups in Burton

Group	origin	76 Club	Paradise	Town Hall	Drill Hall	Vaults	Rolleston YC	Notes
Sean Tyla & the Tyla Gang		77						
Second Hand Band			76					
Settlers, The				76				Burton Grammar School 70
Sex Pistols	London	76						
Shabby Tiger		75						
Shanghai		75,76(x2)						
Sharks		74		74*				*SU -Chris Spedding
Show Bandits, The							74	
Showaddy Waddy	Leicester							Jubilee Hall 75
Simple Minds	Glasgow	79						
Sir Nata	Derby							Continental Club 77
Skid Row	Eire	72						
Skin Alley	UK/USA	72						
Skweela			76					
Sky Rocket								Continental Club 76
Skyye				76*				*support Sassafras
Slack Alice	East London		75					
Slik	Scotland							Midge Ure
Slik	Scotland						77	
Slowbone		76						
Smoke								Sharpes & Knights 71
Snaffu		73						
Soft Boys		79						→ Cryer
Sons and Lovers	Nottingham	72						
Sore Throat & the Spiders		79						
Sound	Hinckley							Peel Croft, S & K's 71
Source of the Power, The		70						
Spangled Mob								Jubilee Hall 75
Spasm								Adams 74,75 ->Maxim
Speed Limit			79					
Speed Trap		79						
Speedometers		79						
Spencer Mac								Hatton Youth Club 71
Spice of Life								Eton Park Club 73
Spider	Burton?							Leander Club 75
Spirit	Stoke							BTR Club 70
Spirit of John Morgan								Hatton Youth Club 71

Appendix 3... 1970s Groups in Burton

Group	origin	76 Club	Paradise	Town Hall	Drill Hall	Vaults	Rolleston YC	Notes
Split Enz	New Zealand							76 Club ??
Stackridge	Bristol	72						
Stan Webb Band	Birmingham	75						→ **Chicken Shack**
Starry Eyed and Laughing	Northampton	75						
Static Granny Band	Walsall		76					
Steve Gibbons Band	Birmingham	75(x2),76		75*				*SU
Steve McGuire Band			79*					*Murials
Stevensons Rocket							76	
Stonewall Jackson		70						
Straight Eight	London	79						
Straits, The		79						
Stray		77	76					
Stress			76					
Stretch		75						
Strider		74,77						
Strife		75,76,78						
String Driven Thing	Scotland	73,74		74*				*SU
Stripjack		77						
Stroll On	Burton						74	
Sundance		74(x2)						
Supercharge		76		75*				*SU
Superdrive			76					
Supersonic		79						
Supertramp		72(x2)					73	
Sutherland Brothers & Quiver	Scotland			73*		72		*SU
Suzi Quatro	Detroit, USA	73						
Sweet Sensation		75						Jubilee Hall 75, Adams 76
Sweet Wine								Adams Disco 76
T2								70s
Tea, The	Switzerland	76						
Thin Lizzy	Dublin	73						
Tickle							78	← Bollards
Tiddlywinks								Eton Park Pop Festival 70
Tiger			76					
Tim Rose Band	USA	75						
Tir Na Nog	Dublin							Hatton Youth Club 71
Titus Groan	London				70			

Appendix 3... 1970s Groups in Burton

Group	origin	76 Club	Paradise	Town Hall	Drill Hall	Vaults	Rolleston YC	Notes
Tony Capstick				72				Barley Mow Folk Club 75
Topper	East Anglia						77	
Train	USA, (Liverpool?)	77	76					
Trapeze	Wolverhampton	70,72(x2),73		71				Eton Park Pop Festival 70
Trapeze	Wolverhampton	74,76,77(x3)						Hatton Youth Club 71
Trax								Adams Disco 75
Trickster		79						
Trilogy			76					
Tristyn Day		71						
True Explosion								Rugby Club 74
U Boat		77						
UFO	London	72,73,74						
Ultravox		77						
Unicorn		72(x2),73						
Upp		74,75(x2)						
Upp		76(x2)						
Uriah Heep	London							Hatton Youth Club 71
Van der Graaf Generator	Manchester Uni							Hatton Youth Club 71
Vapour Trails		78						
Vibrators, The	London	76						
Vinegar Joe		72						Rt Palmer + Elkie Brooks
Wally	Harrogate	75						
Walrus		72						
Warhorse		73(x2)						
Warren Harry		78						
Watt Roy Turner Band		74						
Western Union		70						Eton Park Club 73
Weston Green	Burton							1970's
Wham Bam Thankyou Mam		72						
Wheels	Nottingham				76			
Wild Heritage	Midlands		70					
Wild Turkey		72(x2),73(x2)					72	
Wild Turkey		74						
Winkies, The	London	74						Jubilee Hall 75
Witchfynder		78						
Woman (Ray Phillips)		75,77						← Budgie
Woody Woodmanseys U Boat		77						← David Bowie